Joseph
THE LIFE, TIMES AND PLACES OF
THE ELEPHANT MAN

I am Yours Truly
Joseph Merrick

Contents

Acknowledgements

This book has only been made possible with the help and support received from many people. Forgive me if I have unintentionally missed someone out! So here's a big "thank you" to all my friends who I have not sent Christmas cards to, and have not seen. You have all been so understanding.

I would like to start by thanking Gary Burks, the Superintendent Registrar at the City of London Cemetery and Crematorium, for assisting me in my recent research to locate the burial plot of Joseph Merrick. Without Gary's help I would not have been able to pinpoint to actual burial site. Thank you.

My research began at Welford Cemetery in Leicester. With the help of the wonderful and knowledgeable volunteer staff, George Mackness and Barbara Boulter, I was able to locate the grave of Joseph Merrick's mother, his grandfather and all his aunts, uncles and cousins who are buried in the cemetery. Their help and advice was invaluable and the book would not have even got off the ground without their help. I would also like to thank Bob Jones of the Ashby Museum who provided photographs of specific establishments in Ashby, and of course the priceless help of the Leicester, Leicestershire and Rutland Records Office in Wigston Magna and specifically archivist Jenny Moran.

My good friend Sarah Bicknell, schoolteacher, re-enactor, seasonal volunteer at Leicester Cathedral and gin drinking partner for reading one of my very first chapters on New Year's Eve 2015; Vicky McNabb, my neighbour and close friend, for dissecting a segment of the book over a bottle of wine, and to Richard Mackinder, my boss, who so kindly provided and trusted me with his excellent information and research on the Wombwell Menagerie and who is a relation to George Wombwell; the Very Reverend David Monteith, Dean of Leicester, and the Reverend Pete Hobson, for their help and advice on services in the Church of England. I would also like to thank all the volunteers and staff who I work with at Leicester Cathedral for putting up with me going on and on about my book. You have all been so patient.

Some of the excellent photographs you see in this book were provided by Marc Haynes of darkestlondon.com, who so graciously gave me permission to use them and Christian Jaud for his timeless photographs of Bedstead Square, probably the last photos taken of Joseph's final residence. These are two gentlemen I have never met but I thank you with all my heart.

Dave Andrews, Radio Leicester presenter, gave me airtime on his History show and thank-yous must also go to Lucky Dog Theatre Productions, who performed their play Mr Merrick, The Elephant Man at Leicester's Guildhall in April 2016. Philip Hutchinson and Tony Carpenter gave myself and fellow historian Neil Bell an opportunity during the Q&A session to answer questions on Joseph, his family and life in Leicester.

I have come across many interesting stories and people during my research, including Ken Stewart, who kindly let me use his research and photographs on the Merrick family in Australia, a vital asset in my book. Sandi Carter, a great niece of Tom Norman, who verified my family relationship to Mr Norman - we now acknowledge ourselves as cousins. Another new cousin, Valerie Howkins, a granddaughter of Tom Norman who I have enjoyed speaking to and visiting her Museum of Memories in King Street, Great Yarmouth is a woman who wants to see her grandfather's reputation restored, something I hope I have been able to achieve in this book.

Pat Selby, another wonderful lady, Joseph Merrick's second cousin, who invited me into her home and provided me with cups of coffee and photographs. You are a wonderful lady, funny, kind and entertaining. Thank you.

Christine Anderson, my best friend, who I dragged around

Leicestershire looking for materials and who listened to me whittle on and on about my book, gave me so much support and encouragement. Christine and the Rutland and Derby public house in Leicester became my sanctuary during days of stress. So Christine, thank you so much, I could never wish for a more wonderful best friend.

I would like to thank Michelle Merrick, related through marriage to Charles Barnabus Merrick and who has appeared in documentaries on Joseph, from the bottom of my heart. I wrote to Michelle in early 2016 and she kindly telephoned me and I explained what I was doing. Thank you Michelle for trusting me, I couldn't have done it without your blessing. Michelle has provided explanations on her family history, photographs and corrected some of my errors.

I have to of course thank my family, my older brother Andrew Vigor, who offered to read my chapter on the workhouse but never got around to it - the thought was there!; my mum and Dad, Lynda and Stuart Vigor, who for the past year listened to me drone on about my book. My two wonderful children, Elizabeth and Andrew Mungovin, thank you both for being so patient and understanding. It's been hard and I know if I wasn't at work I had my nose in research and my fingers were superglued to the laptop. Your Dad who has been great ferrying you both here, there and everywhere - thank you Jim for your help, support and understanding.

Last, but certainly not least, Neil R.A. Bell, fellow historian, author of Capturing Jack the Ripper: In the Boots of a Bobby in Victorian London and a fantastic friend. Without Neil's help and advice this book would never have been conceived. Neil planted the seed in my mind and from then on it grew and grew. Thank you for picking me up when I've been down and ready to jack it in. Your knowledge on Victorian history is priceless, thank you for reading and re-reading my chapters, rectifying mistakes, suggesting extra research, driving me down to London, giving up your time and generally giving me the confidence to do this. Thank you so much.

JOANNE VIGOR-MUNGOVIN

Foreword

It is always a great thing when people write books that help to keep Joseph's memory alive and I was delighted when Joanne approached me to access my family history research.

I know a couple of my documents challenged some of her pre-conceptions but she listened and, I am pleased to report, made amendments to her work where necessary.

I feel that, in the past, films have been made that distort the truth for dramatic effect, and books have been written that provide the facts leaving the reader to use what social history knowledge they have of Georgian and Victorian cities and apply it to the characters. In this book Joanne has taken social history down to street level which enables the reader to understand the lives and times as they affected each individual.

Joanne's ancestor, Tom Norman, ran side show attractions, and we tend to look back on his trade with 21st Century eyes. It is easy for us to demonise the man but that would take us far from the truth. With Tom Norman, Joseph was able to make a living from his affliction and keep himself out of the workhouse without having to fall on the benevolence of his aunt and uncle, even though they were offering him shelter.

With diligent research and sensitivity Joanne takes the reader through the ancestors who formed the background to Joseph's life, the local social history that affected his life and the strength and humility he showed as he led that life.

I am privileged to have played a small part in the creation of this book.

MICHELLE MERRICK,
Cousin to Joseph Merrick through marriage

INTRODUCTION
A Tale of Two Cities

"Can you imagine the kind of life he must have had?"

"Yes, I think I can."

"I don't think so. No one could possibly imagine it!
I don't believe any of us can!"[1]

Joseph Merrick, better recognised as 'the Elephant Man', was born in the industrial town of Leicester in the late summer of 1862.

Born without any indication of the affliction yet to come, Joseph lived at home first with his mother and father then, after his mother had passed away and his father remarried, with his uncle, being admitted into the Leicester Union Workhouse at the age of seventeen.

It was after four long years living in this institution that Joseph contacted a local music hall proprietor to propose that he exhibited himself as a novelty or freak. And so began the life of The Elephant Man.

The majority - if not all - of the books, plays, and the one and only film of his life focus on Joseph Merrick's time spent in London. Leicester, the town of his birth, is barely touched on. In fact, if you asked the general public the question "Where was Joseph Merrick born?", most would probably say London; not many would know he was a Leicester resident.

I wanted to put the two stories of Joseph Merrick together; my

---

1   Extract from *The Elephant Man* directed by David Lynch, 1980.

own 'Tale of two cities', if you like.

Leicester is an extremely ancient city, probably one of the oldest in the country. Look beyond the new shopping centres, fancy condos and exquisite unique shops, and you will find a long history dating back to the Romans and probably earlier. The town was named *Ratae Corieltauvorum* – the walled place of the Coriani.

Although only officially a city since 1919, the history of Leicester is rich and eventful, including the legend of King Leir (who according to the fable gave his name to the town of Leir-cestre and is buried in a vault under the River Soar), the knighting of King Henry VI in the Church of St Mary De Castro in Leicester's castle grounds during the Parliament of Bats in 1426, the Battle of Bosworth in 1485 where the town welcomed two kings in two days, the seize of Leicester in 1645, and more recently the re-interment of King Richard III at Cathedral Church of St Martin in March 2015.

The principal purpose of this book is to present Joseph's early life and family: what was going on in the environs around him when he was growing up, the sights he might have encountered, what his family were achieving. I've tried to concentrate my research on Joseph's milieu, spending less dissecting his deformity.

Genealogy has always aroused my interest with a passion. I've managed to trace my own maternal line, the Warrens, to 1799, and my fifth-generation Great Grandfather Richard Ward Warren's house still stands in Friar Lane in Leicester.

My paternal line became extremely thought-provoking, as when researching Tom Norman, the showman who exhibited Joseph and was portrayed as 'Bytes' in the 1980 film *The Elephant Man*, I discovered that we are cousins, despite not having an inkling of our relationship when starting this book. Tom Norman is actually my fifth cousin, three times removed.

Tom was much-maligned and criticised for taking advantage of those poor freaks such as Joseph Merrick. Scores of them, unwelcome and banished by their own relations, were appreciative of the chance to achieve some degree of independence, their only alternative being starvation or the workhouse.

My research on Joseph's genealogy began with his maternal side, the Pottertons, a fascinating family with accounts of suicide, train crashes, infant mortality and - please excuse the outdated expression - the mentally defective and deformed.

Although these descriptions are not used nowadays, they were commonplace a century ago, and sometimes still used less than thirty years ago, written on birth and death certificates and in newspaper articles, so they are words I have employed in this book. Obviously they are not the words I would choose to use now, so please do not take offence.

The Merricks are another noteworthy family. Joseph's grandfather re-established himself in Leicester after leaving his children from his first marriage in the East End of London. One of his sons was deported to Tasmania for stealing pork at the tender age of sixteen.

So, as well as his cousins in Leicester and London, Joseph also had - and still has - cousins on the other side of the world.

At the time of writing, the diagnosis of Joseph's deformity is Proteus Syndrome. But until his remains can be fully tested and DNA extracted, Joseph Merrick continues to be a medical enigma.

Ladies and gentlemen, in the absence of the Lecturer with your indulgence I would like to introduce Mr Joseph Merrick, the Elephant Man. Before doing so I ask you please to prepare yourselves – Brace yourselves up to witness one who is probably the most remarkable human being ever to draw the breath of life.

- Tom Norman.[2]

---

2   *The Penny Showman: Tom Norman, Silver King.* With additional writings by his son George Norman (1985).

CHAPTER 1

Thurmaston is a Very Poor Village, Generally Speaking

Joseph's family on his mother's side, the Pottertons, originated from the Northamptonshire village of Ashley, close to the county border with Leicestershire. The family were agricultural labourers by trade.

Joseph's direct lineage can be traced back to 1799, when William Potterton was born to Michael and Catherine.

By 1828 William was working at West Langton, a small village just in Leicestershire. Here he met and married Elizabeth Robinson, who hailed from a neighbouring village of Cranoe. The couple were married in Cranoe's 12th century St Michael's Church on 7 July 1828, under the curacy of John Davies. The ceremony was witnessed by Robert Robinson, Elizabeth's brother.[1]

The couple went to live in East Norton, where Elizabeth gave birth to her first son John, who was baptised on 7 February 1830[2] in the village church of All Saints. Sadly, John did not survive, and by 1834 William and Elizabeth had moved to Stoughton Grange, a large country house estate just outside the town of Leicester, where William continued his agricultural profession.[3]

---

1   Marriage certificate of William Potterton and Elizabeth Robinson. Originally shared by LindaHolmes55, 20 October 2014.

2   Baptism records of John Potterton.

3   The house and estate at Stoughton Grange was owned by George Anthony Leigh Keck, a landowner and Conservative MP who had inherited the estate in

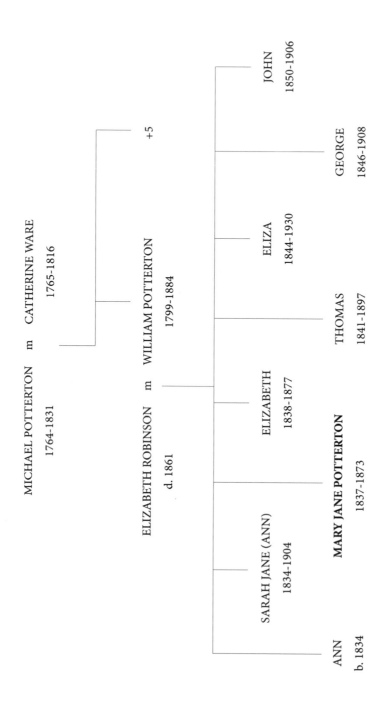

MICHAEL POTTERTON
1764-1831

m

CATHERINE WARE
1765-1816

+5

ELIZABETH ROBINSON
d. 1861

m

WILLIAM POTTERTON
1799-1884

ANN
b. 1834

SARAH JANE (ANN)
1834-1904

MARY JANE POTTERTON
1837-1873

ELIZABETH
1838-1877

THOMAS
1841-1897

ELIZA
1844-1930

GEORGE
1846-1908

JOHN
1850-1906

It was at Stoughton Grange that the family briefly settled and grew. By 1834 William and Elizabeth had two daughters: Ann, born about 1834,[4] and Sarah Jane presumably also born in 1834 as she was baptised at the village church of St Denys in Evington on 8 June 1834.[5] Another girl, Mary Jane, was born in 1837, followed by Elizabeth in 1838 and Thomas in 1841.

By 1844, William and Elizabeth Potterton had moved their family to Thurmaston, a village just four miles north east of Leicester. The family continued to grow, and Elizabeth gave birth to three more children. Eliza arrived in 1844, George in 1846 and finally John in 1850.

It would be reasonable to assume William and Elizabeth were not highly educated, because their wedding certificate does not hold their signatures. However, this did not stop them seeking out a decent education for their children, and the couple did send them to the local school, Thurmaston National School, which opened in 1844. The opening was reported in the *Leicester Journal*, with the school being described as a 'school for the education of the poorer classes'. Explaining that the school had been built through local subscriptions, the newspaper continued:

> The site, which is situated nearly opposite the church, has been given by Mr T Allen, and principal inhabitants of the neighbourhood have contributed the requisite sum for the erection of the building'.[6]

Those who contributed to the building did so in the hope that a 'Christian education would make the poor willing to accept their

---

1797 at the age of 23, and who would control the house and land for 63 years until his death in 1860. Leigh Keck enlarged the estate's vast acres by buying land in Knighton from the Craddock family. By 1832, Leigh Keck had retired as an MP and spent the next 30 years as a country squire, taking care of the house and making it one of the finest houses in Leicestershire. Information from *Stoughton: Images of a Village* (Soar Valley Press).

4   1841 Census.

5   Baptism certificate of Sarah Jane Potterton. Originally shared on ancestry.com by LindaHolmes55, 18 October 2014.

6   *Leicester Journal*, 16 August 1844.

lowly place in society as God's will'.[7]

With the country in the throes of the Industrial Revolution, the mid-1800s was a time of great social unrest, with reports of machine-breaking, riots and Chartist demonstrations.

The Church of England was also being challenged by the increasing power of other denominations such as the Baptists, Methodists, Unitarians, Roman Catholics and atheists, and when the Reverend Edward Hatch Hoare, Perpetual Curate of Thurmaston, applied in September 1842 for funds to the National Society for promoting the Education of the Poor in the Principles of the Established Church (The National Society), his fears were emphasised when he wrote:

> Thurmaston is a very poor village, generally speaking... It is a village too, which is full of that most dissatisfied (and certainly not wholly without reason) class of persons. Frame work knitters and from its nearness to Leicester it catches the disaffected and revolutionary spirit, which I am sorry to say, prevails there to a very considerable extent. Several of the inhabitants are avowed Chartists and many more secretly favourable to them. Yet for the sake of education they suffer their children to go to the church Sunday school and if a daily school can be added I doubt not that they will send many of them there also.[8]

The school replaced the weekly lessons which had been held at the local Wesleyan Chapel. Originally built in 1792, the chapel was on Thurmaston's Melton Road, and was used for children's writing classes on a Monday evening.

A professional curriculum was introduced at a fee of 2d, but poor attendance was common until the fee was abolished in 1891.[9] It seems to have been a fee the Pottertons could afford, because in 1851 Elizabeth, Thomas, Eliza and George are all recorded in the census as 'scholars'. John was only three months old at this time; Sarah Jane was 18 and working as a servant in Conduit Street in Leicester, and Mary Jane was 14 and also working as a servant,

---

7   *Thurmaston National School 1844-1868* (1979).

8   Ibid.

9   *Memories of Thurmaston* (2007).

probably in the local Manor House.

The family seemed to do well for themselves in Thurmaston. In 1847, William was awarded £1 at the annual Agricultural Society meeting, recommended by Sir A.G. Hazelrigg for having raised five children under the age of 12 without receiving parochial relief.[10] And two years later William was again recommended, this time by C.W. Packe Esq, MP of the Leicester Agricultural Society, and awarded £5 for "maintaining 5 children under 14 plus one child over, and buried two,[11] and not received parish relief within five years ending 16th September 1849."[12]

It was clear that the Potterton family, though poor, were able to look after themselves. And as the years passed the children grew, and began to spread their wings in readiness to fly the nest.

Sarah Jane and Ann were the eldest surviving children of William and Elizabeth. Born in 1834, there is no record of Sarah Jane in the 1841 census, and no record of Ann, who would have been aged seven in 1841. They could be two different sisters, or perhaps more likely, the same person. A Sarah Ann Potterton is recorded in the 1851 census record as a housemaid at 83 Upper Conduit Street in Leicester. She died in 1904, a spinster, and is buried in Welford Road Cemetery. The cemetery records list her as Sarah Ann Potterton of 8 De Montfort Street.[13]

Elizabeth, the third daughter (assuming Sarah Jane and Ann are indeed the same person), was born in Evington in 1838. By the time she was 23 years of age Elizabeth was working as a housemaid in the village of Knighton, just a few miles south of Leicester, and almost seven miles from her home in Thurmaston. Many employers of housemaids searched for staff sometimes as far as twenty miles away, in order to stop friends from visiting and thereby reducing socialising. Days off were relatively unheard of, perhaps one

---

10 *Leicester Mercury*, 4 December 1847.

11 The second of the two children is presumed to be Ann, as there is no record of her after 1841.

12 *Leicester Journal*, 26 October 1849.

13 Welford Road Cemetery records.

afternoon a month, which probably made even socialising with neighbouring servants extremely difficult. It was a pretty lonely life for a young girl away from home.

Elizabeth may have answered an advert similar to this placed in the *Leicester Journal* in 1859:

> Wanted, a single handed butler, a ladies' maid and an upper house maid who have filled similar situations. Liberal wages for good servants, with respectable characters.
>
> Apply by letter to M.R. Leicester Post Office.[14]

Elizabeth's household was relatively small compared to those of her neighbours. She lived and worked at Stoneygate Grove, in a large house on the affluent London Road area in Knighton. The head of the house was Mr Thomas Sargent, a retired hosier. There were two other servants: Sarah Gibbes, the head housekeeper, and William Brown, the groom. A household with three servants had an average income of £500 (£40,000 today).

Next door, in Stoneygate House, were the Toller family. Richard Toller was a Clerk of the Peace and lived there with his wife, their six children and six servants. On the other side, living in The Stoneygate House, was Liberal MP, hosiery manufacturer and philanthropist John Biggs, a three-time mayor of Leicester.[15]

Life as a domestic servant was not easy. Elizabeth was the only housemaid. Her earnings would have been between £12 and £18 per annum. She would have to rise at 6.00am in the summer and 6.30am in the winter. Before breakfast, duties would have included the sweeping and dusting of the living areas and the clearing of fire grates, then the lighting of fires and taking up hot water to the master of the house. After breakfast, the servants' rooms would have to be cleaned and the rest of the house, such as the hall and kitchens, swept and cleaned.

Elizabeth was expected to dress for lunch and dinner with a clean

---

14 *Leicester Journal*, 19 August 1859.

15 In 1840, 1847 and 1855. A statue of Biggs was erected in Welford Place in Leicester, such was his standing within the then town.

mop cap and apron. Her breaks in the afternoon were used to mend linen and clothes and, in the midst of all that, she was expected to answer the door to visitors.[16] Breakfast for Elizabeth was usually served at around 8.00am, once the household had eaten, and usually consisted of bread and butter, tea and ale. Lunch was often served with cold meats, vegetables and fruit pie. Tea, which was around 4.00pm, would usually again be bread and butter, but this time with fruit cake. And finally supper, served after 9.00pm, was yet again cold meats and fruit pie.

There is not much left now of the old Knighton village. An old timber-framed cottage dating back to 1600 stands near the parish church of St Mary's, and The Craddock Arms public house, which was originally The Bull's Head, is still *in situ*. Knighton Hall, home to the Craddock family, and the small cottage on Chapel Lane designed by Henry Goddard in 1838 as a schoolhouse for the Craddocks are probably the only other buildings Joseph's Aunt Elizabeth would recognise today.

Sometime between 1861 and 1871 Elizabeth left her position in Knighton, and moved back to Thurmaston to live with her brother George and their father. It may have been because her mother had passed away, or perhaps her employer died; there is no record of Thomas Sargent after 1861. Knighton was developing and became part of the ever-growing industrial town of Leicester. Even John Biggs' house had been demolished in 1866. This was followed by the other Stoneygate Houses in the 1870s, resulting in the creation of the Clarendon Park area. The other servants with whom Elizabeth had worked had also moved on: in 1871 William Brown, the groom, was a shoe finisher living with his wife and young family in Leicester.

In June 1877, at the age of 39, Elizabeth married John Potterton, her first cousin once removed, and six years her junior.[17] Elizabeth was not John's first wife; he had previously lived in the Potterton's ancestral village of Ashley, Northamptonshire, where he had

16 *The Duties of Servants: The Routine of Domestic Life* (1894).

17 John was the son of Elizabeth's cousin George, and without wishing to get too complicated, John's grandfather was Elizabeth's father's brother.

married Betsy Freestone on 5 December 1867. Sadly, Betsy died the following year aged 29, and is buried in Ashley parish church.

Following their marriage John and Elizabeth themselves moved into Thurmaston Lodge, the gatehouse to Thurmaston Hall on Humberstone Lane,[18] a large estate comprising 31 acres which was originally built for William Herrick Esq.[19]

Sadly, on 29 December 1877, just six months after they married, Elizabeth died of cerebral disease apoplexy - a stroke - and she was buried on 1 January 1878 in unconsecrated ground at Leicester's Welford Road Cemetery.[20]

A year later John married again, this time to Ann Ross, nee Warren, of Cranoe in Leicestershire. Ann happened to be Elizabeth's first cousin on her mother's side, and had previously been married to a James Ross, with whom she had tied the knot on 1 November 1862 at St Alkmund's church in Derby, the couple going on to have three children.[21]

In 1881 John was working as a dyer, with the family living at 51 Leir Street in Leicester. John and Ann produced six children: John (b. 1881), William Henry (b. 1882), Lizzie (b. 1883 but who died eight months later in July 1884),[22] Arthur (b. 1886) and Gerald and Horace, both recorded as being born in 1888, it being reasonable to assume they were twins. Sadly, the pair died in infancy, Gerald at three weeks[23] and Horace aged 15 months.[24] At some point before Gerald and Horace's births, the family had moved to Twycross Street. I can find no record of Ann's children from her previous marriage

---

18 Nothing is left today of the Hall itself, and where it once stood is now Northdown Drive. Only the gardener's cottages remain, still on Northdown Drive, but the lodge where Elizabeth and John lived on Humberstone Lane still stands.

19 William Herrick was a solicitor, magistrate and town Clerk of Leicester. It was William's ancestor, Robert Herrick, who built his house on the original Grey Friars site in Leicester, the location where King Richard III was buried in 1485.

20 Plot uS 22 C u39421 (Welford Road Cemetery).

21 Select Church of England Parish registers 1538-1910.

22 Plot cL 877 C c25433 (Welford Road Cemetery).

23 Plot cL 877 C c29328 (Welford Road Cemetery).

24 Plot cL 877 C c30516 (Welford Road Cemetery).

except in 1891, when her son Francis James Ross married. At this time he was living on Leicester's Lyndale Street.

Ann died on 11 April 1888, just two months after the birth of her twins and the shattering loss of Gerald. She was buried with her cousin (and John's second wife) Elizabeth Potterton in Welford Road Cemetery. John must have purchased the plot, because when Ann was buried it was listed as a family grave.[25]

In 1889, one year after the death of his third wife, John remarried yet again, this time to Mary Ann Thompson from Burton-on-Trent. Then something strange seems to occur. Twelve years later, in the 1901 census, John had married a fifth wife, Mary Ann from Harston. He still has his children with him from his marriage to Ann. Mary Ann Thompson is not found on any records until 11 June 1909, when she was admitted into the Borough Asylum in Leicester, and then in 1911 when she was admitted as an inmate into the town's Swain Street Infirmary Workhouse. She stayed there until she died in 1918, aged 75. Mary Ann is buried in Welford Road Cemetery in an unmarked common grave, nowhere near her husband John.[26]

John himself died in 1902, and was buried on 9 June with his third wife Ann in the family plot in Welford Road Cemetery.[27]

Eliza was the youngest of the daughters born to William and Elizabeth Potterton. Born in Thurmaston in 1844, like her sisters she went into service and at the age of seventeen was working for the Cowling family, bootmakers at 14 High Street, Leicester.[28] In 1870 Eliza married Henry William Hewitt, of the Hewitt family organ

---

25 Plot uS 22 F u61683 (Welford Road Cemetery).

26 Ancestry.co.uk

27 Plot uS 22 F u91836 (Welford Road Cemetery).

28 1861 Census.

29 Record of marriage. Henry had a tendency to build cheaper organs, made up of disused parts of other organs pre-dating 1880 and re-installing them after a few adaptations. This made the apparatuses very old but also unique to Hewitt. The organ in St Marks Church, Isle of Man, built by Hewitt is very distinctive in that the keyboard starts with GGG, which was common before church organs had pedals. Many of Henry's organs still survive today in churches around the country, and eleven of them can been seen and heard in the following churches

makers from London, in Leicester.[29] They had three children during their marriage,[30] and Henry had a workshop at 10 Glebe Street, Leicester, in the Highfields area of the town.[31] The family lived at this address between 1871 and 1891.[32] Many of Henry's organs still survive today in churches around the country, and eleven of them can be seen and heard in Leicestershire alone.[33] Eliza Potterton Hewitt died in 1930, aged 76.

Thomas Potterton, the eldest of William and Elizabeth's three surviving sons, was born in Evington in 1841. Whilst still living at home Thomas followed in his father's footsteps for a while and worked as an agricultural labourer for one Thomas Allen. In 1856 he won the second prize of £1 in a ploughing competition, at which he ploughed half an acre of land with a pair of horses without a driver within four-and-a-half hours, and no less than four and half inches deep.[34] In 1857 Thomas was rewarded for his loyalty to his employer, when the Agricultural Society presented him with £1 for having worked eight years with Allen.[35]

Thomas married Naomi Bosworth of Arnesby, a tiny village in Leicestershire, on Christmas Day 1868. The young couple settled in Leicester and Thomas worked on the railways. At the time of writing, no records have been discovered of the couple having any children. In 1871 Thomas and Naomi lived only a few doors away from his sister Eliza on Upper Conduit Street. 1881 saw Thomas's

---

in Leicestershire: the Baptist Church in Sutton-in-the-Elms, the Primitive Methodist in Ratby, the Baptist Church in Cosby, the Free Church in Desford, the Baptist Church located in Earl Shilton. As well as the Primitive Methodist Church, Aylestone Park, the Baptist Church in Carleym Street, the Medbourne Road Chapel, the Presbyterian Church, Leicester, St Peters Roman Catholic Church and St Stephens Presbyterian Church, all in Leicester.

30 Henry born in 1870, Harriett in 1873 and Eliza in 1874.

31 www.culturevannin.im/special/church_organ/An introduction.pdf.

32 1891 Census.

33 www.organ-biography.info/index.php?.id=Hewitt_HenryWilliam_1845.

34 *Leicester Journal*, 14 November 1856.

35 *Leicester Mercury*, 5 December 1857.

employment take the couple to Bedford, where they settled at 52 Edward Road. However, it wasn't long until they returned to Leicester, taking up residence at 74 Mere Road, Highfields. Here Thomas died of malignant tumours of the spleen in June 1897, aged 56 years.[36] He is buried in Welford Road Cemetery.[37]

John Potterton, the youngest child of William and Elizabeth, was born in Thurmaston in 1850. Most of the Potterton children attended Thurmaston National School, but John, at the tender age of 10, was employed as a carter. This wasn't to be his chosen career, because by the age of 20 he was working as a railway service fireman at St Andrew's-the-Less, East Bramwell near Cambridge, a choice of career in which he was soon joined by his brother Thomas. John married Christina Chambers in 1878, and the young couple returned to Leicester, settling at 16 Waring Street.

John's career on the railways seems to have lasted about twenty years. Sadly, those twenty years had their ups and downs, as working on the railways wasn't easy employment. A parliamentary enquiry concluded that engine drivers were working ninety to one hundred hours a week - not the sort of working conditions that would lure potential workers nowadays. Even back then, employers had to make the job attractive to potential employees. However, the railways had security and betterment, wage increments depending on length of service, and housing. Companies expected employees to stay with them; it truly was a 'job for life' back then.

A description of a Railway Fireman can be found in Charles Dickens' work *Dombey and Son*, a story about the personal and business dealings of the firm of 'Dombey and Son, Wholesale, Retail, and for Exportation':[38]

> He was dressed in a canvas suit abundantly besmeared with coal dust and oil, and had cinders in his whiskers, and a smell of half slacked ashes all over him. He was not a bad looking fellow, nor even what

---

36 Death certificate, 17 December 2015.

37 Plot cK 532 F c39977 (Welford Road Cemetery).

38 Dickens's original title for this novel.

could be fairly called a dirty looking fellow, in spite of this, in short, he was Mr Toodle, professionally clothed.[39]

Working on the railways was hard and dangerous, and claimed lives of hundreds each year. In 1878, John very nearly became one of those hundreds.

On Friday, 29 August 1879 a mail train from Scotland was timed to arrive at Leicester at 1.52am. It was late, and when it did finally arrive was split in two. The first carriage, which accommodated the bulk of the passengers and Pullman cars, made it to St Pancras safely, albeit a little late.

The second half of the train, manned by John Potterton, consisted of a locomotive, tender, two meat vans, fish van, luggage van and two passenger carriages, carrying approximately thirty passengers in total. This train was due to have arrived at London's St Pancras at 4.15am. The second locomotive passed Mill Hill station near Hendon 35 minutes after the first passenger train. Just before Hendon, near Colin Deep Lane, was a sharp curve, and in a moment of disaster, the engine and tender left the rails and went over the embankment close to the up line.

The engine became embedded in soft clay, and the tender in descent was thrown some distance. The two passenger carriages went over the embankment, and the post office car and three other carriages were hurled down the embankment near the down side of the line. By the time Mr Flewitt, the stationmaster at Hendon, arrived at the scene, most of the passengers had got out of the train, suffering from shock but otherwise uninjured. Staff at the nearby Midland Hotel had come to the aid of the shaken passengers, giving them some brandy as they did so. Within an hour a new train had arrived, taking the passengers and mail to complete their journey to St Pancras.

John Potterton and his fireman, Paul Cooley, were sent back home to Leicester. John had suffered only minor injuries to his hands and

---

39 *Dealings with the Firm of Dombey and Son: Wholesale, Retail and Exploration* by Charles Dickens (1848).

head, whilst Paul had scalded his leg. It wasn't until later that John's injuries were noticed as being more serious than first thought. On the Saturday, the day after the crash, he was unable to get out of bed; both hands were cut and bruised, and he had severe concussion, clearly due to the fact that he had a scalp wound on the right side of his head.[40]

John's own account of the derailment, given to the *Leicester Journal*, read as follows:

> The first half of the mail left Leicester 15 minutes late, and I followed with the second half 28 minutes late. All went well until between Mill Hill and Hendon. It was just beginning to get light but I could not see any distance in front of the engine. We were running at a rate of between 45 and 46 miles per hour, as near as I can say, when suddenly I saw just a few yards in front of the engine that the line had given way, that the rails had slipped out very wide, and that the ballast had been washed away. I had no time to say anything, but I shut off the steam and were off the rails in a moment. The engine sank deep into the ground, ploughing up the way, and after running for about twenty yards, as near as I can say, rolled down the embankment which is about 10 feet deep and lay on the right side. The engine dragged the front part of the train with it, but the great portion was hurled over to the down lines, blocking it completely. I was covered with coal and debris, but I held onto the engine, which was shattered and broken almost to pieces. I was turned quite round, but with what I do not know, and I found myself in a huge heap of rubbish, just in front of the firebox. I got out as quickly as possible, then became very faint on account of the great pains in both hands, which had been aerated and torn by the debris. I found that the stoker had got out before me, and had been badly scalded on the thigh. I do not know how we escaped being killed. I took upon it as miraculous. There was a great deal of confusion, but I was too ill to take notice of it.[41]

Despite this shocking incident, the crash didn't seem to have halted John's career, and his family life initially thrived. They moved from Waring Street to Coalville for a few years, with two of his children,

---

40 *Leicester Chronicle*, 6 September 1879.

41 *Leicester Journal*, 5 September 1879.

John and Eliza, being born there. However, by 1891 the family had grown to six, with 10-year-old Edith, 8-year-old John, 6-year-old Eliza and 3-year-old Richard living with John and Christina in a small terraced house at 66 Berners Street, back in the Highfields area of Leicester.

This area was, at this time, one of the most respectable areas of Leicester. The houses built here were created as 'second class' housing, not working class dwellings.[42] The housing was a mixture of terraced, semi-detached and detached properties. The reason given by the authorities for the description as 'second class' was that in 1864 no street had been built to link the semi-main thoroughfare of Sparkenhoe Street to the larger London Road, so the area was difficult to approach.

During these years a disease known as phthisis was rife in Leicester, and lengthy discussions about this 'wasting away' disease had gone on as far back as 1851. Adolescents and young adults were chiefly struck down, with overpopulation, poor housing, overcrowded living space, crowded ill-ventilated factories, poverty and poor nutrition all being blamed.

The Medical Officer of Health, in the Borough of Leicester Health reports of 1908, stated that:

> This disease is the cause of so much economic loss to the nation, and so much domestic sorrow and loss to the family, attacking its victims as it does during active working years of life that no other diseases approaches it in importance. As, moreover, phthisis must be regarded as largely a preventable disease, it is only fitting that it should be considered at some length.[43]

Phthisis is probably known better by its two other names, tuberculosis and consumption. It is caused by the bacterium known as tubercle bacillus - mycobacterium tuberculosis.

The disease affects various parts of the body, mainly the lungs, and

---

42 *We are South Highfields: Life in Our Area Past and Present.* Edited by Penny Walker (2012).

43 *In Sickness and in Health: A History of Leicester's Health and Ill health 1900-1950* by Clive Harrison (1999).

is commonly spread through the air via coughing. By 1900 there was a massive increase in the cases of phthisis in Leicester, with 210 deaths in that year. By 1905 this had increased even more to 353 deaths, yet by 1917 that number had slightly reduced to 342.[44] To be affected by phthisis, you were destined to waste and dwindle away. Puccini, in his 1896 opera *La Bohème*, romantically yet graphically describes the point of death of the character Mimi from consumption, another term for phthisis. Rodolfo, whose affection for Mimi is clear, confesses his fears for his love to his friend Marcello, in Act III, when he sings:

> In vain I'm hiding all my torture that racks me
>
> I love Mimi, she is my only treasure,
>> I, I love her, but I have fear, I have fear
>
> Mimi's so sickly, so ailing! Every day she grows weaker
>
> That poor unhappy girl is condemned
>
> A terrible cough shakes her chest, already gaunt cheeks, blood red
>
> And my room's a squalid hovel, with no fire
>
> Remorse assaults me - I am the cause of the fatal illness
>> that is killing her

Mimi spends her last moments with Rodolfo. She has a short-lived respite known as spes phthisica (state of euphoria), where she feels she may recover; however, she does not and her final words are 'my hands are much warmer... I'll sleep now'.[45]

Instances of phthisis declined after 1910, when many old workshops were replaced by modern factories with improved ventilation. Around this time there was also an interest in hereditary predisposition, and in an attempt to break the cycle of phthisis being passed from parent to child the less ill were taken out of the unhealthy environment into sanatoriums, where they received good air, healthy food and medical care. But the sanatorium was for the rich, not the working class. The idea of a sanatorium was first mooted

---

44 Ibid.

45 *La Bohème* Act 4. Composed by Giacomo Puccini.

by Leicester authorities in 1900, yet it wasn't until 1914 that it was given the go-ahead. In 1903 the 'hospital isolation of consumptives' was tried out on a ward at Groby Road Isolation Hospital. A Ministry of Health report of the same year clearly laid out the intentions of these Isolation Hospitals, stating:

> It should be clearly understood that patients are not admitted with the object of curing them, but rather in the hope of benefitting and instructing them - by a practical object lesson - as to the best mode of life for them to adopt. It is hoped that the knowledge thus imparted will extend beyond those actually treated at the hospital. It is hoped, also, that an increased appreciation of the value of fresh air as a preventative, as well as a curative of consumption, will be similarly diffused.[46]

All this unfortunately came a too late for John Potterton's family, for in 1898 they lost one of their sons, also John, to phthisis at the age of 15. This was not the only tragic brush with the illness, for in 1906 another son, Richard, was also lost to phthisis. Young John Potterton died whilst the family were living at 31 Haddon Street; no occupation is listed on his death certificate, so we can't make a guess as to how he caught the disease. As mentioned above, there was a particular interest at the time with family relationships and phthisis, and to how the extent of hereditary and interpersonal infection was a cause. The chief medical officer produced a report for the sanitary committee in 1904, after conducting a survey of 176 phthisis-affected families in Leicester:

> ...in over 60 per cent of the cases there was a history of other members of the family or household having already been attacked by this fell diseases. How far these figures should be taken as an inherited tendency to consumption is a debated point. The more modern view is that very many, if not most, of the cases should be regarded as having occurred through direct infection from one person to another living in the same house. Evidence is accumulating to support this view but there is no doubt that a constitutional weakness or similar

46 *In Sickness and in Health: A History of Leicester's Health and Ill health 1900-1950* by Clive Harrison (1999).

tendency of consumption often is inherited, though actual infection
afterwards is necessary before the disease can develop.[47]

John Potterton Jr died on 29 June 1898, with his mother present
at his bedside. There is no record of a post mortem, and the death
was certified by Dr R J Braye. He was laid to rest in a family plot at
Welford Road Cemetery in Leicester, not far from his young cousins
Gerald, Horace and Lizzie Potterton, and their mother Ann.

After young John's death, the family moved to Ashby-de-la-Zouch,
an ancient market town in north west Leicestershire and home to
Ashby Castle, the purpose-built seat of one of the most powerful
English politicians in 15th century England, Lord Hastings, who was
executed by King Richard III in 1483.[48] In the 19th century it was an
industrial town, and although surrounded by coalmines, was not a
coalmining town in itself, but with its main industries being leather,
cotton and glue.[49]

Ashby-de-la-Zouch has also given birth to notable people over
the years. Frederick Bailey Deeming, infamous murderer and Jack
the Ripper suspect, born there on 30 July 1863, was executed on 23
May 1892 in Melbourne, Australia, for the murder of his wife Emily.
Deeming had also murdered his first wife Marie and their four young
children in Rainhill, Liverpool. The press soon caught on to the fact
he was being suspected of being Jack the Ripper,[50] as the following
article in the *Pall Mall Gazette* shows:

> Reuters this morning forwards the following messages – The detective
> Cawsey, who has charge of Deeming alias Swanston… before leaving
> Albany secured the assistance of four marines, who were passengers
> by the vessel, to assist him in watching the prisoner during the
> voyage to Melbourne. Cawsey has stated to several persons on board
> the steamer that he feels convinced that Deeming is Jack the Ripper.[51]

47 Ibid.
48 www.english-heritage.org.uk.
49 Ashby Museum, North Street, Ashby-de-la-Zouch, Leicestershire.
50 www.casebook.org/dissertations/dst_deeming.html.
51 *Pall Mall Gazette*, 29 March 1892.

John Potterton Sr had a complete career change on moving to Ashby-de-la-Zouch, becoming the landlord of the King's Head in Market Street. Whether the family decided to relocate after young John's death to obtain a better way of life is not known, but by then daughter Eliza was 15-years-old and apprenticed to a local milliner. Her sister Edith and young brothers Richard and Frank were all living with them at the pub, and were there to enjoy the celebrations of King Edward VII's coronation in 1902. Yet by 1906 the family were back in Haddon Street in Leicester, this time at number 35.

It was here in the November of 1906 that John Potterton was admitted into the Borough Asylum, dying of heart disease on the 13th, aged 56. Just a few weeks later, on 6 December, his son Richard died of phthisis pulmonalis at the family home in Haddon Street, aged 18. His occupation at the time of his death was butcher's assistant. Christina was again present at her son's death.

After the death of her husband and son, Christina moved the remainder of her family - Edith, Eliza and Frank - to 53 Buxton Street, still in the Highfields area of Leicester. Edith, by 1911, was a servant at Mill Farm in Gaddesby, in rural Leicestershire. Eliza was working as a barmaid and Frank a cycle shop assistant. Christina died in January 1929. Just ten months later, on 11 October 1929, her daughter Eliza died aged 44 at the Leicester Frith Homes from acute peritonitis and phthisis.[52]

How and why Eliza Potterton ended up at the Leicester Frith, a Home for the 'mentally defective', remains a mystery, although at 15 years of age Eliza was working as a millinery assistant in Ashby. A mercury solution was commonly used in the process of turning fur into felt, with hatters breathing in the fumes which led to the

---

52 The Leicester Frith Homes Hospital where Eliza died was opened in August 1923 for the 'mentally defective'. It housed 30 male and 30 female children as well as 60 female adults. Half of these women had transferred from the Cross Corners home in Belgrave, having previously lived at Sunnyholme - a residential care home for girls from the workhouse who were unable to look after themselves - until its closure in 1916. Sunnyholme closed in 1916 and the girls were transferred to Cross Corners. In 1925, the residents were moved to the new Leicester Frith, and the matron superintendent, Miss Nellie Russam, moved with them.

accumulation of mercury in the body, causing symptoms such as trembling, loss of coordination, slurred speech, memory loss, depression and anxiety. The phrase 'mad as a hatter' stems from the effects of mercury poisoning, and perhaps this was the cause of Eliza's illness.[53]

John and Christina Potterton, together with their children John Jr, Richard and Eliza are all buried in the family plot, which is now sadly unmarked.

George was the seventh child of William and Elizabeth. When his mother passed away in 1861 George remained at the family home at Allen's Lodge with his elderly father. In 1862 he was recommended the sum of £1 by his employer and landlord, Thomas Allen, for 'being a boy under the age of eighteen who had been employed for the longest period with one master', and who had 'uniformly borne a good character'.[54] This was recognition for George's having established a career as an agricultural labourer.

George married Catherine Taylor from Weedon in Norfolk in 1873. The couple had eight children, Catherine (b. 1875), George (b. 1877), Sarah (b. 1878), John Thomas (b. 1880), James Leonard (b. 1882), Mary Eliza (b. 1885), Thomas Henry (b. 1887) and Lily Naomi (b. 1888).

Tragedy struck at the beginning of 1884. On Sunday, 3 February, at their home at Allen's Lodge, George's wife Catherine found blood on her father-in-law's bedroom floor. On entering the room she saw William Potterton lying on his bed. She called for her husband, who found his father lying on his left arm and elbow with his head over the side of the bed, in his hand holding a razor.

George shouted, "Oh dear father, what have you been doing?" receiving the reply, "Oh my boy, don't you take it away, I've not done cutting yet, don't take it away."

Dr A.W. Emms, surgeon at nearby Belgrave, was sent for. William was alive and able to speak. He wasn't aware that he had done anything to himself. He had a wound nearly four inches long to the

53 www.cas.org/news/insights/science-connections/mad-hatter.
54 *Leicester Journal*, 26 September 1862.

front part of his throat, and had lost a considerable amount of blood. William haemorrhaged whilst Dr Emms was making arrangements to get him to the Leicester Infirmary, so he stitched the wound there and then. William died the next day without ever realising what he had done to himself.

The inquest before Mr Coroner Dean was held at the Harrow Inn in Thurmaston on Tuesday, 5 February. The investigation concluded that William Potterton committed suicide while in a state of temporary insanity. He was buried with his wife Elizabeth at Thurmaston Parish Church.[55]

George Potterton ended his days at the Leicester Borough Asylum. He was admitted on 16 April 1908, and died aged 64 on 25 April 1910. Two months earlier, on 10 February, his son Thomas, who had been paralysed since birth, had also been admitted into the Asylum. There he stayed for a considerable period before he died on 15 September 1925.

George's widow Catherine died in 1933, and is buried with her husband and their son Thomas and daughter Mary Eliza in the family grave at Welford Road Cemetery.[56]

Mary Jane Potterton was the second daughter born to William and Elizabeth, in the village of Evington, Leicestershire, in 1837.

It is possible that she attended Thurmaston National School from the age of nine. From the age of around 14 she went into service, and then later worked for Baptist Richard Jacques, a tallow maker and soap boiler of 41 Cank Street, Leicester.[57]

Originally from Shepshed in Leicestershire, Jacques lived and worked in Tottenham Court Road in London until filing for bankruptcy in 1840 and returning to Leicester.[58] It may have been

---

55 *Leicester Chronicle*, 9 February 1884.

56 Welford Road Cemetery burial records.

57 Non-conformist and non-parochial registers, 1567-1970.

58 *Perry's Bankrupt Gazette*, 1 February 1840.

while working with Jacques that Mary Jane came under the influence of the Baptist Ministry.

Although christened into the Church of England in St Denys Church in Evington, and later marrying at the Anglican Church in Thurmaston, Mary Jane taught as a Sunday School Teacher[59] in one of the eight Baptist churches in Leicester. Exactly which one is not recorded, although it was probably Archdeacon Lane Chapel because it was here that the Merricks are recorded as having communion on a regular basis.[60]

Mary Jane Potterton was destined to become the mother of Joseph Carey Merrick.

---

59 *The True History of the Elephant Man* by Michael Howell and Peter Ford (Kindle Edition 2011).

60 Communion & Members Register for Archdeacon Lane Baptist church. Nos. 287 & 288, July 1872.

CHAPTER 2

At Present, Intelligent People Do Not Have Their Children Vaccinated

- George Bernard Shaw

The origins of the surname Merrick have their roots planted in the rugged landscapes of Wales. It derives from the forename Meunc, Welsh for Maurice, and is taken from the Latin name of Mauntius meaning Dark.[1]

Joseph Carey Merrick's ancestors may have originated from Wales, but his great-great-great-grandfather Barnabus Merrick, who was born in 1690, lived in Spitalfields in London's East End with his wife Anna, who was born in 1691.[2] Barnabus lived to the grand old age of 84, and Anna 82. Both were buried in that iconic East End place of worship, Christ Church in Spitalfields.

The name Barnabus seems to be a prevalent family name given to the firstborn son in early Merrick family history. Four generations were named Barnabus, and in future generations the name often appeared as a middle name.

Barnabus and Anna's son, born in 1740, was therefore also named Barnabus. He and his wife Mary, born in 1734, spent their entire married life living around the Shoreditch and Whitechapel districts. This area was a slum of Georgian London. Housing planning

1   www.houseofnames.com/merrick-family-crest.
2   Ancestry.co.uk.

regulations were in force at the end of the 17th century, specifying that city lanes had to be at least fourteen feet wide. However, there were little effective guidelines to deal with pillars, buttresses, bulging walls, overhanging upper storeys and gables, bollards and pumps, and this all limited pedestrian and vehicular access. The area was densely packed, with tall narrow houses that over-extended backwards to enclosed courtyards, which were entered by passages often measuring only a shoulder's width.[3]

Barnabus and Mary Merrick had five children. Their first born, a boy, came into this world on 2 August 1763 and was predictably named Barnabus.[4] Six years later, when their second son Silvester was born, the young family were living in George Yard,[5] off Whitechapel High Street, an area made infamous a century later during the Jack the Ripper crimes of 1888 with the horrific murder of Martha Tabram there on 7 August of that year.[6]

The Merricks were back in Shoreditch by the time their daughter Mary was born in 1772, at Holywell Street,[7] but once more at George Yard two years later where their daughter Hannah was born.[8] When their last child James was born in 1776, the Merricks were now living in Grey Eagle Street, Spitalfields.[9] This was an area well known for French silk weavers.

Eldest son Barnabus Merrick, born in 1763, married Martha Box at St Ethelburga's Church, Bishopsgate, on 26 August 1785.

In a settlement record dated 10 December 1803 regarding the examination of a Sarah Molce, Barnabus (or Barnaby as he is described in the report) is recorded as a loom broker. According to the same settlement record, Sarah Molce's husband was Barnabus'

---

3   www.sarahwise.co.uk/Dissitation/labyrinthinelondonPDF.

4   Baptism record of Barnabus Merrick, 1 October 1781.

5   Baptism record of Silvester Merrick, 9 July 1769.

6   *Capturing Jack the Ripper: In the Boots of a Bobby in Victorian England* by Neil R.A. Bell (2014).

7   Baptism record of Mary Merrick, 8 March 1772.

8   Baptism record of Hannah Merrick, 10 April 1774.

9   Baptism record of John Merrick, 29 September 1776.

apprentice, but had been ill-treated by his master and had fled to sea, leaving his pregnant wife destitute:

> The Examination of Sarah Molce wife of James, Middlesex, to with this examination on the oath, faith that she is the wife of James Molce now at sea and was married to him at Shoreditch church on 8th day of December 1802. That the said husband hath informed her and which information she believes to be true that when he was of the age of 14 years or thereabouts he was bound an apprentice by the trustees of Langbourn Ward School to Barnaby Merrick of Grey Eagle Street in the parish of Christchurch in the county of Middlesex, loom broker, and served his said master there about 18 months. When being ill-treated by his master he left him and went to sea and did not return to his said master. He hath not gained any other settlement – and this examination being pregnant by her said husband hath become chargeable to the parish of St Leonard's, Shoreditch aforesaid.[10]

Barnabus Merrick died the following year, on 21 March 1804, and was buried at Christ Church, Spitalfields.[11]

When Barnabus Merrick died on 21 March 1804 he left a vast legacy to his children and grandchildren, and even his housekeeper. The family were not poor, and had a number of business and properties.[12]

His eldest surviving son, a fourth-generation Barnabus, had been born on 23 April 1792 and baptised at Christ Church, which obviously dominated the life of the Merricks during that period.[13]

However, he was not the firstborn son. His elder brother, obviously also named Barnabus, had been born in 1791 but died after a year. When another son was born shortly afterwards he was christened Barnabus, in keeping with family tradition. The family would be joined by five further children: Martha Elizabeth (b. 1794), John (b. 1795), Martha Mary (b. 1796), William (b. 1803) and Joseph (b. 1805).

---

10 Settlement papers of Shoreditch Poor Law Union, 10 December 1803.

11 Death record of Barnabus Merrick.

12 Will of Barnabus Merrick, transcribed by Michelle Merrick.

13 Baptism records of Barnabus Merrick.

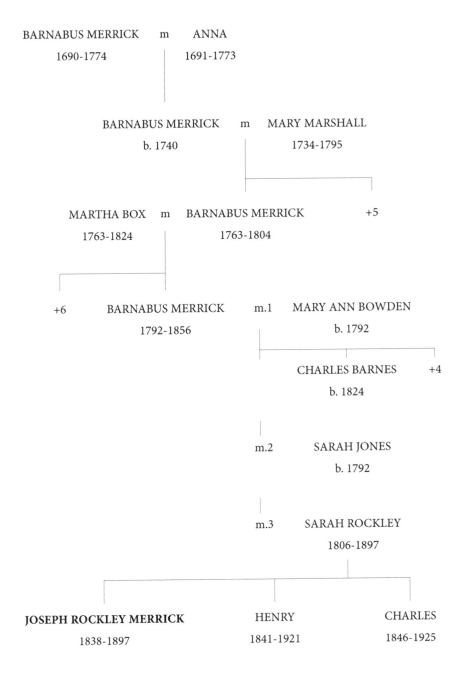

BARNABUS MERRICK   m   ANNA
1690-1774   1691-1773

BARNABUS MERRICK   m   MARY MARSHALL
b. 1740   1734-1795

MARTHA BOX   m   BARNABUS MERRICK   +5
1763-1824   1763-1804

+6   BARNABUS MERRICK   m.1   MARY ANN BOWDEN
1792-1856   b. 1792

CHARLES BARNES   +4
b. 1824

m.2   SARAH JONES
b. 1792

m.3   SARAH ROCKLEY
1806-1897

JOSEPH ROCKLEY MERRICK   HENRY   CHARLES
1838-1897   1841-1921   1846-1925

Barnabus was married three times, firstly to Ann Bowden, who had been born in 1792 at Holywell Mount.[14] Together the couple had five children: John Barnabus (b. 1816), William George (b. 1818), Ann Martha (b. 1820), Charles Barnes (b. 1824) and Mary (b. 1826).[15] Ann must have died not long after the birth of Mary, because on 3 June 1826 Barnabus married Sarah Jones at St Ethelburga in Bishopsgate, with his status on the marriage banns recorded as a widower.[16] There doesn't seem to be any children from this union, and we are unsure as to what happened between Barnabus and Sarah because by 1837 he had tied the knot for the third time to Sarah Rockley, from Bulcote in Nottinghamshire.[17]

Barnabus and Sarah settled in Leicester and had three children. Breaking with the tradition of naming the firstborn son Barnabus, their first son, born in 1838, was named Joseph Rockley Merrick. Henry followed in 1840, and Charles Barnabus in 1846.

While Barnabus was raising a new family with Sarah in Leicester, his children from his first marriage were fending for themselves back in the grim East End of London. Charles Barnes Merrick, Barnabus' and Ann's fourth child, particularly found himself in trouble, when he was accused of stealing 6lbs of pork valued at 3s from Jane Wing of John's Row on 5 March 1839. Although Charles said he saw two boys go and take the pork, a witness, George Stocksley, accused Charles. He was found guilty and transported for seven years on a convict ship.

Charles was first detained in Parkhurst Prison, but immediately found himself in trouble again with the prison authorities when he attempted to steal the sum of £15. For this he received an additional sentence of three months, which was added to his seven-year transportation service.

---

14 Baptism record of Ann Bowden. Holywell Mount had been a burial ground for centuries, and was used heavily between 1664 and 1666 to bury plague victims. However, by Ann's birth it had been cleared for housing due to large amounts of murders and muggings.

15 ancestry.co.uk.

16 Record of Banns at St Ethelburga, 3 June 1826.

17 1851 Census.

Charles was shipped out on the *Runnymede*, departing London on 11 November 1839 and arriving in Van Diemen's Land, better known today as Tasmania, on 28 March 1840.[18]

On arrival Charles claimed he was 17-years-old, but in reality he was actually sixteen. His description was as follows: 4ft 11in, brown hair, clean shaven, hazel eyes, fresh complexion with freckles, long visage with a small mouth, nose and chin. After serving his sentence in Tasmania, on 4 July 1846 Charles was awarded his free certificate.[19]

As Charles was being transported to Tasmania, on a passage probably unknown to his father, Barnabus Merrick had established himself in Leicester with his new wife.

The Merricks settled in Nelson Square, not far from London Road. The streets around Nelson Square were bustling with shops, auctioneers, public houses and even professors teaching foreign languages to private paying students. Other businesses nearby included Sketchley & Co., mangle and clasp makers, and the Trafalgar Brewery, owned by Thomas Goddard.[20]

Barnabus bought his trade with him, and continued working as wood turner. His wife Sarah had their three sons to look after. By 1851, Barnabus had moved his family to Lower Charles Street, another respectable area in the same district. He was still working as wood turner.[21] Here, the Merricks were surrounded by piano makers, merchants and bakers. The residents of neighbouring households held middle-class jobs.[22]

On 12 April 1856, Barnabus died at the Hospital Cottages at Leicester Union Workhouse[23] from heart disease and dropsy. He was 64-years-old.[24]

---

18 www.convictrecords.com.au.

19 Members.iinet.net.au/~kjstew. See Appendix Four.

20 *Leicester Journal*, 25 February 1848.

21 1851 Census.

22 1851 Census; *Leicester Mercury*, 13 April 1850.

23 Welford Road Cemetery records.

24 Members.iinet.net.au/~kjstew.

His widow, Sarah, and the eldest son Joseph moved to 20 Lee Street, which seemed to be quite a prosperous thoroughfare. New houses in Lee Street were advertised as having extensive rooms for businesses and outbuildings, with two well-built tenements adjoining.[25] The area was relatively new, and respectable. There was a grocer's shop on the corner,[26] and the Lion and Lamb public house at number 21, opposite the Merricks' new house.

By this time the other two boys had left home.

The second son, Henry, had joined the army and was stationed at the Barracks on Sadling Road in Maidstone. One of two army barracks in Maidstone, it was used for training the cavalry's young horses, and was later to become the Army's riding school.[27]

On 27 January 1865 Henry married Jane Moffatt in Leith, on the Firth of Forth in Scotland. Their first child, Charles Henry, was born in Sheffield in 1866. By the time he was five-years-old, in 1871, the family moved into 1B Broad Street, next to the Red Lion public house in Spalding. Henry had left the army by this stage and was working as the Service Club manager for the Chelsea Pensioners.[28]

At some point between 1881 and 1892 Henry Merrick moved his family to the south coast, to Poole in Dorset, where he became landlord of the Bull's Head on High Street.[29] His wife Jane had passed away some time within those ten years, and at the age of 52 Henry married for a second time, on 4 December 1892 to twenty-year-old Sarah Jane Orchard,[30] a sister of one of his servants, Eliza Orchard.[31] The marriage lasted only four years, possibly even less than that, as Henry filed for divorce in 1896 when Sarah admitted adultery with one William Tollerfield.[32]

25 *Leicester Journal*, 3 July 1857.

26 *Leicester Mercury*, 24 January 1852.

27 History of Maidstone via Wikipedia, 2016.

28 1881 Census; www.chelsea-pensioners.co.uk.

29 1891 Census.

30 Marriage register.

31 1891 Census.

32 Divorce records 1858 -1914.

Henry married for the third and final time in 1899 at the age of 59, to 24-year-old Matilda Hunt of Blandford in Dorset.[33]

Matilda seems to have come from rather a troubled background. Her father Henry Hunt had been incarcerated at Dorchester Gaol in 1877 for stealing, when Matilda was just two-years-old.[34]

When she was sixteen, Matilda was living at the Trewint Industrial Home for Girls at 190 Haverstock Hill in Hampstead, London.[35] Trewint had been established in 1850 in Hackney, east London, with the intention of rescuing young girls who were under the influence of 'evil parental example or unmanageable'. In 1889, Trewint moved to 190 Haverstock Hill. It became a certified school, and took in girls from workhouses and elsewhere who were over 14 and thought to be 'naughty, tiresome and unmanageable, committed petty theft, were deceitful, untrustworthy or untaught in household duties'. Payment of 3s 6d a week was required from parents or patrons, to be paid quarterly in advance. Suitable clothing had to be provided, along with a certificate of health. The girls were taught needlework, reading, writing and rudiments of arithmetic, as well as laundry work and cleaning. They stayed for one year, after which suitable situations were found for them.[36]

If Matilda had been found suitable employment, it may have been with the Coghill family near Hastings, as one Harry Coghill left £100 in his will to a servant named Matilda Hunt in 1895.[37] If her employer had died, it may explain Matilda's return home and her subsequent marriage in 1899 to Henry Merrick.

The couple continued to live at and run the Bull's Head in Poole, until Matilda died in October 1905 at the age of 30. Henry went to live with his son Charles and his wife, who were still living in Poole at Tatnam Road,[38] and later to 4 Bosworth Road, Leicester, where he

33 Marriage register.

34 *Dorchester Prison Admission and Discharge Registers*, Ref NG PRI D3 4.

35 1891 Census.

36 *London Daily News*, 3 February 1890.

37 *Morning Post*, 1 November 1897.

38 1911 Census.

died on 15 March 1921 aged 81.[39]

The youngest son of Barnabus and Sarah, Charles Barnabus Merrick, had remained in Leicester and, at the age of fifteen, was living not too far away from his mother and brother as an apprentice hairdresser to Stephen Walker of 56 Churchgate.[40] At 22 years of age Charles married Jane Bosworth at All Saints Church, Highcross Street in Leicester.[41] The young couple moved to 144 Churchgate. Here they were soon joined by Charles' mother Sarah and their own first child, Charles Henry, who was born in 1869. By 1870, Jane had given birth to another son, Arthur Gilbert, who was born in August 1870 but sadly died after just two weeks.[42] A third son, also named Arthur Gilbert, was born in October 1871.

In December 1872, Charles applied for, and received, a loan of £50 from the General Charities Trustees acting on behalf of the Sir Thomas White's charity,[43] which had been established as far back as 1542 to provide loans to new and young businesses.[44] No doubt a cause for celebration, the money would probably have been invested into Charles' hairdressing business, but the sense of good fortune ahead for the family was short lived. In the same month Charles and Sarah's third son, the second Arthur Gilbert, sadly died aged only 14 months. He was buried alongside his brother in Welford Road Cemetery.[45]

Another son, Albert, was born in 1875, followed by a daughter, Emma Ada, in 1876. Again tragedy struck, as Emma passed away a year later, in July 1877. She is also buried in Welford Road Cemetery

---

39 England & Wales National Probate Calendar (Index of Wills & Administrations) 1858 -1966.

40 1861 Census.

41 my.ancestry.co.uk.lindaholmes55.

42 Plot URI 3042 C u24611.

43 *Leicester Chronicle*, Saturday 21st December 1872.

44 This charity still runs today, and Sir Thomas White is honoured in Leicester by being one of four statues on the City's famous Clock tower. See www.stwcharity. co.uk

45 Plot URI 3042 C u29382.

with her two baby brothers.[46] By this time Charles and Jane's nephew, Joseph Carey Merrick, had moved in with them,[47] and with Charles' mother also living there, the house would have been a busy one. The family was ever-increasing and another daughter, Alice, was born in 1879. In that year Charles was presented with a summons and fined ten shillings for neglecting to have his children vaccinated.[48]

Another son, John Ernest, came along in 1881. Once again Charles made an application to the Sir Thomas White charity and was awarded £40.[49]

The family moved to 248 Belgrave Road, continuing to grow with the birth of two more sons, George Perry (b. 1885), and Walter Edward (b. 1886) adding to the bursting household. Unfortunately, the two youngsters passed away very quickly. George breathed his last in April 1886, aged only one year, and Walter died that August at the tender age of only nine weeks. The two boys were buried with their other siblings at Welford Road Cemetery.[50]

Things took another turn for the worse that year, when Charles was again summonsed for neglecting to have his children vaccinated within three months of birth and fined ten shillings.[51]

In 1840 a Vaccination Act had been introduced to provide free vaccinations to the poor. This outlawed 'inoculation', which at the time meant 'variolation' inoculation of smallpox material. In 1853 it became compulsory for infants to be vaccinated within the first three months of life; if the parents defaulted they would be fined or imprisoned,[52] and this led to the founding of the Anti-Vaccination League in London.[53] In 1867 vaccination became compulsory for all

---

46 Plot URI 3042 C u38432.

47 *The True History of the Elephant Man* by Michael Howell and Peter Ford (Kindle Edition 2011).

48 *Leicester Daily Mercury*, 26 May 1879.

49 *Leicester Chronicle*, 11 March 1882.

50 Plot URI 3042 C u57310 and u58109.

51 *Leicester Chronicle*, 27 February 1886.

52 www.ministryofethics.co.uk/?p=9&q=2.

53 www.thehistoryofvaccines.org/content/articles/history-anti-vaccination-movements.

children up to the age of 14,[54] and opponents focused their concern upon the infringement of personal choice and liberty.[55]

The Anti-compulsory Vaccination League was founded in 1867, with smaller leagues being set up in the towns and cities throughout England in response to this new law, and pressure from this anti-vaccination movement was increasing. In 1885 a huge anti-vaccination demonstration was held in Leicester, attracting around 100,000 people. Banners were raised, as well as a child's coffin and an effigy of Dr Edward Jenner, the forerunner in promoting the smallpox vaccination.[56] The local newspaper, the *Leicester Chronicle* described the size of the demonstration in Leicester, commenting: "...nothing approaching the demonstration of Monday in magnitude nor in its representative character has ever been organised in the days that are past."

The paper goes on to say that:

> The affair was unique, being one of the largest. Windows of houses along the line of the routes were filled, as well as balconies and other elevated positions. Banners labelled with cartoons baring the words 'Leicester's baby hunter', followed by a starved looking pony, with bandages around its body, through which blood was made to appear, supposed to represent the source from which lymph is extracted. Then came a coffin, bearing wreaths of flowers and drawn on a bier to represent 'another victim of vaccination'.[57]

A Royal Commission was appointed in 1896 to investigate the anti-vaccination grievances, as well as hearing evidence in favour of vaccinations.

In 1898 a new act removed cumulative penalties, and introduced a conscientious clause allowing parents who did not believe vaccination was safe or effective to obtain a certificate of exemption. The Act also introduced the concept of the 'conscientious objector'

54 www.ministryofethics.co.uk/?p=9&q=2.

55 www.thehistoryofvaccines.org/content/articles/history-anti-vaccination-movements.

56 Ibid.

57 *Leicester Chronicle*, 28 March 1885.

into English law.[58]

Charles and Jane Merrick had no further offspring. They had brought nine children into the world and buried five of them. The hairdressing business flourished and would continue through four generations;[59] eldest son Charles Jr became the barber for the Leicester Union Workhouse,[60] and in 1896 he was involved in a coroner's inquest into the death of one of its inmates, as the *Leicester Chronicle* reports:

Singular death at the Workhouse
An Infirmary patient's escapade

The borough coroner has received intimation of the death at the workhouse of an inmate named John Dawson, 48 years of age, which occurred under unusual circumstances. The deceased was admitted to the workhouse infirmary from the prison on Welford road on May 28th and had since been under medical treatment. He appeared to be almost demented. On Tuesday last he managed to get through one of the windows of the lavatory, and jumped down on to the lawn outside, where he was found subsequently. He did not appear to be injured by the jump, and no bones were broken, but the patient afterwards developed pneumonia and in consequence of his escapade the coroner decided to hold an inquest. Deceased is described as having come from London, but an effort made to trace any of his friends has up to the present be unavailing.

The inquest on the body was held on Tuesday afternoon at the old town hall before the borough coroner. Mr R Harvey – In briefly relating to the facts the coroner said the deceased went on all right at the Workhouse Infirmary until the 4th of this month. At eight o'clock in the evening of that day the ward in which he was placed was locked up as usual by the nurse, and early on the following morning deceased was seen to go into the lavatory. Shortly afterwards - about quarter past seven – the attention of Charles Henry Merrick, hairdresser, who was at the workhouse on business, was drawn to the deceased, whom he found lying on the lawn below the lavatory

---

58 National Library of Medicine.

59 *The True History of the Elephant Man* by Michael Howell and Peter Ford (Kindle Edition 2011).

60 *Leicester Chronicle*, 4 January 1896.

window. Merrick asked him whether he had fallen down. He replied he had jumped out, and added that he was tired of life. Dawson was taken back to the ward but died on Sunday morning.

The first witness was Mr D Elpatrick, assistant medical officer at the Workhouse, who attributed the death to pneumonia from exposure – Nurse Coe of the workhouse infirmary, deposed to seeing deceased in bed apparently all right at eight o'clock on the evening of the 3rd – John Booth, an inmate of the infirmary, who occupied a bed next to the deceased, said he saw him go into the lavatory shortly before half past six on the morning of the 4th. Charles Henry Merrick, hairdresser, 144 Churchgate, found the deceased lying on the ground with only a nightdress on.[61]

Jane Merrick lived out her last years at the family home of 9 St Margaret's Street in Leicester, dying there in January 1916 at the age of 68. Her husband Charles Barnabus Merrick died at Balfour Street, Leicester in November 1925, aged 79. They are buried next to each other in Welford Road Cemetery,[62] with their children and Charles' mother Sarah Merrick all nearby.[63]

Joseph Rockley Merrick remained at home and worked as a warehouseman at one of the town's factories until his marriage in 1861. He may have laboured at one of Leicester's many boot and shoe factories, an industry which manufactured more footwear goods than anywhere else in the country.[64] Between 1851 and 1861, the number of people employed in the shoemaking trade in Leicester rose from 1,393 to 2,741,[65] and many companies, such as F. Bostock, shoe manufacturers,[66] were setting up business in and around the Cank Street area of Leicester, an area where Mary Jane

61 *Leicester Chronicle*, 16 June 1896.

62 Plots u0 557 F u102847 and u0 556 F u115054

63 Welford Road Cemetery records.

64 www.le.ac.uk/ebulletin-archive/ebullitin/news/press-release/2000-2009/ 2008/narticle.2008-10-35-html.

65 www.british-history.ac.uk/vch/leics/vol4/pp314-326.

Potterton was living and working at that time.

This is pure speculation, as we do not yet know how Joseph's parents did meet. However, what we do know is that Joseph Rockley Merrick and Mary Jane Potterton were married on 29 December 1861, at the Anglican Parish Church of St Michael and All Angels in Thurmaston, the village where Mary Jane grew up.[67] Joseph was 22 and Mary Jane was 25.

Months later, this union bore its first child, a child who was to become, as one person put it, "probably the most remarkable human being ever to draw the breath of life".[68]

66 *Leicester Mercury*, 22 October 1859.

67 Marriage certificate of Joseph Rockley Merrick and Mary Jane Potterton (via my.ancestry.co.uk.lindaholmes55).

68 A quote by Tom Norman published in *The True History of the Elephant Man* by Michael Howell and Peter Ford (Kindle Edition 2011).

CHAPTER 3

There Were Two Young Women Among Them, and They Knocked Backwards

St Michael and All Angels Church, in the Leicestershire village of Thurmaston, came under the vicarage of the Reverend E.W. Woodcock. It was here, on 29 December 1861, that Joseph Rockley Merrick and Mary Jane Potterton were married, witnessed by the bride's father William and her sister Elizabeth.[1]

Looking at the dates, it is possible that Mary Jane was already eight weeks pregnant when she married. If so, such a situation would not be ideal for a young girl in the nineteenth century. It would be seen as hugely shameful, and most unmarried pregnant girls either found themselves on the streets, in the workhouse or would simply put an end to the shame and commit suicide. However, being only eight weeks pregnant, it is most likely Mary Jane did not even know she was with child as early pregnancy symptoms were not recognised during this period, and it was more common for a woman to know she was expecting from around the fifth month.

The newly-married couple settled into 50 Lee Street, not too far from Joseph's mother at number 20.

Lee Street was just off the Belgrave Road in the Wharf Street area of Leicester, and was later remembered by many locals as 'the Slums'.

---

1 Marriage certificate of Joseph Rockley Merrick and Mary Jane Potterton (via my.ancestry.co.uk.lindaholmes55).

After WWII the principal area of unfit housing in Leicester was indeed situated in this region east of Wharf Street, but before the war there had been other areas of the city which were considered to be far more depraved. But because these districts were cleared pre-1939, their existence had faded from the memory of many of the recent local inhabitants of Leicester, which is why the Wharf Street neighbourhood is, somewhat incorrectly, remembered as the epicentre of Leicester's slum districts by modern day historians.[2]

Lee Street as it was in the 1800s does not exist anymore, apart from a very small section now known as Lower Lee Street. Number 50, where Joseph and Mary Jane Merrick had settled, would have been where the Lee Street multi-storey car park is now located.[3] Good quality housing was available for rent in Lee Street during the Merricks' time there, and was often advertised as having 'both kinds of water', meaning 'soft and hard'.

This was a period when water remained a scarce and an unreliable utility. Spring water was hard and moderately safe to drink, but came from relatively shallow wells and was liable to contamination from leaking or overflowing cesspools, often being the cause of local outbreaks of typhoid or cholera. Hard water was not useful for the weekly wash, as it curdled the soap, so many good quality houses came with large rainwater storage tanks to collect water for the use of washing clothes.[4]

In one local newspaper, the *Leicester Journal*, the houses in Lee Street, specifically numbers 86, 88, 90 and 92, were advertised with two-storey workshops, a kitchen and a yard and hard and soft

---

2   *The Slums of Leicester* by Ned Newitt (2009).

3   Built in the 1960s, Lee Circle and its fellow car parks which circle the city centre were an attempt to cope with the growing number of cars coming into Leicester. It is said to have been the first automatic multi-storey car park in Europe and it housed, at the time, what was reputed to be the largest supermarket in the UK, the first Tesco outside London. It also hosted a bowling alley and for a short period Lee Circle was the place to be seen. Information from www2.le.ac.uk/conference/previous/curiouser/eccentric-leicester-tour/lee-circle-car-park-le1.

4   *Victorian and Edwardian Services (Houses) 1850-1914.*

running water.[5] A few doors down, at numbers 78, 80, 82 and 84, yards and gardens could be found, all again with hard and soft water pumps.[6]

During the first few months of their marriage, Joseph Merrick was working full time as a warehouseman.[7] Working hours were long, so to relax many people went out and visited the local theatres. There were plenty of music halls around to delight in. One such theatre in Leicester was Steven's New Circus, on the Fleur de Lis grounds in Belgrave Gate, a very short walk from the Merricks' abode. Steven's New Circus was a large wooden building which could hold up to two thousand people. In 1862 it was renamed the Alhambra Music Hall, refitted with a new stage, and opened every evening at 7pm. The cheaper seats in the gallery cost tuppence,[8] a small extravagance when you consider the average earnings for a warehouse man in the 1860s was only 25s.[9] The Merricks could probably just afford the cost, but not on a regular basis. There were also plenty of public houses in and around the Wharf Street neighbourhood, and two of these stood in Lee Street, The Lion and Lamb[10] and The Painter's Arms.[11]

According to Joseph Dare, a domestic missionary working amongst Leicester's poor, there was an abundance of highly questionable working class pursuits. In his annual Reports of the Leicester Domestic Mission, written between 1846 and 1877, a whole range of activities came under fire. Dog fighting, pigeon flying, rat hunting and the rat pit, bare knuckle fighting, swimming nude and general frivolous activity in the Abbey Meadows area of Leicester came to Dare's attention.[12] One such 'frivolous' activity was reported in the

5   *Leicester Journal*, 21 February 1862.
6   *Leicester Journal*, 11 September 1863.
7   1861 Census.
8   arthurlloyd.co.uk.
9   www.logicmgmt.com/1876/living/occupations.htm.
10 *Leicester Chronicle*, 5 January 1856.
11 *Leicester Journal*, 10 February 1854.
12 *Working Class Life in Leicester: The Joseph Dare Report.* Edited by Barry Haynes (1991).

Leicester Chronicle:

> 'Sunday bathing near the pasture and Abbey Meadow'

To the Editor of the Leicester Chronicle.

Sir, - Allow me to call your attention to the disgraceful proceedings which occur every Sunday during the summer months in the Pasture and Abbey Meadow. Complaints have been made for years, both by people living in the neighbourhood, and also by pedestrians from other parts of the town; in fact, that beautiful promenade is completely closed to the respectable inhabitants, except they are prepared to mingle with crowds of men in a state of nudity, who shamelessly expose their persons in the presence of both males and females; and there are, unfortunately, even females who, by frequenting these and other such places, have familiarised their minds which such scenes, and consequently lost all that belongs to womanly purity. I do not think that sanitary considerations require the continuance of such immoral practices. There are times and places more suitable for the necessary ablutions without offending public decency in the manner thus described. I also think that the inhabitants of the mother part of the town have a right to be heard in such a case, for the sake of their wives and daughters, as well as against the closing of that only place of recreation in that part of town.

Would it not be sufficient to allow full scope to the bathers until nine o'clock, and after that time instruct the police to prevent any further intrusion on that day.

Hoping you will give this insertion.

I remain yours
A Moral Reformer[13]

There was one activity the whole family could enjoy: the bi-annual fair in Humberstone Gate was free entertainment which everyone could delight in. The original May Fair was granted on 2 April 1473 by Edward IV, brother of the much-maligned King Richard III. In the grant, Edward IV noted the fair would be 'free to all, including strangers to the town. Free from tolls, stall age, pickage [sic] and other customs belonging to the King and his heirs [sic].' [14] Originally,

13 *Leicester Chronicle*, 30 July 1859.
14 *Medieval Leicester* by Charles Billson (1920).

the Fair was to be held three days before the feast of St Philip and St James, on the First of May, and for three days after. Later the Fair turned into the Great Pleasure Fairs, and later still became the Leicester May and October Fairs. On 10 May 1862, the May Fair was advertised in the *Leicester Mercury*:

Notice is hereby given

That the Leicester May fair will be held on Monday the 12th day of May next, for the sale of Horses, Beasts and sheep; and on Tuesday, the 13th and the following days, for the sale of cheese.

By Order

Saml Stone, Town Clark [sic]
Welford Place. April 23rd 1862[15]

The stalls and shows occupied a strip of wasteland on the south side of Humberstone Gate called No Man's Land, and the booths overflowed in to East Gates and Cheapside. The stalls would sell goods and novelties, with a cattle fair held on the Monday,[16] and a cheese fair which was held on 13 May in the Market Place. This specific year, 1862, the dairies were congratulated on their superb cheese and dairy products, and some of the farmers made at least 76s to 79s, a tidy sum of money.

In Humberstone Gate there was always a menagerie and theatre,[17] although in 1862 there doesn't seem to be any newspaper reports of a menagerie attending the carnival, and it was reported in the *Leicester Chronicle* that:

This year 1862 especially saw the lack of shows, bazaars and similar exhibitions although it was still visited by a large crowd of people.[18]

The October Fair of 1862 was a complete contrast. Edmond's Menagerie, previously known as Wombwell's, had arrived in Leicester on Thursday, 9 October 1862. The procession consisted of

15 *Leicester Mercury*, 10 May 1862.
16 *Leicester Chronicle*, 17 May 1862.
17 *Medieval Leicester* by Charles Billson (1920).
18 *Leicester Chronicle*, 17 May 1862.

twelve caravans, a band which was being drawn by a dwarf elephant, two camels and a dromedary. The menagerie entered the Market Place through Leicester's principal thoroughfares of Highcross Street and High Street, but unfortunately due to the tremendous size of some of the vehicles and narrowness of some of Leicester's roads, a street lamp in Hotel Street which was suspended from Messrs Cort and Paul was purposely bent to accommodate the parade. The spectacle proceeded on its route along Wellington Street, Waterloo Street and London Road, all the way down to Humberstone Gate. A report in the *Leicester Chronicle* goes on to say that 'thousands of men, women and children assembled in different parts of the route to witness the unusual arrivals'.[19]

The Pleasure Fair closed the following Monday, 13 October. However, Edmond's Menagerie returned to Leicester during its circuit tour, having just been to the south Leicestershire town of Market Harborough on Tuesday, 21 October 1862, and the nearby village of Kibworth the following day. The menagerie arrived in Leicester on Thursday, 23 October and settled at the Campbell Street ground near the Campbell Street railway station, before heading off on the last leg of its tour to Ibstock, Whitwick and Melbourne, finally arriving at Ripley on Tuesday, 28 October.[20]

It was at the May Great Pleasure Fair in 1862 that a terrible accident befell Mary Jane Merrick, according to Joseph Carey Merrick in his autobiography, which he believed contributed to his affliction:

> The deformity which I am now exhibiting was caused by my mother being frightened by an Elephant: My mother was going along the street when a procession of Animals was passing by, there was a terrible crush of people to see them and unfortunately she was pushed under the Elephant's feet which frightened her very much; this occurring during a time of pregnancy was cause of my deformity.[21]

---

19 *Leicester Chronicle*, 11 October 1862.

20 *Leicester Journal*, 17 October 1862.

21 *The Autobiography of Joseph Carey Merrick*
    (See Appendix One).

On Saturday, 17 May 1862, the *Leicestershire Mercury* reported a disturbance in Humberstone Gate during the Fair. Three youths named Smith, Brown and Raven were charged with pushing people about the fairground. The article goes on:

> Inspector Smith stated that he was standing on the Coalhill about half-past or a quarter to 11 o'clock last night, and saw the three defendants and another come round the corner into Humberstone Gate, Smith and Brown got their hands out and were pushing people.[22]

Although the article doesn't mention any kind of animal which may have been in the way and frightened the spectators, Inspector Smith continues:

> There were two young women among them, and they knocked backwards, and a child one of them had flew out of her arms, and was hurt against a stall.[23]

It is not suggested that the babe in arms was Joseph Carey Merrick as he wasn't born then, but the article reports that a commotion did take place. If Mary Jane had been caught up in this incident, she may later had combined her memory of it with seeing elephants at the menagerie at the later October Fair of 1862 and used it to explain her son's condition.[24]

According to one source, Mary Jane did believe in 'Maternal Impression',[25] a theory which thrived all the way through the Middle Ages to the Renaissance, and well into the 19th century until it started being doubted by physicians. Physician and anatomist William Hunter concluded after his clinical study that "a pregnant woman's emotions were unrelated to vascular birthmarks."[26] By

---

22 *Leicestershire Mercury*, 17 May 1862.

23 Ibid.

24 *The True History of the Elephant Man* by Michael Howell and Peter Ford (Kindle Edition 2011).

25 *Measured by Soul: The Life of Joseph Carey Merrick (also known as 'The Elephant Man')* by Jeanette Sitton and Mae Siuwai Stroshane (2012).

26 Vascular Anomalies Centre (VAC) History (bostonchildrens.org).

the end of the 19th century Maternal Impression was canned as nonsense by the medical community.

On 5 August 1862, just seven months after getting married, Mary Jane gave birth to her 'perfect baby boy'[27] at the marital home of 50 Lee Street. The child was named Joseph Carey Merrick. Joseph was one of the most popular boys' names in Victorian England,[28] and he was probably named after his father. Carey came from the Particular Baptist Minister William Carey, founder of the Baptist Ministry movement, who also became minister of the Harvey Lane Baptist Church in Leicester in 1789.[29] The church has since been demolished along with his cottage, although a museum dedicated to William Carey can be visited at the Central Baptist Church on Charles Street in Leicester.[30]

Whether Joseph was born prematurely or Mary Jane was pregnant when she said "I do", Joseph was born a healthy little boy.

It must still have been a worry for the young parents, in an age when infant mortality was high. Most Victorian women gave birth at home. Those who could afford it, the middle and upper classes, hired a nurse who would stay with them for a period of three months, but having a midwife was dependant on finances, so help often mostly came from family and friends.[31] Having her mother-in-law, Sarah, just a few doors down must have been very reassuring to Mary Jane. Her own mother had died in the late summer of 1861,[32] just a few months before Mary Jane and Joseph had married, and her sisters were making independent lives for themselves. Victorian England was a very difficult time to give birth, with little or no aftercare for the working class, and the new mother was expected to be back to her home duties within a few days. And with the absence of a doctor

27 *The True History of the Elephant Man* by Michael Howell and Peter Ford (Kindle Edition 2011).

28 www.baby2c.com.

29 www.wmcarey.edu/carey/leicester/memories.pdf.

30 www.central-baptist.org.uk.

31 logicmgmt.com/1876.

32 Death register.

during birth, women who did suffer complications often went unnoticed.

New mothers were traditionally honoured with a tea party after the baby's birth. This was a celebration for female friends and family only.[33] Gentleman never called upon the new mother; they paid their respects to the father, and as The Painter's Arms was directly opposite his home, it would have been the ideal place for the new father Joseph Merrick to go and 'wet the baby's head'. The ladies, of course, would bestow the new mother with homemade gifts, more often that not useful items such as nappies, clothing and bathing supplies, but the grandmother would give something silver.[34] Traditional Victorian silver gifts included a silver sixpence which would be kept as an initial nest egg for the child, silver cups and napkin rings. The giving of a silver Apostle spoon has its roots in the Tudor period and is thought to be the origin of the phrase 'born with a silver spoon in its mouth'.[35]

In addition to Mary Jane's mother-in-law Sarah living close by, just seven houses along at 65 Lee Street lived the Green family, comprising John Thomas Green and his wife Emma, and their children, Jane, Emily and William. Emma Green was of a similar age to Mary Jane, and was the daughter of the landlord at The Painter's Arms. With three children of her own, she was experienced in the labours of childbearing, and may well have assisted Sarah Merrick in giving comfort to Mary Jane in the period before and after her son's birth.

During the years in which the Merricks lived at Lee Street, Joseph probably played with the Green's children. William Green was born in 1862, the same year as Joseph, and it is most likely the pair would have played together in the alleyways and passageways adjoining Lee Street. Children like Joseph and William played in the streets with homemade wooden toys, hoops, marbles and skipping ropes.[36]

33 www.victoriana.com/partyplanning.html.

34 Ibid

35 www.christeningsilver.com/christening-gifts-a-history.

36 www.thebowesmuseum.org.uk.

Marbles were usually made out of clay balls, nuts or pebbles. Hoops and sticks consisted of hitting a wooden hoop with a stick to keep it rolling as you ran alongside.[37]

Children would be shepherded out straight after breakfast, which generally included porridge made with milk, toasted bread with a little butter and preserves.[38] After an exciting morning causing havoc in the neighbouring districts, Joseph and William would return to their homes for lunch and a wash. Joseph would have eaten sandwiches with paste or leftover meat, watercress and cheese, or soup made from meat and vegetables.[39]

Straight after lunch, Joseph and William would go straight back out to play. The two boys would amuse themselves with games such as 'Follow the leader' or 'Oh great King or Queen', where one player stands on a stool or box or anything which represents a throne. The other participants must pass before the throne one by one; each child stops in front of the King and must say "Oh great King, I worship thee and bow down before thee" in a very solemn manner. The King will then make the ugliest faces and strange poses to make his subjects laugh. The player who laughs takes the role of the next King/Queen.[40]

However, the fun didn't last forever, and in Leicester you always had to be tucked up in bed before the '9 o'clock osses'.[41] A Leicester tale not dissimilar to the 'bogeyman', but told to children through generations and generations, linked itself to the night farm labourers who would come into the town with their horse and carts to collect waste products to use as manure on the surrounding farmland. These were called the night soil men. Leicester had a local bylaw which stated that the night soil men could not come into the town to collect the waste until after 9 o'clock at night, and as child labour was so cheap, any child caught wandering the streets of the town

---

37 www.judgeslodging.org.uk.

38 www.logicmgmt.com/1876/living/occupations.htm

39 Ibid.

40 www.judgeslodging.org.uk/resourses/victorianoutdoorgames.

41 "Osses" - slang for Horses.

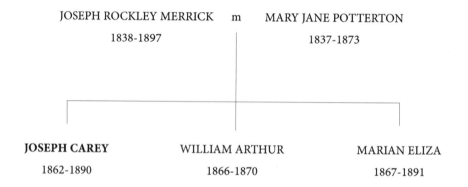

JOSEPH ROCKLEY MERRICK   m   MARY JANE POTTERTON

1838-1897   1837-1873

JOSEPH CAREY   WILLIAM ARTHUR   MARIAN ELIZA

1862-1890   1866-1870   1867-1891

after 9 o'clock would also be collected up and taken back to farms as labour.[42]

By 1865 Mary Jane was pregnant again, and Joseph Sr must have seen an advert in the *Leicester Journal* advertising property auctions at The Craven Arms Hotel on Humberstone Gate in Leicester. One of the properties was Lot 4, messuages[43] or tenements with palisades, gardens in the front, yards, buildings and back gardens. One of the plots included 119 Upper Brunswick Street.[44] Joseph Sr bought the property and soon the Merricks found themselves on the move. According to plans of dwellings in Taylor Street, which linked to Upper Brunswick, these houses were two bedroomed, and had a kitchen and a living room.[45] Things were looking like they were going in the right direction for the Merricks, as Joseph Sr gained a new job as a stoker on a steam engine in a cotton factory.[46]

Mary Jane gave birth to their second son on 8 January 1866.[47] They named him William Arthur, possibly after Mary Jane's father William.

While the Merricks had moved to Upper Brunswick Street, the Greens had remained in Lee Street and moved a few doors down the road into number 40. The Greens had nine children altogether, but by 1870 their relationship had severely broken down. John was drinking heavily, and by 1874 had embarked on an affair. Knowing Emma would never divorce him, his hatred for her intensified so dramatically that in 1876 he purchased a hand gun, with the intention of shooting his wife.[48] The results were reported in a local

---

42 The '9 o'clock horses' - Abbey Pumping Station Museum, Leicester.

43 A dwelling house together with its outbuildings, curtilage and the adjacent land to its use (via www.thefreedictionary.com/messuage).

44 *Leicester Journal*, 9 June 1865.

45 *Home Sweet Home: A Century of Leicester Housing 1814-1914* by Dennis Calow (2007).

46 *The True History of the Elephant Man* by Michael Howell and Peter Ford (Kindle Edition 2011).

47 Birth certificate of William A Merrick.

48 *Foul Deeds and Suspicious Deaths around Leicester* by Kevin Turton (Kindle Edition 2005).

newspaper:

> PC Kendall said that on Monday, about 5 O'clock, he was in Belgrave Gate, with constable Hickinbottom, when a boy came up and told them that Tom [sic] Green had shot his wife.

> PC Hickinbottom said he accompanied last witness to prisoner's house and saw the prisoner standing in the doorway. He said 'I am the man' before he had been addressed. He was told to go inside, and in his right hand pocket was found the pistol produced, which was warm, and bearing the nipple produced. Before he was charged he remarked 'that's what I done it with'. The cap and bullet were subsequently found and the prisoner, on being charged with 'grievous bodily harm' replied 'grievous bodily harm – is that all. She dared me to do it'. The deceased was then lying in a pool of blood surrounded by neighbours, and upon his return to the house he saw Dr Meadows in attendance.

> By permission of Dr Meadows, he asked the deceased when was the last time the prisoner threatened her before and after it had been repeated several times she replied 'yesterday'. She also said 'My husband shot me'.

> During that time, she repeated several times 'Oh I am dying'.[49]

Emma Green died at the Leicester Infirmary on Tuesday, 22 August 1876. John was convicted of her murder, and was hanged on 20 December 1876 in Leicester, his executioner being the noted William Marwood.[50]

Just over a year after the birth of young William Merrick, a little sister to he and Joseph came along. On 28 September 1867 Mary Jane and Joseph Sr were blessed with a daughter, Marian Eliza.[51] Sadly, the joy of Marian's birth may have been over shadowed by the fact that she was born less abled, for according to her death certificate Marian had been 'a cripple from birth'.[52] An anonymous letter published in

---

49 *The Leicester Chronicle and Leicestershire Mercury*, 26 August 1876.

50 *Foul Deeds and Suspicious Deaths around Leicester* by Kevin Turton (Kindle Edition 2005).

51 Birth certificate of Marian Eliza Merrick.

52 Death Certificate of Marian Eliza Merrick. Registration District of Barrow-upon-Soar.

the *Illustrated Leicester Chronicle* on 27 December 1930 claimed that Mary Jane was herself also a cripple,[53] this though has never been proven. It was common in the census records to register in the far right hand column whether the resident was crippled, deaf, dumb or even an imbecile, yet this was never recorded against Mary Jane's entries.

It must have been an extremely happy time for Joseph to have a little sister and brother. Helping his mother with the babies, singing nursery rhymes and reading stories to keep them quiet whilst Mary Jane got on with her chores, although some of those stories may have been a little gruesome, as is sometimes the way with little boys. Sinister folklore stories were popular in the 1800s, with one local Leicester story being very menacing, the tale of 'Black Annis'. Black Annis, or Anna, was said to be in the habit of crouching among the branches of the old pollard oak (the last remnant of the forest) which grew over the cleft of the rock over the mouth of her cave or "bower", ever ready to spring like a wild beast on any stray children passing below.[54] Maybe a bit too disturbing for five-year-old Joseph to be telling his little brother and sister, but older siblings do tend to enjoy scaring younger brothers and sisters, and I doubt Joseph was any different.

It was around this time, in 1867, when Joseph was five years of age, that he suffered a severe fall which caused his hip to become infected, leaving him being unable to walk without the use of a cane.[55]

There were plenty of hazards around the Victorian home that caused accidents, and the common staircase was one of them. Houses were put up quickly, and one area of design which was overlooked was the staircase, sometimes too narrow or too steep, with irregular steps, a child could easily fall running up and down.

---

53 *The True History of the Elephant Man* by Michael Howell and Peter Ford (Kindle Edition 2011).

54 'County Folk-Lore. Leicestershire and Rutland' by Charles James Billson F.R.H.S (William Kelly) in the *Leicester Chronicle* of 3 October 1874.

55 *Measured by Soul: The Life of Joseph Carey Merrick (also known as 'The Elephant Man')* by Jeanette Sitton and Mae Siuwai Stroshane (2012).

As one newspaper reported in 1865:

> On Tuesday last, an accident occurred to a little girl, about eight years of age, the daughter of James Morton, who is in the employ of Mr J H Ward, resides near the Wharf. It appears that the child had come into town to get some hose to seam, and was in the act of bringing them down the stairs when her feet slipped, and she accidently fractured her leg. She was taken to the surgery of Mr Griffs, where the proper means were used to reduce the fracture, and she is now progressing favourably.[56]

Joseph's fall at five years old coincides with his memories regarding his afflictions, commenting in his autobiography: "It was not perceived much at birth, but began to develop itself when at the age of 5 years."[57]

It may have been Joseph's fall which first triggered his disease, and his accident is similar to the 1938 case of another young boy who then suffered a sudden onset of disease. Harry Raymond Eastlack, a healthy active five-year-old boy from Philadelphia in the United States, was out playing with his sister when he broke his leg. Not long after, bone growths began to develop on the muscles in Harry's thigh. The condition began to spread around his body, and by his mid-twenties his whole vertebra had fused together. By the time Harry died, just four days before his 40th birthday, his body has completely ossified. He died of pneumonia, his jaw had locked, leaving only his lips to move. Harry suffered an extremely rare condition called Fibrodysplasia Ossificans Progressiva, a mutation of the body's repair mechanism which causes fibrous tissue, muscle, tendons and ligaments to ossify when damaged,[58] and affects approximately one in two million people. Bridges of extra bone develop across joints, progressively restricting movement and forming a second skeleton that imprisons the body in bone.[59]

---

56 *The Leicester Chronicle and Leicestershire Mercury*, 5 January 1867.

57 *The Autobiography of Joseph Carey Merrick*
    (See Appendix One).

58 Disturbing Disorders: FOP (Stone man syndrome) on www.thechirurgeons apprentice.com.

However, a recently-found newspaper article written in 1889 suggests that Joseph's afflictions didn't start to appear until he was in his teens:

> He is decidedly short and rather slight and speaks in a very intelligent manner. His accent shows plainly that he is not a Cockney. As a matter of fact, Merrick was born in Leicester some 29 or 30 years back. The disease only began to manifest itself noticeably when he was in his teens.

It must be noted that it is only assumed the reason that Joseph walked with a stick was because of a fall, and there are no surviving medical records to tell us why Joseph had a limp when he was a child. In Victorian England, there was a crippling childhood illness known as osteoarticular tuberculosis, which is related to tuberculosis, a condition in which the tuberculosis bacillus directly infects the bones and joints. In children, the joints are richly supplied with blood, and this makes them more vulnerable to a number of infections that are carried in the circulatory system. Unfortunately, in Victorian England this condition was not linked to consumption,[60] and during these years tuberculosis was rife in Leicester. Adolescents, young adults and children were struck down, and it was this disease which claimed the lives of three of Joseph's cousins.

The problems and pain his hip would have caused him as a young boy are unthinkable, and if you were able to afford it, pain relief could be bought over the counter in the form of commercial mixtures and formulations containing laudanum and tinctures of opium. Opium was widely used to control diarrhoea, coughs, pain. One of the most popular remedies, introduced in 1857, was Collis Browne's Chlorodyne, which according to the advertisement '... assuages pain of every kind, affords a calm, refreshing sleep without

---

59 www.ifopa.org.

60 *Health, Medicine and Society in Victorian England* by Mary Wilson Carpenter (2010).

61 The Victorian Web: Victorian Drug Use.

62 *Leicester Trade Directory 1870.*

headache, and invigorates the nervous system when exhausted'.[61]

In 1868, just a couple of years after Joseph's fall and despite the hardship of bringing up a family of three children with two of them being disabled, the family moved to 161 Birstall Street. Joseph Sr had set himself up as a haberdashery proprietor at 37 Russell Square in the Wharf Street area of the Leicester.[62] The business was obviously doing well, as the properties in Birstall Street were a little more lavish than those the Merricks were used to. An advert in the *Leicester Journal* on 7 May 1869 showcased an auction for dwellings in Birstall Street. These houses had parlours, living rooms, kitchens, cellars, three bedrooms, hard and soft water pumps, complete gas fittings and with no water rates,[63] these homes must have seemed like pure heaven. With three bedrooms, the boys could share one, Marian would have her own room, and their parents would have the privacy many married couples craved.

Apart from being a full time mother to three children, Mary Jane Merrick may have helped out at the haberdashery shop whilst her husband continued to work in the cotton mills, possibly with help from son William, who was nearly five years old, and also Joseph if he wasn't at school. As an educated woman herself, and a Sunday school teacher, Mary Jane would have wanted the best education for her children. Under the Education Act of 1870, local authorities were required to set up school boards to provide elementary education for children aged 5 to 13 years. It has been suggested that Mary Jane sent Joseph to Syston Street Board School,[64] located in the street adjacent to where the family was living at that time. Although Syston Street was the first board school in the area, and within a stone's throw of Joseph's house, it wasn't opened until 1874. Instead, Mary Jane may have sent her two eldest children, Joseph and William, to

---

63 *Leicester Journal*, 7 May 1869.

64 *Measured by Soul: The Life of Joseph Carey Merrick (also known as 'The Elephant Man')* by Jeanette Sitton and Mae Siuwai Stroshane (2012).

65 *The City of Leicester: Schedule of Schools* (www.british-history.ac.uk/vch/leics/vol4/pp335-337).

66 Archdeacon Lane Baptist Chapel Records (Leicester, Leicestershire & Rutland Record Office: N/B/179/101-169 (DE2380)).

the type of school in which she herself had been educated, a National School. Leicester's first National School was founded in 1814, and situated near St Nicholas' Church on Holy Bones, St Nicholas' Street in the town.[65] The school has long since gone, but St Nicholas' Church remains and is now next to the Holiday Inn Hotel on St Nicholas' Circle.

Alternatively, Mary Jane may have sent them to one of the local church schools. Archdeacon Lane Baptist Church was where the family worshipped,[66] and it had an infant school attached which was opened in 1838. Sunday Schools were set up to meet the needs of poor children, especially those whose parents had sent them out to work. It is not suggested that Joseph had been sent out to the mills to earn a crust, but he may have gone with his mother when she was teaching. In 1835, five Baptist churches and one congregational Sunday School established the Leicestershire and Rutland Sunday School Union, which had twenty schools in Leicester affiliated to it by 1840. Girls were taught reading, sewing and seaming, and boys reading, writing and accounting.[67]

Even with his crippled and diseased hip, Joseph probably didn't stand out amongst his peers, and, unless, his facial deformity had deteriorated badly by this point, he probably didn't become a subject of ridicule. The widespread childhood disease of the 20th century, rickets, caused twisted and bent limbs. Rickets was linked to many of the large industrial towns and cities, of which Leicester was obviously one.

By the winter of 1870, when Joseph was eight years old, William four and Marian three, an epidemic of scarlet fever swept through the schools in Leicester, a dreadful and potentially fatal disease with deadly consequences. The epidemic was at its highest in the old overcrowded part of the town, and once the initial symptoms had passed, especially if it was a mild case, parents sent their children

---

67 Ibid.

68 www.nhs.uk/conditions/scarlet-fever/pages/introduction.aspx.

69 *Leicester Chronicle*, 19 November 1870.

back to school or let them play out on the streets. However, this was one of the most infectious stages of the illness, with weeping open spots, coughing and sneezing, and cross infection was inevitable.[68]

In November 1870, Councillor Crossley stated there were 700 to 1,000 cases in Leicester,[69] and sadly William Arthur Merrick, Joseph's little brother, became one of those statistics when he fell dangerously ill. All his mother could do to nurse him was to keep him cool, and comfort him.

William would have started with sickness, a headache, shivering and a sore throat. These symptoms were followed by a rash all over the body which was mostly visible on the neck and shoulders, and a white fur coating his tongue, which gives the disease its nickname of 'strawberry tongue'.[70] The worst cases of scarlet fever ultimately lead to death. Symptoms appear very quickly, breathing being loud and difficult, the temperature very high, and the child may convulse and hallucinate. There was no treatment for scarlet fever during this period as antibiotics had not been discovered, and because of this it was one of the most feared diseases in Victorian England. Death could occur within one to two days, and sometimes before the characterised rash had appeared.

All Mary Jane could do was keep William in bed and mop his brow with cold water to help with his temperature. She may have given the following mixture if she was unable to obtain medical advice, common of the period:

> 36 grains of sesquicarbonate of ammonia
> ½ ounce of simple syrup
> 6 ounces of water would have been given
>> every three hours and the throat kept clear with the mop.[71]

Sadly all this proved useless, and on 21 December 1870, Joseph Merrick's brother William died. Mary Jane went to the registry office the following day to notify them of her son's death, and signed the

70 patient.info/health/scarlet-fever-leaflet.

71 *Domestic Medicine, Section 4: Eruptive Fever in Cassells Household Guide* (n.d. - c.1880s).

72 Plot Us 22 C u25333, Welford Road Cemetery.

certificate with an 'X'. He was buried on Christmas Day 1870 aged only four years.[72]

Ginns funeral directors, now Ginns and Gutteridge, may have performed the funeral. Based on High Cross Street, Ginns funerals are listed in the local trade directory for Leicester in 1855:

Ann Ginns and Sons
Coffin makers and funeral undertakers
55 High Cross Street
Leicester
Funeral completely furnished in town and
County on the most reasonable terms.
N.B. Superior hearses and mourning coaches for hire.
The oldest establishment in the Trade.[73]

It has been suggested that tragedy first struck the family much earlier, in 1864, with the death of a son called John Thomas Merrick from smallpox. According to a relatively recent article in the *Leicester Mercury*, John Thomas died at only three-months-old, and is buried in Welford Road Cemetery.[74] The same child appears in a recent book about Joseph Merrick - "John Thomas born 21st April 1864 and died of small pox at only 3 months",[75] and a new memorial erected on 10 May 2014[76] by the Friends of Joseph Carey Merrick at Mary Jane Potterton's grave also states John Thomas was her son.[77]

Although there was indeed a John Thomas Merrick born on 21 April 1864, he was born to Jane Merrick of 11 Lee Street,[78] not to Mary Jane and Joseph Merrick of 50 Lee Street. He did indeed die at

73 *Leicester Daily Mercury*, 7 February 1876.

74 *Leicester Mercury Online*, 17 December 2012.

75 *Measured by Soul: The Life of Joseph Carey Merrick (also known as 'The Elephant Man')* by Jeanette Sitton and Mae Siuwai Stroshane (2012).

76 www.fojcm.com/#!events/c1339.

77 Plot uS 22 C 30268, Welford Road Cemetery.

78 Birth Certificate for John Thomas Merrick.

79 Death certificate of John Thomas Merrick; 1871 Census.

80 Plot uA 303 C u14355, Welford Road Cemetery.

three months of age, at his home at 4 Lee Street,[79] and is buried also in Welford Cemetery, away from the Potterton grave.[80] There are no birth records at the General Register Office to connect Mary Jane and Joseph Merrick to this child, and there doesn't seem to be any connection beyond the coincidental name and address.

Mary Jane continued to work in the haberdashery shop after William passed away. Just before his death in December 1870, Joseph Sr advertised their Birstall Street home as being for sale. An advert appears in the *Leicester Chronicle* in November 1870:

> Freehold land and Houses, to be sold by auction by Messrs Porter and Taylor. At the Bull's Head Hotel, Market Place on Thursday 24th November 1870 at six for seven o'clock in the evening.[81]

The article goes onto to read:

> Lot 6: A messuage situate and being 161 Birstall Street, Leicester occupied by Mr Merrick.[82]

The family continued to live there until at least July 1872,[83] then sometime between 1872 and 1873 the house in Birstall Street was sold and the Merricks went to live in their new home at 51 Cranbourne Street,[84] which was located at the back of Birstall Street.

The hours would have been long for Mary Jane in the haberdashery shop in Russell Square. She would have started work at 6.00am in the summer and 8.00am in the winter, not closing until well into the evening. The shop would have been open on Saturdays, with half day Sunday closing.[85] Having a husband working full time, and with two disabled children to look after and bring up, it must have been challenging, but with a successful business and a comfortable income Mary Jane may have been able to afford a 'maid of all work',

81 *Leicester Chronicle*, 12 November 1870.

82 Ibid

83 Communion & Members Register for Archdeacon Lane Baptist Church, Nos. 287 & 288. July 1872.

84 Death Certificate of Mary Jane Merrick.

85 logicmgmt.com/1876/overview/Victorian shopping/shops.htm.

86 Ibid.

maybe a young local girl seeking her first employment who would undertake all the household duties whilst Mary Jane and Joseph Sr went to work. Small local shops were often staffed by family, and perhaps an apprentice.

Large or small, bright and airy, decorated with the goods on sale or dark and dingy, these shops catered for all social classes.[86] 37 Russell Square, where the haberdashery was located, was obviously quite a large premises. Prior to Joseph Sr taking the shop, it was owned by a dressmaker, and in 1851, ropemakers Lee resided there with ten members of the family living under the same roof.[87] However, even with a successful business and a better standard of living, the Merrick family could not be saved from one more tragedy, and one which was to devastate young Joseph.

Spring in 1873 came late, and May was a particularly cold month as polar winds swept through the country. The warmer days brought overcast skies, heavy rain and low temperatures. With average temperatures of 12°C and frosts, May was one of the coldest months of the first part of 1873,[88] and must have been the saddest for the Merrick family. Mary Jane fell ill, and on 29 May 1873, just three years after the death of her second son, the mother of Joseph Carey Merrick died of bronchial pneumonia at her home in Cranbourne Street.[89]

The flooding of houses and the damp conditions, together with the cold temperatures, would not have helped his mother's condition. Victorian doctors understood the pathology of pneumonia as involving the inflammation of living tissue, promoted by the predisposing inherited acquired factors of damp, cold, dusts and other lung diseases. Bronchitis in most cases is caused by a bacteria or virus, predisposing factors such as prior lung disease, smoking, emphysema, tuberculosis, air pollution and adverse weather

---

87 1851 Census.

88 *Leicester Journal*, 6 June 1873.

89 Death Certificate of Mary Jane Merrick.

90 *Oxford Journals: Social History of Medicine. Epidemics and Infections of the Nineteenth Century* (www.ncbi.nlm.nih.gov.DMC/articles/PMC2663978).

conditions,[90] and flooding was a particular problem in Leicester, as this letter in the *Leicester Journal* confirms:

A WORKING MAN ON THE STATE OF DRAINAGE OF LEICESTER

TO THE EDITOR OF THE LEICESTER JOURNAL

Sir, - I have got another person to write this foe [sic] me, being no scholar myself, but I am very much injured by the state of the drains, I live in the low parts of your town, and I depend for my living upon the sale of milk and butter. A few days ago my cellar was rapidly filled with filly water rushing up the drains and spoiling everything in the cellar. The milk and cream were ruined. I took it with good heart, and I cleaned all up well, and hoped for the best; but about two o'clock four mornings after we had to go down to the cellars where the milk was floating in the puncheons and turned sour and bad by the stink of the mess that came up the sewer. A few more such troubles and I must give up all hope of getting a living.

Sir, its seems very hard that not only we, but hundreds besides, of poor men here should be flooded out every time a flush of rain falls. If it does no harm to their goods, it does harm to their health, and I think it is the reason of so many people being in bad health in these parts.

Sir, everybody says, as the water could be quite easily let off. If the plan of the surveyor was followed. It does not seem right that some of us should be half ruined if it can be helped, and I am confident that the people cannot enjoy good health as long as their cellars are flooded with stinking filth.

Sir, I hope the corporation will cause these low parts to be drained, for it is doing great damage.

A HARD WORKING MAN, THAT HAS NEVER YET TAKEN A PENNY FROM POOR'S RATES.[91]

It wasn't until 1881 that the Improvement Bill gave Leicester Corporation the power to build essential flood defences to protect the town and the outlying regions.

---

91 *Leicester Journal*, 20 June 1873.
92 Death Certificate of Mary Jane Merrick.
93 Plot uS 22 c u30268, Welford Road Cemetery.
94 Death Certificate of Mary Jane Merrick.

At only 36 years of age,[92] Mary Jane was buried on 1 June 1873 in a common grave in Welford Road Cemetery Leicester alongside her late son William Arthur.[93]

Present at her death was Catherine Taylor, who was living at the time at number 58 Cranbourne Street.[94] Catherine would go on to marry Mary Jane's brother George, and it was Catherine who would witness the suicide attempt by Mary Jane's father William Potterton in 1884.

Although Mary Jane and William's grave was originally a common one, in later years the plot would be registered as a family grave. Mary Jane was joined by her sister Elizabeth after her untimely death in 1877, followed nine years later by their cousin Ann in 1888, and finally in 1902, John Potterton, the husband of her sister Elizabeth and her cousin Ann.[95]

After the death of his wife, Joseph Merrick Sr moved out of the family home in Cranbourne Street. It is not clear whether he sold or rented the house out, or the exact date he relocated, but with his two surviving children, Joseph Jr and Marian, Joseph Sr moved to Luke Street,[96] only two streets away from his brother Charles' home on Churchgate.

In April 1872, the houses on Luke Street were advertised in the *Leicester Journal* as having an entry yard, a garden, two storey workshops and out buildings.[97] Living not too far from his brother, Joseph Sr may have relied on his sister-in-law Jane, or even his mother Sarah, to help out with his children whilst he went out to work as a stoker.

---

95 Welford Road Cemetery records: Mary Jane Merrick (Plot uS 22 C u30268); William Arthur Merrick (Plot uS 22 C u25333); Elizabeth Potterton (Plot uS 22 C u39421); Ann Potterton (Plot uS 22 F u61683); John Potterton (Plot uS 22 Fu91836).

96 Communion & Members Register for Archdeacon Lane Baptist Church, No. 258, July 1873.

97 *Leicester Journal*, 5 April 1982.

98 BDCA: Breakdown Crane Association. The Major Makers: Appleby Brothers. Written with the kind help of John Steeds, a great-grandson of Charles James Appleby. See www.bdca.org.uk/makers.html.

At the bottom of Luke Street was the London Steam Crane and Engine Works, an engineering company established in 1866 by the Appleby Brothers, who had another engineering works on Emerson Street in London. The Appleby Brothers were the first company to deliver engine powered, purposely manufactured breakdown cranes to the British railways. They were joined in Leicester by Joseph Jessop, who had supervised the construction of the Leicester works.[98]

The residence in Luke Street may have been a temporary measure, as Joseph Sr later moved his family once again, this time into lodgings with the Wood-Antill family at 4 Wanlip Street.[99] John Wood-Antill was a policeman and his wife Emma a needlewoman. They had two children, Annie and Florence.[100] Annie was born in 1863, one year before the couple married, and Florence in 1873.

Still mourning the loss of his mother, this further upheaval must have weighed heavily upon Joseph Jr's young shoulders. In a passing reference to his mother, and his father's pending remarriage, Joseph pinpointed this time in his life as the moment which shattered his idyllic outlook on the family unit, when he wrote:

> After she died my father broke up his home and went into lodgings; unfortunately for me he married his landlady; henceforth I never had one moment's comfort.[101]

99   *The Autobiography of Joseph Carey Merrick* (See Appendix One).

100 1871 Census.

101 *The Autobiography of Joseph Carey Merrick* (See Appendix One).

CHAPTER 4

The Wicked Stepmother of the East

The small village of Mountsorrel stands between Leicester and Loughborough in north west Leicestershire, and it was here John Wood-Antill was born in 1844. Coming from a modest background, his father laboured as a stocking weaver and his sisters were hired as framework knitters.[1] John Wood-Antill may have craved for something a little more adventurous, with better prospects, and so he joined the police.

The first police force in Leicester, and one of the first in the country outside London, was founded in 1836 as Leicester Borough Police.[2] This new force's base was in Town Hall Lane, at the Guildhall, an address now known as Guildhall Lane. John, however, worked in the Belgrave Road neighbourhood of Leicester, a slight distance from the Town Hall. His beat was not too far from his own home on Wanlip Street, and very close to the Merrick family on Cranbourne Street.

An article published in the *Leicester Chronicle*, shows that PC Wood-Antill regularly patrolled Cranbourne Street:

> WILFUL DAMAGE – a boy nine years of age, named Samuel Thomas Clay, was charged with wilfully damaging a wall belonging to Mr George Harrison – P.C. Antill said he was on duty in Cranbourne street about half past eight o'clock on the Saturday night, and saw the defendant and another boy on a wall, throwing the coping off, and pulling out the spikes. When he went towards them, they dropped

1   1851 Census.
2   leics.police.uk/about-us/our-history.

off the wall and ran away - prisoner threw down the spikes produced on the ground. He followed and caught him, and afterwards brought him to the station - Mr White, agent to Mr Harrison, said he saw the wall on Saturday between five and six o'clock. It was then alright. He had seen it again this morning, and found that four yards of the coping was off – Defendant said the two boys on the wall were named Porter and Taylor.[3]

The youngsters who had been arrested and charged faced a fine of 7s 6d, or they could serve seven days' imprisonment,[4] pending the magistrate's decision. However, not all of John's arrests were as simple or painless. In July 1870, he was assaulted whilst on duty. Again, the *Leicester Chronicle* reports.

ASSAULTING THE POLICE – John Merchant was charged with assaulting P.C. Antill in the execution of his duty. – Complainant said he was on duty on the Foresters ground[5] on Tuesday, about the middle of the day. There were a great many people clearing away. Defendant was there, and was drunk and fighting. He dispersed the crowd, and sent the parties off the ground, but they came on again. When the defendant got outside, he picked up a stone, and was going to throw at his head, but he stopped him, apprehended him, and he threw himself down, and kicked him several times about the legs. Brought him to the station – John Joyce corroborated as to the kicks - fined 21s, or fourteen days' hard labour.[6]

Almost a year to the day that Mary Jane Merrick passed away, John Wood-Antill died, not as a serving officer in the Leicestershire Police Force, but as a carter.[7] John breathed his last on 31 May 1874 from that plague of the age, phthisis, at his home on 4 Wanlip Street. John left behind two very young children, and a wife, Emma. However, her widowhood didn't last long, because seven months later, on 3 December 1874, Emma Wood-Antill married her lodger, Joseph

3   *Leicester Chronicle*, 17 June 1871.

4   Ibid.

5   Annual Demonstration of the Ancient Order of Foresters - see www.foresters friendlysociety.co.uk.

6   *Leicester Chronicle*, 2 July 1870.

7   Death certificate of John Wood-Antill.

Rockley Merrick,[8] at Archdeacon Lane Baptist Church. Joseph Sr was still an active member of the church,[9] and a photograph recently discovered possibly shows him playing the organ at the very church he married Emma.[10]

Joseph Sr, who seems to be a bit of an entrepreneur, ran a lamp and oil dealership from the house at 4 Wanlip Street,[11] as well as maintaining his haberdashery business. By 1877, he had moved his new family to the house attached to that haberdashery shop at 37 Russell Square. Russell Square still survives to this day, but is now a lot smaller than it once was, the shops gone with flats and maisonettes built in their place, with only one side of the Square's original buildings standing amongst the new estate of St Matthew's. Merrick's original haberdashery shop has also long gone from its position on the corner of Junction Street and Russell Square,[12] replaced by a bland warehouse.

Just over twenty years after the Merricks had resided in the area, another young industrialist moved into 23 Russell Square,[13] a gentleman by the name of George Oliver Love from Bethnal Green in London. He moved up to Leicester to set up a baker's shop, and married a young local girl by the name of Caroline Beatrice Thornhill.[14] George Oliver Love was an alias, for his actual name was George Joseph Smith, the infamous serial killer and bigamist known for the Brides in the Bath murders.[15]

The two older children in the new family, Joseph Carey Merrick

---

8   *The Autobiography of Joseph Carey Merrick* (See Appendix One).

9   Communion & Members Register for Archdeacon Lane Baptist Church, No. 253, July 1873.

10   Photograph of Archdeacon Lane Baptist Church Harvest Festival. Ebenezer Smith and J. Merrick (organ). Leicestershire and Rutland Records office, Long Street, Wigston.

11   *Commercial and General Directory and Red Book of Leicester and Suburbs 1875.*

12   Goad Insurance Plan of Leicester 1892 sheet 28-1.

13   archive.org/stream/trialofgeorgejos015895mbp/trialofgeorgejos05015895 mbp_djvu.txt.

14   Marriage index.

15   content.met.police.uk/article/brides-in-the-bath-murders.

and his stepsister Annie Wood-Antill, would have been old enough to go to school. Although the Education Act of 1870 had not stipulated a school leaving age, school boards were given the power to make attendance compulsory in their area and to determine their own leaving age. Syston Street Board School opened in January 1874, and by September of that year the new by-law set up by the Leicester Board was brought into operation, laying down compulsory attendance for all children aged between five and thirteen.[16]

If Joseph had attended the newly-built Syston Street, he would have only been there for about twelve months.

At 13-years-old Joseph left school, and just like many other children of his age, attempted to bring money into the home. He writes in his autobiography that nothing would "satisfy [my] step mother until she got me out to work".[17]

Many hard-working families were often up against intense household poverty. Emma came into the marriage with two young daughters, and Joseph Sr with two less-abled children. Joseph was at school, but as soon as he reached the school leaving age, like most children, he would have been expected to find employment and contribute to the family purse. Even basic additional household tasks such as fetching wood or water were effectively allowing for a higher standard of living. It must have also been very hard work for Emma, who has been described as the 'Wicked step-mother of the East',[18] to have two extra children to look after. Marian, Joseph's little sister, may not have been able to work or even attend school. There is no record suggesting the type of disability she suffered from, only what has been written on the census record of 1881, which states 'deformed from birth'.

Joseph Sr and Emma must have had some compassion towards the two children, as both Marian and Joseph could have been quite easily admitted into the workhouse or an institution for children

16 *Education in Leicestershire 1540-1940*. Edited by Brian Simon (1968).

17 *The Autobiography of Joseph Carey Merrick* (see Appendix One).

18 Podcast: Joseph Merrick, The Elephant Man with Jeanette Sitton (25 July 2015): www.casebook.org/podcast/listen.html?id=108.

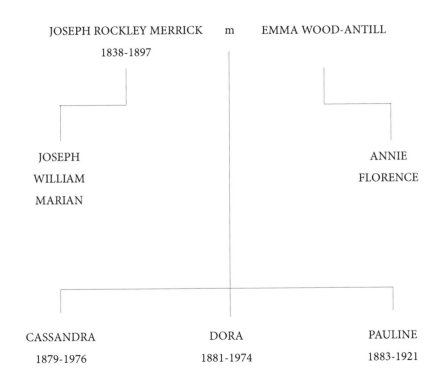

JOSEPH ROCKLEY MERRICK   m   EMMA WOOD-ANTILL

1838-1897

JOSEPH

WILLIAM

MARIAN

ANNIE

FLORENCE

CASSANDRA

1879-1976

DORA

1881-1974

PAULINE

1883-1921

with physical or mental disabilities. Many disabled children were financially supported by the poor laws, which paid for them to receive the sought-after education and training provided by these institutions. The 1834 Poor Law Amendment Act, along with subsequent amendments, provided the destitute with the right to ask for poor relief. While it was first intended that this would entail entering the workhouse, in later years local poor law guardians were empowered to provide funds for disabled children to be educated in specialist institutions.

One such establishment was the Nazareth House in Cardiff, which catered for Roman Catholic girls, especially those with physical or mental disabilities. And disability was not considered a barrier to education. A girl born without arms was taught to write with her mouth. Sarah Donovan, a young patient at the home, was described as a cripple but was helped to find employment by using her needlework skills.[19]

However, Joseph and Marian stayed at home, and in 1875, when Joseph was old enough to leave school, he found employment with Freeman's cigar manufacturers.[20]

In 1875 there were two Freeman cigar manufacturers in Leicester. There was T. Freeman & Co. on Churchgate,[21] the same street on which Joseph's uncle Charles Barnabus Merrick lived and worked. The foreman of that cigar factory was a Henry Smart, who lived on Birstall Street,[22] the same street where Joseph had lived at with his parents when his mother was alive back in 1872. The other Freeman's cigar manufacturers were located on Lower Hill Street,[23] the road running parallel to Lee Street, Joseph's birthplace. From where the Merricks were living in Russell Square, the walk to Lower Hill Street would have been a few minutes' walk, so Joseph most

---

19 remedianetwork.net.

20 *The Autobiography of Joseph Carey Merrick*
(See Appendix One).

21 *Leicester Mercury Online*, 27 July 2011.

22 *Leicester Daily Mercury*, 27 December 1876.

23 *Leicester Chronicle*, 10 March 1877.

probably worked at the latter as it was nearest to his home.

Making cigars was a fiddly business. Before Joseph could make and roll the cigars they were prepared by his work colleague, who would take the leaves one by one, fold them and strip off the stalks with very quick and dexterous movements. The leaves would then be laid out smoothly[24] and handed to Joseph, who was the cigar maker.[25] Joseph would be seated on a low stool in front of a low workbench which had three sides with raised edges, the other facing his work colleague open. Joseph started by smoothing out the leaf in front of him and cut it into a long cigar shape, similar to the shape of the side of a hot air balloon. A few fragments of tobacco leaf were spread on the balloon-shaped leaf, consisting of various small cuttings, and then he would roll the leaf to form the cigar and place it into a gauge made of iron, cutting it to the given length. After taking it out of the iron guide, Joseph rolled the cigar and twisting the end to prevent the tobacco leaf from loosening. Joseph would have to do this very swiftly, as only a few seconds were required to make the cigar,[26] and a good maker could turn out 1,000 cigars a day.[27]

While Joseph was working at Freeman's, a terrible incident occurred to one of his work colleagues. John Nicholas Higgott, a young cigar bundler, at fifteen-years-old the same age as Joseph, when he died at the neighbouring Gladstone Arms beer house at 38 Lower Hill Street on 28 February 1877. Higgott, who lived at 54 Burgess Street in the north end of the town near St Margaret's Church, suffered from pleurisy,[28] an inflammation of the membrane that surrounds the lungs and lines the rib cage.[29]

In his post-mortem, the surgeon Dr Henry Meadows noticed his

24 *The Penny Magazine of the Society for the Diffusion of Useful Knowledge.* Volume 10 page 470 (1841).

25 *The True History of the Elephant Man* by Michael Howell and Peter Ford (Kindle Edition 2011).

26 *The Penny Magazine of the Society for the Diffusion of Useful Knowledge.* Volume 10 page 470 (1841).

27 *Leicester Mercury Online*, 27 July 2011.

28 *Leicester Chronicle*, 10 March 1877.

29 www.webmd.com/lung/understanding-pleurisy-basics

left lung was slightly smaller than his right and that he died from the formation of a blood clot on the right side of his heart. Although Meadows stated in his report the pleurisy was not brought on by neglect, Thomas East, another of Joseph's work colleagues, and who also worked next to John Higgott in the workshop, said that on several occasions Higgott had only a bit of bread to eat which lasted him all day. On the Monday before he died, Higgott told Thomas his father had made him get up at 5.30 in the morning and had not given him any food. Higgott had been ill for weeks and on his last working day, Wednesday, 28 February 1877, his manager Bernard Rothschild sent him home, but he was so ill he had to be carried to the door of the factory. Rothschild gave him 3d and sent him to the beer house across the road to keep warm before sending for his parents.

John Higgott died at 2.30 that very afternoon in the presence of his manager, Bernard Rothschild. Even though his parents had been sent for between one and two o'clock, his mother didn't arrive until after 2.30 in the afternoon, and his father until after half past three. On one occasion before his death, Bernard Rothschild had caught Higgott crying. Rothschild wanted to send him home but Higgott refused, saying his father would beat him and if he lost any time at work, he would not eat.

Following Higgott's death, the surgeon noted that he was not wearing undergarments such as socks or stockings, even though it was very cold.[30] An inquest was called, and even though no charges were brought against the parents for neglect, the coroner concluded his findings at the inquest stating he "had never seen a person display less regard and more indifference at the loss of a child then the mother in this case has shown."[31]

Joseph worked at Freeman's for about two years until he was 15-years-old,[32] but by then the increasing heaviness and awkwardness of his malformed right arm, hand and fingers made it

---

30 *Leicester Chronicle*, 10 March 1877.

31 Ibid.

32 *The Autobiography of Joseph Carey Merrick*
    (See Appendix One).

almost impossible for him to accomplish the delicate work required in making cigars and had little alternative but to leave.[33]

Joseph Sr helped by securing a peddler's licence for his son, as Joseph would later confirm:

> Being unable to get employment my father got me a peddler's licence to hawk the town.[34]

With a tray of ribbons, stockings, gloves or indeed any items which were easily laid on a tray around his neck, Joseph, at the age of fifteen, would walk the streets of Leicester, going door to door, and sometimes standing at the town's iconic Clock Tower, with his name on a card.[35]

The Clock Tower, built in 1868, was the result of years of campaigning by the East Gates Improvements Committee to erect some sort of memorial or monument in the space once occupied by the old Haymarket buildings, where the people of Leicester met to buy and sell hay and straw. This open space was now dangerous to pedestrians, with its high volume of horse traffic coming into Leicester from the five busy roads of Belgrave Gate, Humberstone Gate, Gallowtree Gate, High Street/East Gates and Churchgate, all meeting at one point.

The improvement committee proposed a structure to be built to protect the public from the traffic:

> Mr Angrave, the chairman having withdrawn, took the chair, and in reply to Mr Carryer, said he might rest satisfied they would have some splendid thing erected where East Gates stood. He had designs himself already. The town had been greatly indebted to three benefactors, Alderman Newton, Sir Thomas White and William Wigston; and he hoped to see a splendid column erected surmounted by those three figures.[36]

33 Ibid.

34 Ibid.

35 *Leicester Mercury*, 4 September 2003.

36 *Leicester Mercury*, 21 June 1862.

Being an extremely busy area of Leicester, the Clock Tower would have been the ideal place to sell his goods. Joseph states in his own memoirs that people would not come to their doors to him as he was lame and deformed,[37] and the mass protruding from his mouth was making communication with those who did not know him nigh on impossible.[38]

But even hawking on the streets had its problems for Joseph. He could not move around the town without having a crowd of people gather round him,[39] most probably jeering and laughing.

It was Napoleon Bonaparte who famously called the English "a nation of shop keepers"; adding 'peddlers' and 'street sellers' to that quote would have made it more complete. Throughout the 19th century, street sellers, peddlers and hawkers were a common sight in villages and towns around England.

The Pedlars Act of 1871 states:

> The term 'Pedlar' means any hawker, pedlar, petty chapman, tinker, caster of metals, or other persons who, without horse or other beast bearing or drawing burden, travels and trades on foot and goes from town to town or to other men's houses, carrying to sell or exposing for sale any goods, wares or merchandise or procuring orders for good, wares or merchandise immediately to be delivered, or selling or offering for sale his skills in handicraft, to have a permanent home address and be of good character before the police will grant them a 12 month licence to sell wares.[40]

With his father owning his own haberdashery shop and lamp and oil dealership, the goods to sell probably came from Joseph Sr himself. However, other stores specifically sold to hawkers and shopkeepers such as G. Brown, manufacturers of 42½ Humberstone Gate, who

---

37 *The Autobiography of Joseph Carey Merrick*
    (See Appendix One).

38 *The True History of the Elephant Man* by Michael Howell and Peter Ford (Kindle Edition 2011).

39 *The Autobiography of Joseph Carey Merrick*
    (See Appendix One).

40 Pedlars Act 1871.

advertised supplying goods to hawkers and shopkeepers.[41] It wasn't just hawkers and shopkeepers trying to get people to buy goods from them, and where hawkers needed licences, beggars did not.

There were many classes of beggars. 'Forney Squarers' made finger rings out of brass buttons. Using large coat buttons, they would stamp two rings out of each button, using the tools they had such as stamps, hammers, files and brushes they would make the rings very attractive to the buyers, selling at two to four shillings, usually to servants. As long as they could afford 'a good cant', they wouldn't even refuse six pence.[42]

'Driss Fencers' were ladies who would purchase a quantity of the commonest lace and prepare it by putting it into a bag containing some yellow sand, swing it backwards and forwards to enthuse the lace with a rich golden colour and thread-like appearance, before it was then well shaken and ironed. The ladies then sold this as pillow lace, which they claimed to have just finished and are obliged to sell at a great loss through some sad misfortune.[43]

Competition was pretty tough for Joseph. Often when he returned home from a day's hawking his stepmother Emma would set his plate before him with the remark that it was more than he had earned.[44] Even though Joseph felt that his stepmother loathed him by making his life a perfect misery, often giving him smaller portions than the rest of the family, his treatment was not exceptional in this era. As we have seen, poor young John Higgott, Joseph's work colleague, was treated much the same.

Women and children suffered greatly from ill health in the 19th century, not due to work but the result of want of food. As in all working class families, the male head of the household had the

---

41 *Leicester Daily Mercury*, 11 January 1879.

42 A 'good cant' consisted of bread, cheese, butter, meat, tea, sugar, flour or any article of clothing.

43 *Working Class Life in Victorian Leicester: The Joseph Dare Reports*. Edited by Barry Hayes (1991).

44 *The True History of the Elephant Man* by Michael Howell and Peter Ford (Kindle Edition 2011).

best of what food was available, and the biggest helpings. Joseph's father was the most important wage earner in the family. As well as receiving small food portions for not meeting his daily quota, it is also said that Joseph was continually beaten with the encouragement of his stepmother.[45]

Whipping was the most common method of discipline; food was scarce and parents expected children to be thankful for whatever was put in front of them. By today's standards the methods of punishment would certainly be considered abusive, but Victorian parents took quite literally the Biblical order of 'spare the rod and spoil the child'.

Augustus Hare, the late Victorian travel writer and historian, recalled that when he was five-years-old he was shut in his room for two days on bread and water to explicitly break his spirit, by an aunt whose little boy had bit and slapped him but he was not allowed to retaliate. A young girl named Ann Taylor was whipped for not being able to remember what T-H-Y spelt. Victorian parents punished their children, not because they didn't love them, but because they wanted to instil proper values and moral codes.[46]

However, it all got too much for Joseph, so whenever he failed to sell the required quantity of goods he spent the little money he had earned on food for himself. When he returned home to Russell Square he received another severe thrashing. Finally, at the age of sixteen he left home for good:[47]

> In consequences of my ill luck my life was again made a misery to me, so that I again ran away and went hawking on my own account.[48]

---

45 *Measured by Soul: The Life of Joseph Carey Merrick (also known as 'The Elephant Man')* by Jeanette Sitton and Mae Siuwai Stroshane (2012).

46 "The Life of Infants and Children in Victorian London" accessed via www.123helpME.com/view.asp?id=22350.

47 *The True History of the Elephant Man* by Michael Howell and Peter Ford (Kindle Edition 2011).

48 *The Autobiography of Joseph Carey Merrick*
(See Appendix One).

Joseph Sr's treatment of his children didn't go unnoticed. On 8 October 1878[49] he assaulted Drusilla Rudd outside her home in Russell Square for criticising his parental skills:

> Joseph Merrick – was charged with assaulting Drusilla Rudd on the 8th inst – Mr James appeared for the complainant, who stated that she lived in Russell Square. On Tuesday evening, while she was talking to some neighbours about the defendants conduct towards his child, Merrick came out and said he would smash her head if she talked about him anymore. He struck her two violent blows on her neck and bruised her collar bone badly. Defendant pleaded provocation – Fined £3 3s and costs or one month's hard labour.[50]

After spending nights in the cheapest of Leicester's common lodging houses, Joseph moved in with his uncle Charles at 144 Churchgate.[51] Charles, a hairdresser and licensed tobacconist, is recalled fondly by Joseph in his memoirs:

> The best friend I had in those days was my father's brother, Mr Merrick, Hair dresser, Churchgate, Leicester.[52]

The hairdressers that his uncle owned was on the west side of Churchgate, directly opposite St Margaret's church, and is now part of major road known as St Margaret's Way. Joseph may have continued hawking his father's haberdashery items, and he may have been allowed to keep a small amount of the takings as housekeeping for his uncle, but with a new baby on the way, Joseph Sr and Emma were moving house and selling the businesses. The haberdashery business was sold, with a shoemaker named Pratt living in the premises by 1881,[53] and the lamp and oil dealership was advertised to rent.[54]

---

49 Suggests the year Joseph left home.

50 *Leicester Journal*, 18 October 1878.

51 *The True History of the Elephant Man* by Michael Howell and Peter Ford (Kindle Edition 2011).

52 *The Autobiography of Joseph Carey Merrick* (See Appendix One).

53 1881 Census.

54 *Leicester Daily Mercury*, 1 January 1879.

Joseph's father and stepmother had two more children, Cassandra (b. 1879) and Dora (b. 1880), and they moved to 30C Roughton Street in the Belgrave area of the town, an area of well-built house close to the tramway.[55] As the years passed, the family moved to Justice Street, and Emma gave birth to another daughter, Pauline, born in 1883.

Although the haberdashery business had long gone, Joseph Sr still worked in the hosiery industry, becoming a warehouseman, then a stationary engine driver to a stoker in a dye works.[56] He seemed to have been in continuous employment, and worked hard for his family.

Hosiery dominated employment in mid-Victorian Leicester. Up until the mid-19th century, little technological advance was made in the industry and the equipment used by the framework knitters was similar to that used by their 16th century ancestors. This began to change on 13 July 1865, when the foundation stone for the behemoth that was to become the Corah Hosiery factory was laid by Mr Edwin Corah. On 14 June 1866 Miss Jennie Corah started the new beam engine. With steam-powered machinery, it beckoned in a new age for the local industry.

The Corah Building, known as the St Margaret's Works, formed a large complex in the north of Leicester, near St Margaret's church and just a stone's throw from Joseph Sr and Emma Merrick's home.

The brick and stone warehouse was designed in bold Italian style by local architect W. Jackson of Loseby Lane, with a huge boiler and engine house adjoining the factory and a 140ft chimney looming high over the works.[57]

New factory-based work offered substantially improved wages for hosiery workers, with Corah claiming a 25 per cent rise in salaries. Working in a factory rather than framework knitting for small businesses demanded more discipline, but on a positive side,

55 *Leicester Journal*, 12 November 1880.
56 1861, 1871, 1881 and 1891 Census records.
57 www.corah-leicester.co.uk

also shorter hours and better pay.[58] In the 1870s Corah extended its range of products, and the 'St Margaret's' brand became the first registered trademark for knitted goods in Britain,[59] being worn even by Royalty. In 1878 Princess Alexandra and her children were photographed on board the royal yacht wearing St Margaret's jerseys.[60]

The Merrick family seemed settled, but on 19 March 1891 Joseph Sr's first born daughter Marian Eliza Merrick died aged 24 at the family home of 28 Justice Street.[61] She had been 'crippled from birth' and her cause of death was recorded as Myelitis Convulsions - spinal cord seizures which are well documented in literature dealing with multiple sclerosis. The seizures are characterised by tonic clonic spasm in the extremities and often accompanied by painful dysesthesias.[62] Present at the time of her passing was neighbour Dinah Preston of 30 Justice Street.[63] Marian was buried at Belgrave Road Cemetery in Leicester.[64]

Six years later she was joined by her father,[65] when Joseph Rockley Merrick died on 30 January 1897, aged 58, of chronic bronchitis.[66] His death was followed by that of his mother, Sarah Merrick - Joseph's grandmother - who died at 28 Justice Street on 7 February 1897, aged 92.[67] Sarah was buried in Welford Road Cemetery on 11 February with her grandchildren, the young children of Charles and Jane Merrick.[68]

---

58 *The Story of Leicester* by Siobhan Begley (Kindle Edition 2013).

59 www.knittingtogther.org.

60 *The Story of Leicester* by Siobhan Begley (Kindle Edition 2013).

61 Death Certificate for Marian Eliza Merrick.

62 US National library of Medicine, National institute of Health.

63 Death Certificate of Marian Eliza Merrick.

64 Information from Marian Eliza Merrick's grave.

65 Ibid.

66 Joseph Carey Merrick Tribute Website (www.josephcareymerrick.com).

67 *Leicester Chronicle*, 13 February 1897.

68 Plot uR1 3042 C u80478,Welford Road Cemetery.

Emma went on to marry her neighbour, George Preston,[69] the widower of Dinah Preston who had nursed Marian Eliza Merrick during her final moments.

69 Marriage index.

CHAPTER 5

The House on the Hill

A teenaged Joseph Carey Merrick spent two years living at 144 Churchgate, Leicester with his Uncle Charles and Aunt Jane, his cousins and his grandmother Sarah. It was Christmas Day 1879, a day for reminiscing, and no doubt Joseph's mind turned to happy memories with family, his mother, father, sister and brother. Amongst those memories was undoubtedly a sad one, as Joseph's little brother William had been buried on Christmas Day nine years earlier.

Joseph must have loved the excitement of decorating a Christmas tree, and singing the most popular Christmas carols, 'Good King Wenceslas', 'I saw three ships' and the jolly tune of 'Jingle Bells', probably known better by Joseph as 'One horse open sleigh',[1] and the pleasure of opening Christmas cards, a delightful tradition which became popular with the introduction of the half penny stamp, and the sheer thrill of pulling a Christmas cracker, a Christmas treat invented in 1843 by London sweet maker Tom Smith.[2]

Due to the success of the large factories and mass production, games and toys were made in large numbers and sold at affordable prices which targeted the middle classes, but not so for the poorer children. In their Christmas stocking, which became a popular tradition around the 1870s, all they could expect would be an apple, orange or a few nuts if they were lucky.[3] Christmas Day fare had its

1 www.girlguideingstaffordshire.org.uk/a-victorian-carol-book.pdf.
2 www.historic-uk.com/HistoryUK/HistoryofEngland/A-Victorian-Christmas.
3 Ibid.

regional variations; in the northern counties of England roast beef was popular, while in the southern counties and London goose was eaten. The poorer classes often made do with rabbit. Although turkey had been in England from around 1526,[4] it was still very expensive. It was reported in the local paper, the *Leicester Daily Mercury*, that "Fishmongers and poulterers [sic] made great demands on the poultry yard and game preserves",[5] so it wouldn't be surprising if a well-bred goose was on Joseph's table that Christmas.

The evening and night of Christmas Eve, according to the paper, passed off very quietly in Leicester.[6] Groups of carol singers paraded the streets, many of whom were youths spreading their Christmas cheer. There were also a couple of companies singing around the town. Again, the *Leicester Daily Mercury* reports:

> They rent in the air, with "Christians awake" and we venture to avow that whoever came within sound of their voices, be they Christians, Jews, mussulmans [sic] or pagans, would never be able to sleep.[7]

These bands of merry singers were often joined by the 'waites', bands of people led by important local leaders, who only sang on Christmas Eve, a night once known as 'waitnight' because the Biblical shepherds were watching their sheep whilst waiting for the Angels.[8] However, it was described in the local newspaper that the town was getting too big for them to trail around in one night.[9]

Because of the wealth generated by the industrial revolution in the Victorian age, the middle classes of England and Wales were able to take two days off at Christmas - Christmas Day and Boxing Day - and some grocers even closed on Christmas Eve, not reopening until 29 December.[10] A newspaper article sums up Christmas 1879 as

---

4   www.britishturkey.co.uk.

5   *The Leicester Daily Mercury*, 26 December 1879.

6   Ibid.

7   Ibid.

8   www.whychristmas.com/customs/carols/history.shtml.

9   *The Leicester Daily Mercury*, 26 December 1879.

a delight hailed by thousands... all classes of shop keepers laid in extra stock in anticipation of a larger trade, and on the whole it may be taken that their hopes were not blighted.[11]

The busy gentlemen of Leicester may have still have needed to visit the barbers for a cut or beard trim, and if money was to be made there is little doubt a hairdresser like Charles Merrick was in no position to refuse, with a growing and extended family for which he probably felt he needed every penny he could earn. As Charles Dickens writes in his famous novel *A Christmas Carol*, "Christmas is a poor excuse every 25th December to pick a man's pockets."[12] Even though it sounded as thought the shopkeepers were doing well, and industry was booming, appeals were made on behalf of the unemployed and poor of the town. On Christmas Day in the St Mark's Parish to the East of Leicester town centre, the clergy and church wardens assisted one hundred families with meat, coal and clothing, and one hundred poor children were provided with a Christmas dinner at the Mission Rooms in New Humberstone, a village just outside of the town centre. There was also an increase in the number of people received at the Union Workhouse that Christmas. The previous year, in 1878, eight hundred received Christmas dinner. This year of 1879, 1,145 inmates ate their Yuletide feast, the largest number since 1857, and it was just four days after the wonderful celebrations of Christmas of 1879, his last as a member of the family unit, that Joseph Merrick added his own name to those workhouse statistics.

On Monday, 29 December 1879,[13] Joseph declared himself to the Leicester Union Workhouse for the first time. Life with his Uncle Charles and Aunt Jane was never going to last forever; they had a growing family and more mouths to feed, and if Joseph's deformities were intensifying, obtaining work would be difficult. In an era when

10 *Leicester Journal*, 19 December 1879.

11 *The Leicester Daily Mercury*, 26 December 1879.

12 *A Christmas Carol* by Charles Dickens (1843).

13 *Workhouse Registers (Index Admissions and Discharge)*, Leicestershire, Leicester and Rutland Records Office: T615 107.

boys where considered men at the age of 12, Joseph must have thought it was time to move on and support himself the best way he could.

After Joseph had eaten his dinner,[14] possibly prepared for him by his grandmother or Aunt Jane, he set off from the home he'd known for two years on a dark, wintery afternoon.

December 1879 was frosty, and north winds whistled their way through the streets of Leicester as Joseph trekked the mile walk to the workhouse. Making his way along Churchgate, up the narrow streets and dimly lit alleyways, Joseph would have passed many inns and taverns, inside which people would be drinking, dancing and singing.

Joseph packing his bags and leaving for the workhouse may have been an amicable decision, and his uncle may have accompanied him to the workhouse, but it wasn't the last time Uncle Charles or Aunt Jane would be in touch with Joseph.

Two years after Joseph left Charles and Jane's home in Churchgate, in 1881, Jane gave birth to a son named John Ernest. It is not known when, but sometime after the birth of John Joseph sent a copy of Daniel Defoe's *Robinson Crusoe.* Inside he wrote:

John Ernest Merrick
From his cousin
Joseph Merrick[15]

The mile-long walk would have taken Joseph up to the Clock Tower, turning into Gallowtree Gate and onto Granby Street. This would have taken him to London Road, and along Conduit Street all the way to Sparkenhoe Street and the looming gates of the workhouse, known locally, and rather ominously, as 'the house on the hill'.[16] The

---

14 Workhouse registers refer to last meal eaten before being admitted. *Workhouse Registers (Index Admissions and Discharge)* Leicestershire, Leicester and Rutland Records Office: T615 107.

15 Letter and inscription published with the kind permission of Michelle Merrick. Sadly, there is no date in this book to indicate when Joseph inscribed it, however the signature matches exactly the only other known signature of Joseph Merrick, which is held at the Royal London Hospital Museum.

streets around the workhouse may have been hospitable in Joseph's younger years due to family visits with his mother to his aunts, uncles and cousins on Upper Conduit Street, listening to stories and adventures of train journeys or the sound of his Uncle Hewitt's organ playing, but those days were gone. That side of his family had moved away, and his mother was now dead. Joseph, at the age of seventeen, was about to start life on his own.

When Joseph arrived at the workhouse, he was greeted by a gate through which 'only one could enter and one could leave'.[17] Until the next weekly Board of Guardians meeting, Joseph was permitted into the male receiving ward, where he would have the extravagance of a dip in clean warm water, his clothes stored and disinfected and where he would be given a workhouse uniform.[18] The night Joseph arrived, he must have been overwhelmed at the numbers of people coming and going. As well as all the inmates, there were an extra two hundred people visiting and being entertained there. The night in question, 29th December 1879, was the annual distribution of prizes to the workhouse children. 1,400 people were present, two hundred of them were guests.[19] It is not known if Joseph saw any of this, in fact it is very doubtful as he was in the receiving ward and the celebrations were being held in the dining hall. However, he may have heard the comings and goings, but located in a separate building Joseph would have just had to imagine the entertainment that was going on without him.

As Joseph was being cleaned and re-clothed in the cold-stoned floor and walled receiving ward, in the dining hall, walls and passageways were still decorated with the Christmas evergreens. The master and matron, Mr and Mrs Dickinson, were present at the festivities, as was the Lord Mayor of Leicester, John Bennett. The first part of the evening was dedicated to sacred music, with a solo

16 *Leicester Chronicle*, 27 December 1879.

17 *Leicester Journal*, 21 November 1851.

18 *Indoor Paupers: Life inside a London Workhouse by 'One of Them'* by Peter Higginbotham (Kindle Edition 2013).

19 *Leicester Journal*, 2 January 1880.

sung by a Mr Chandler and the choir singing the anthems 'The Jewry is God Known' and 'Let us now go', and the chorus 'And the Glory'. The children of the workhouse also sang hymns. The young boys sang 'Lord of all Power and Might', and the girls resonated 'Seek and Ye Shall Find'.

In between the performances, the Mayor distributed prizes, with the accolades principally books. After the prize giving, Mayor Bennett gave a speech:

> When Mr Chamberlain asked me to say a few words to the children tonight, I confess I felt a great deal perplexed as to what to say. I felt it would not be right to preach contentment to the children who are in the workhouse, because if I were there myself I should wish as soon as possible to get out of it. (Laughter from the audience.). The mayor continued - As I was walking along the streets, I noticed on one of our lamp posts that the foot passengers were requested to keep to the right. I dare say you have often seen the confusion that has resulted from neglecting this precaution. A boy coming up the street meets a boy coming down, and instead of being on the right side, goes tumbling right against the other person, or the two moved first one way and the other till one says 'I beg your pardon' or laughs out right and stops while the other goes on. It is very desirable therefore, that in our crowded thoroughfares everybody should observe the rule, as much as possible keep always to the right. But it is important all should keep to the right in walking along the streets, and it is still more so that we should all adopt a manly and honourable course in walking along the course of life. Boys and girls, be truthful and straight forward and open in your conduct, and let no one have a reason to accuse you of being sneakiest or untruthful or deceptive. It is easy enough to do and say what is right when it answers our purpose, but it is harder to do and be so when interest seems to point in the opposite direction. If by telling a lie you can get something which you most desire, while by telling the truth you will not get it, by will to deny yourself the pleasure rather than wound your conscience. It is a very bad plan to have to carry a restless and uneasy conscience. If you are wrestling with a sweep, whether you threw him or he threw you, you would be sure to be made black and sooty. New bad company and bad habits of all sorts always have a sooty, blackening influence. Guard against them as you would against the plague. With gold you may buy bread, or clothes or houses or lands;

but you cannot buy good character or a tender conscience, or a wise heart, but you may have them without gold. I have just told you to guard against bad habits, but there are just two against which I will specially warn you. One is the vulgar and degrading practice among boys and girls of using bad and obscene language. Oh, what offensive and coarse and meaningless words are often used in Leicester. It is sad indeed to hear it as we pass along the streets, and since I have been mayor I have had words written down and passed up to me on the bench by witnesses who were ashamed to use them in public. Now this is a habit against which everyone can guard, and I hope that every boy and girl who is here tonight will resolve that they will never use such coarse vulgarities. Do not imagine it is a sign of manliness, for nothing would be a more foolish mistake. It is low and vicious, and a sure proof of want of self-respect. The other habit against which I wish to warn you is the practice of selfishness. How many whom we meet are its victims. They must have the biggest and best of everything, let who will go without, the best ball, or doll or book or dress or seat at school or place in the factory whoever else suffers for it. This is not as it should be. God has put us into a world where there are many poor and afflicted and ignorant, and one reason I think, is that we may have the opportunity of doing them good. We should not despise the poor, but seek every opportunity we can of helping them. One day a gentleman saw two boys going along the street. Their clothes were ragged and tied together with pieces of string. One of the boys seemed very happy over a bunch of withered flowers which he had just picked up. 'I say, Billy, wasn't somebody really good to drop these 'ere posies just where I could find 'em and they're so pretty and nice?'

Think of that when you are tempted to selfishness or greediness. Run on an errand to help a poor widow, carry a basket and help a lame man, read a book to some poor blind person and do something that is truly kind, that you may show at this Christmas time you want to help forward the reign of peace and good will. Now I must stop. I want to show you that even in a workhouse you may be useful. I want you to be civil, to be industrious, to be attentive to your lessons and when you go into trade or service, try your very best to succeed.

I conclude with wishing every boy and girl a very happy and glad and joyous New Year.[20]

---

20 *Leicester Journal*, 2 January 1880.

The evening was then concluded with more music and singing by the choir.[21]

Joseph didn't have to wait long until he was welcomed into the workhouse. The next Board of Guardians meeting took place on Tuesday, 30 December 1879, the day after Joseph arrived at their gates. Present were Messrs Freston (Chairman), Whitehead and Deacon (Vice Chairmen) and the guardians Harding, Keites, Hall, Skillington, Brewin, Carr, Beal, Wilford, Sharpe, Wells, Grey, Broughton, Carter, Taylor, Crow, Watson, Pipes, Stroud, Stretton, Bland, Hames, Lennard, Finn, Prentice, Cox, Collin and Wright. The finances and expenditure from the following week was discussed, as well as the use of utilities. In the year to date, it was stated, 139,000 gallons of water had been used, and 34,000ft of gas. The Union school had educated 100 boys, 93 girls and 82 infants. Messrs Sharpe and Harding reported favourably on the condition of the workhouse, schools and Infirmary, and a communication was read out from the Local Government Board, acknowledging the receipt of a letter from the guardians informing them they have 'resolved to give to the paupers 6oz of bread and a pint of gruel for supper instead of 8oz of bread during the winter months'.[22]

On the day the Board met, there were approximately 1,180 inmates, and Joseph Merrick was now one of them. After the meeting, and after being examined by the Medical Officer, Joseph was given a classification to determine his place of accommodation. The class system determined in which apartment or ward he would reside, as well as the particular diet he would receive, amounts rather than type of food. Joseph was designated Class 1, dietary for able-bodied men and women. After 1834, Union workhouses segregated the different classes in the dining hall, and every workhouse had a set of scales available to every inmate who could demand, in front of witnesses, to weigh their food if they felt their meals fell short.[23]

---

21 *Leicester Journal*, 2 January 1880.

22 Ibid.

23 *The Workhouse Encyclopaedia* by Peter Higginbotham (Kindle Edition 2013).

The workhouse gates didn't loom over Joseph for long, as just 12 weeks later, on 22 March 1880, he left at his own request. Perhaps he thought with spring here and the weather improving, he might have a better chance of getting a job.

A few days before entering the workhouse on 29th December 1879 he had been caught hawking without a licence, and although he was discharged with a caution,[24] the lack of a licence meant that Joseph was unable to return to being a hawker. It was perhaps therefore little surprise that only two days after his departure he was forced to return to the workhouse, on 24 March 1880. This time, instead of listing 'hawker' as his profession, his reason for re-entering the workhouse was given as 'No work'.[25]

It's unclear whether Joseph resided in the workhouse or the workhouse infirmary. In his own account he writes "I then went into the infirmary at Leicester, where I remained for two to three years",[26] and even Tom Norman, Joseph's future manager, later recalled that when he was introduced to Joseph he was given a release form he believed was issued by the Leicester Infirmary where Joseph was an inmate.[27]

Joseph remained at the Leicester Union Workhouse for four years and four months. The original workhouse was built in 1838, then demolished and substantially rebuilt in 1850. It was three storeys high with two mock lookout towers. The two gatehouses guarded the entrance and the narrow gates allowed only one person to enter or leave at a time. When described in the *Leicester Journal* in 1851, there were twenty different accommodation blocks and apartments:

- Harmless insane women
- Single women, 2nd class

---

24 *Leicester Chronicle*, 3 January 1880.

25 Workhouse registers refer to last meal eaten before being admitted. *Workhouse Registers (Index Admissions and Discharge)* Leicestershire, Leicester and Rutland Records Office: T615 107.

26 *The Autobiography of Joseph Carey Merrick* (See Appendix One).

27 *The Penny Showman: Tom Norman, Silver King.* With additional writings by his son George Norman (1985).

- Aged, well behaved women
- Aged infirm women
- Married women under 60, 2nd class
- Single, well behaved men
- Harmless insane men
- Tailors' shop
- Single men, 2nd class
- Married men under 60, 2nd class
- Married men under 60, well behaved
- Boys' school
- Schoolmaster's sitting room
- Aged, well behaved men
- Aged infirm men
- Single women, well behaved
- Married women under 60, well behaved
- Schoolmistress' sitting room
- Girls' school
- Infants' school

The apartments were situated on either side of the long corridor and the doors kept locked, so that each class was kept separate from the others.[28]

On his second admittance to the workhouse Joseph was again categorised as Class 1.[29] The diet for Class 1 was for persons of moderate health or constitution, but with little exercise or exertion. The daily allowance of food was 12 to 18 ounces of sustenance per day.[30]

The daily menu for Class 1 inmates was commonly as follows:

---

28 *Leicester Journal*, 21 November 1851.

29 Workhouse registers refer to last meal eaten before being admitted. *Workhouse Registers (Index Admissions and Discharge)* Leicestershire, Leicester and Rutland Records Office: T615 107.

30 *The Workhouse Cookbook: The Workhouse Dietary* by Peter Higginbotham (2008).

Day	Breakfast	Dinner	Supper
Sunday	6oz bread 1½ pints Gruel	5oz cook meat ½lb potatoes	6oz bread 1½ pints of broth
Monday	6oz bread 1½ pints Gruel	1½ pints soup	6oz bread 2oz cheese
Tuesday	6oz bread 1½ pints Gruel	5oz cooked meat ½oz potatoes	6oz bread ½ pints Broth
Wednesday	6oz bread 1½ pints Gruel	1½ pints Soup	6oz bread 2oz cheese
Thursday	6oz bread 1½ pints Gruel	5oz meat ½oz potatoes	6oz bread 1½ pints broth
Friday	6oz bread 1½ pints Gruel	14oz suet/ rice pudding	6oz bread 2oz cheese
Saturday	6oz bread 1½ pints Gruel	1½ pints soup	6oz bread 2oz cheese[31]

Being admitted into the infirmary with nurses and ward assistants may have been a bit more comfortable for Joseph. It must have been tremendously daunting for the 17-year-old. After being unable to move around his hometown of Leicester without crowds gathering around him,[32] so living in cramped quarters surrounded by more able-bodied men must have been quite intimidating. He would no doubt have wondered how he would be received by the other inmates, whether they would mock him, trip him up, bully or play tricks on him. Although Joseph is described in Tom Norman's memoirs as 'having a will of his own',[33] it would not have been easy for the unusual-looking teenager to get away from a bully's intimidation.

In his book *Indoor Paupers*, bullying and the taunting of vulnerable

31 Ibid.

32 *The Autobiography of Joseph Carey Merrick*
(See Appendix One).

33 *The Penny Showman: Tom Norman, Silver King.* With additional writings by his son George Norman (1985).

inmates was described by Peter Higginbotham:

> When the laggards descended from their dormitories, they are for
> sure to find the idiots, each in his own corner, begirt by a troop of
> laughing tormentors, and growling, storming, and swearing, it may
> be, each in his own peculiar manner.[34]

Even the Infirmary wasn't free from its troubles and problems. On
29 June 1880, less than four months after Joseph's second arrival,
an inmate in the infirmary named Alfred Harrison was murdered
by David Saleswakam, a fellow infirmary patient, who was then
removed to Broadmoor Criminal Lunatic Asylum.[35]

Even some of the nurses had complaints made against them, and
there was a rather peculiar fatal accident which happened in 1883.
On the evening of 2 March, Sarah White, a 77-year-old patient who
had been an inmate of the Union Infirmary for about two years, was
sitting on her commode next to her bedside. After about ten minutes
the superintendent nurse, Miss Bailey, told her she would get cold
if she stayed there any longer. White then placed one hand on the
nurse's arm and the other on the bed with the intention of settling
down for the night. The nurse's assistant, Eliza Hackett, covered
White up and about twenty minutes later Sarah complained to
Hackett that Nurse Bailey had broken her leg. Dr Bryan, the House
Surgeon, was sent for, and found that indeed Sarah White's left thigh
was broken. Sarah White accused Bailey of throwing her into bed,
but she sadly died eleven days later on 13 March 1883. During the
inquest into her death, Dr Bryan gave evidence as to the injuries the
many ways by which the leg could have been broken, but due to a
good character reference provided by the Guardians, Nurse Bailey
was not implicated, and the jury returned a verdict of accidental
death.[36]

Whichever ward Joseph resided at in Leicester Union Workhouse,
he would later confide in Tom Norman that he didn't "ever want to

---

34 *Indoor Paupers: Life inside a London Workhouse by 'One of Them'* by Peter
Higginbotham (Kindle Edition 2013).

35 *Leicester Chronicle*, 10 July 1880.

36 *Leicester Chronicle*, 17 March 1885.

go back to that place".[37]

The class system Joseph was admitted into might give us an insight into the type of work he was required to do in the workhouse. He was an able-bodied male, but had little exercise and exertion. Oakum picking, bone crushing, corn grinding and stone breaking were given to male inmates.[38] Oakum picking involved very little exercise or physical exertion, and involved teasing out the fibres from old hemp rope, with the end product being sold to the navy or other ship builders.[39] Joseph's right hand was now the size and shape of an elephant's foreleg, measuring twelve inches around the wrist and five inches round one of the fingers, and even though his left hand and arm were no larger than that of a ten-year-old girl's,[40] this task was undoubtedly beyond him. Stone breaking was substantially challenging, and for someone with Joseph's condition, extremely unlikely.

Working conditions were not that favourable, and in 1851 three male inmates at the Leicester Union Workhouse refused to continue working because of the conditions they were employed in. Joseph Swingler, John Sarson and Charles Harris were employed in pumping water to the workhouse, and complained that while working at the pump they became very warm and that they did not have room to walk about during the time they were not at work. They also complained that there was a bad smell arising from the water closets and adjoining pump room. The three men refused to work unless the gate was left open. They were brought up before the Mayor G. Toller at the town hall.[41]

---

37 *The Penny Showman: Tom Norman, Silver King.* With additional writings by his son George Norman (1985).

38 www.workhouses.org.uk/life/work/shtml.

39 Ibid.

40 *The Autobiography of Joseph Carey Merrick*
(See Appendix One).

41 *Leicester Journal*, 21 November 1851. Joseph Swingler, who had committed several similar offences, was sentenced to 21 days' hard labour. Sarson and Harris, who had never previously been charged of any offence, were sentenced to seven days' hard labour each.

Refusing to work because of a medical condition was also common. In 1880, Benjamin Barber, an inmate at the Leicester workhouse was charged at Leicester Town Hall with refusing to work. The task master, Arthur Blockley, stated that grinding maize, the work which had been set for Benjamin, was one of the easiest jobs, but he repeatedly refused to do it, stating he was not well. He was examined by Dr Bryan on several occasions, who declared there was nothing wrong with him, but he continued to put his hands in his pockets and refuse to work, saying to a fellow inmate that "he would not turn the mill for anybody, and would defy any person to make him do so." Benjamin was charged but on being taken into custody soon changed his mind and wanted to work. This seemed to save him from jail, and the case was dismissed.[42]

The daily routine was strict and rigid, and changed slightly depending on the season.

Between 25 March and 29 September, Joseph awoke at 6.00am and had his breakfast from 6.30am to 7.00am. His daily toil would begin at 7.00am and he would not get a break until his dinner hour between noon and 1.00pm. The drudgery would finish at six in the evening, and supper was between seven and eight o'clock, when Joseph would be able to finally retire and go to bed. This changed slightly in the winter months, when rising was an hour later at 7.00am and breakfast was between 7.30am and 8.00am. Work started at 8.00am, but the rest of the working day was timed the same as spring and summer.[43]

Approximately two years into Joseph's stay at the workhouse, around 1882, Joseph underwent an operation to have a growth of flesh which had grown from his upper jaw removed. It was about eight to nine inches long, bearing a resemblance to an elephant's trunk. It made his speech incomprehensible and was forcing his lips back,[44] which would probably make eating and drinking incredibly

42 *Leicester Chronicle*, 13 November 1880.

43 www.workhouse.org.uk/life/work/shtml.

44 *The True History of the Elephant Man* by Michael Howell and Peter Ford (Kindle Edition 2011).

difficult. As Joseph himself remembered,

> I went into the Infirmary in Leicester, where I remained for two or
> three years, when I had to undergo an operation on my face, having
> three or four ounces of flesh cut away.[45]

The Union Infirmary, next to the Workhouse, was a separate
building housing both sexes and not just exclusively available to
those residing in the workhouse. In 1851 the wards in the infirmary
had one toilet for each ward, and one fixed bath in the water closet.
The ground floor was paved with bricks and the building was heated
with hot air by furnaces located underneath the ground floor, with
flues passing upwards through the building. In the wards, the
beds were made of iron with cut loose straw for mattresses. There
were benches with backs, chairs and night stools, woollen jackets
for women, slippers, pieces of carpet on the woman's brick floors,
thermometers and screens. One round towel was supplied twice
each week to the Infirmary wards and each ward had two combs.[46]

In the 18th and 19th centuries, workhouses were essential in
making medical care available to the deprived and underprivileged,
and to those who clearly couldn't afford the fees asked for by doctors
and hospitals. Poorer members of society with contagious illnesses
were also frequently admitted, as were accident and emergency
cases. In 1873, Dr Julius St Thomas Clarke, medical officer and
surgeon at the Workhouse Infirmary from 1867 to 1880, noted in
his medical records that

> Among the accidents admitted were a case of fractured thigh, two
> cases of fracture of the upper arm, one of fractured ribs, and two of
> fracture of the forearm.[47]

The 1842 General Medical Order required Poor Law medical

---

45 *The Autobiography of Joseph Carey Merrick*
    (See Appendix One).

46 *Leicester Journal*, 21 November 1851.

47 *Medical Officer's Annual Report 1873.*

officers to be both qualified in medicine and surgery.[48] During Joseph's time in the workhouse, Dr Clement Frederick Bryan was the medical officer and surgeon. He was appointed in 1880, aged 29, and remained there for a further 34 years. Dr Bryan was also President of the Leicester Medical Society in 1894, and town councillor for the Liberal party in 1896. Unfortunately, Dr Bryan was criticised for his lack of record keeping, and those records he did make have not survived.[49]

Some records by Dr Julius St Thomas Clarke have survived though. In one of his medical reports from 1872, Dr Clarke records that he carried out skin grafting operations on 25 workhouse patients with ulcerated legs. Dr Clarke also performed eye surgery with the assistance of the District Officer, Dr Frank Fullager, this to remove an eyeball, correct squints and remove cataracts.[50] Dr Clarke sent letters to the Leicester Union Board of Guardians praising Dr Fullager's support, and to highlight the advantages of the procedures to both the patients and the organisation:

> The two cases of double squint and the one of single squint in the schools were operated on with considerable improvement. An old man.... also underwent, on two different occasions, the operation for cataract in each eye, the result being that he was enabled to read again and go about as usual. A young man...as also operated on with much success for a severe affliction of the eyelids, and has been thereby enabled to earn his living.... I believe the Board will join me in an expression of thanks to Mr Fullager, not only for the unlimited time he has placed at my disposal in the matters, but also for the hearty co-operation he has shown in his work.[51]

Early Victorian surgery was performed without anaesthetic. It was reported that a surgeon could amputate a limb in two-and-half-minutes - a slow operation when there's little or no pain relief.[52]

48 *Medicine and the Workhouse.* Edited by Jonathan Reinarz and Leonard Schwarz (2015).

49 Ibid.

50 Ibid.

51 *Medical Officer's Annual Report 1873.*

52 Robert Liston: www.historyofsurgery.co.uk/Web%20Pages/0413.htm.

By the mid-1800s to around 1900, chloroform was the accepted form of anaesthetic, and Joseph may have been given a Junker Inhaler to breathe in the chloroform before the commencement of the operation on his upper jaw. The Junker Inhaler was manufactured from 1867 by Krohne and Seseman of London, and was used to deliver chloroform-enriched air at high concentration into a mask. The concentrated vapour from the bottle was diluted by the patient's breath. The air was conveyed by a narrow rubber tube to the vaporiser bottle that contained the chloroform liquid.[53]

This would have rendered Joseph unconscious. Another contraption devised for a mouth operation in 1878 was the nasal intubation, which was developed to increase the depth of insensibility throughout operations on the mouth.

Whichever instrument was used, Joseph would not have felt pain until after the operation, as he would have been given opium and laudanum for pain relief. These two opioids were used up until the late 1800s, as the noted physician William Dale stated in 1871:

> Opium is…. our chief medicine for relieving pain and procuring sleep - our right hand in practice - the physician could ill spare it in his battle with disease and pain.[54]

The operation was obviously a success, and the larger portion of Joseph's growth was successfully removed.

If the surgeon undertaking the operation felt he could not acquire the specialised assistance or the correct apparatus, pauper patients could obtain medical treatment elsewhere. The Poor Law Continuation Act of 1851 legalised the use of voluntary hospitals. Leicester Union subscribed to voluntary establishments for specialist medical treatment and rehabilitation for its pauper patients, primarily the Leicester General Infirmary (now Leicester Royal Infirmary), and later Buxton Bath Charity and Margate Sea Bathing Infirmary. Although not in residence at the same time as Joseph Merrick, a young pauper patient by the name of Elizabeth

53 www.mushinmuseum.org.uk/junkersinhaler.html.
54 www.rpharms.com/museum-pdfs/e-pain.pdf.

Lucas, aged 6, returned to the workhouse from Margate Sea Bathing Infirmary "greatly improved in health and strength, with all abscesses healed."[55]

The medical care at the Leicester Union Workhouse is in stark contrast to the traditional image of workhouse medicine. The lengthy periods of service of its medical officers tells of their commitment and is summarised by Dr Bryan's statement to the Leicester Union Board of Guardians in 1903:

> The Sick Poor... ought to have the best treatment and I do not think anything ought to stand in the way of their receiving such treatments.[56]

In May 1882, soon after Joseph's operation, Leicester's Abbey Park was opened by the Prince and Princess of Wales.[57] Huge stands were erected and visitors from all over the country descended on the town. The Prince and Princess rode in a carriage through the streets, and the opening ceremony was conducted with great pomp and splendour. Afterwards, a sumptuous banquet supplied for the Royal Party by Mr J Crane of Market Place was "served in a manner which reflected upon him the highest credit".[58] Vast amounts of food was served over several courses, and afterwards dozens of toasts and speeches. The Prince expressed his "fervent wish for the prosperity of the town of Leicester" and, praising the "magnificent and enthusiastic reception we have met today", concluded "I do not doubt that before long the town of Leicester will be known as one of the healthiest and beautiful in the Kingdom."[59]

---

55 *Medicine and the Workhouse.* Edited by Jonathan Reinarz and Leonard Schwarz (2015).

56 Ibid.

57 Abbey Park was, and still is, a large recreation park in the grounds of the ruined Leicester Abbey, which had been built by Robert le Bossu, Earl of Leicester in 1143. It is also the final resting place of Cardinal Wolsey who, in November 1530, was en-route from York to London when he was taken ill in the town, and died at the Abbey. The Abbey ruins house Wolsey's memorial and lost grave. See www.leicester.gov.uk/leisure-and-culture/abbey-park.

58 *Leicester Mercury*, 12 January 2015.

59 Ibid.

Although all this excitement was going on outside the workhouse, the residents did not miss out. The children of the workhouse were entertained at a feast provided at the Temperance Hall, and they walked in procession from Market Place. According to the local paper they 'did ample justice to the substantial and tempting fare placed before them",[60] and each was presented with an orange and a medal. The adults didn't go without either. The inmates at the main building had a lavish dinner consisting of roast beef and pudding, and the occupants of the infirmary wards were regaled with lamb and new potatoes. The ailing inmates also had buns and plum cake for tea, and 6d each given to each of them, whilst the other inmates received snuff and tobacco and a pint of ale each. The rifle volunteer band played on the front lawn and, to end the day, a display of fireworks was put out on the front of the house, which must have been relished by inmates and local public.[61]

At that moment, little did Joseph Merrick realise that, in just a few years time, the Princess of Wales would personally visit him in his own apartments in London.

Although life in the workhouse was never meant to be an enjoyable experience, but rather the last resort, it is obvious that the Board of Guardians attempted to give the inmates some sort of standard of living and pride. It gave Joseph a roof over his head when he so desperately needed it, and without the workhouse and the Board of Guardians, he could have well ended up on the streets, dying at a young age from starvation and neglect. The workhouse may not be somewhere you want to end up, but it did give relief, shelter and food to the poor and destitute.

This report from the *Leicester Chronicle* describes the workhouse in 1866:

> That a workhouse is not a place that a man should try to enter, or expose himself to the obligation of entering, but at the same time, when we consider the various characters to be dealt with and the

---

60 Ibid.

61 *Leicester Chronicle*, 3 June 1882.

reproaches and calumnies to which those who undertake the guardianship of the poor are exposed, we say that the Leicester Union Workhouse is a much cleaner, healthier and better conducted establishment then we expected to find it. The order which prevails in every department is astonishing.[62]

Joseph remained at the workhouse for four long years. The last Christmas he spent there was in 1883. Dinner was served at the usual time of 12 o'clock, but for once there was no segregation, as schoolchildren sat with the adults. The boys wore clean collars with maroon coloured neckties, and the girls wore as much jewellery as they could find in their wardrobes. Christmas wreaths decorated the corridors and wards, artwork adorned the dining hall, and an enormous arch extending almost the entire width of the room was placed on a crimson background with dark green lettering forming the words "O come let us adore him, Christ the lord". The banner was brightened by coloured rosettes, stars and mottoes.

The pulpit was decorated by a trellis of evergreen over a crimson ground and white rosettes, and the rafters displayed trophies and baskets of flowers. Windows were full of evergreens and the windowsills covered by paper ornaments. On the far wall was an enormous banner, made by inmates and officers, of evergreen and crimson displaying the motto:

A Christmas Greeting

The peace of the spirit, that flies not away, be with thee and round thee, and o'er thee today.

Beer was served, along with tobacco and snuff. The 157 elderly inmates were given a gift of half a crown donated by Mr Cooper of Corah Sons & Cooper, the hosiery manufacturers, and the children received toys and pictures donated by a local resident, a Miss J A Mackennal of Edina Lodge, Stoneygate. There were enough toys and gifts for each child, and enough parcels for the sick. After dinner the entertainment and festivities continued.[63]

62 *Leicester Chronicle*, 8 September 1866.
63 *Leicester Chronicle*, 29 December 1883.

By now Joseph had spent four years in this institution, whether it be in the infirmary or the house itself, and must have been looking for a way to escape the daily routine and discipline.

He may have seen adverts in the local newspapers advertising penny shows, curiosities and freak shows. Sam Torr was a regular advertiser in the *Leicester Chronicle*, promoting his Palace of Varieties.[64] These adverts may have just lit the spark Joseph needed, because he wrote to Torr, possibly out of some sort of inquisitiveness, and requested that Sam visited him in the Workhouse.[65]

Joseph discharged himself from the Leicester Union Workhouse for the final time on 3 August 1884, two days before his 22nd birthday. He is listed as leaving on his 'own request'.[66]

The legend of the Elephant Man had now well and truly begun.

---

64 *Leicester Chronicle*, 14 June 1884.

65 *The True History of the Elephant Man* by Michael Howell and Peter Ford (Kindle Edition 2011).

66 *Workhouse Registers (Index Admissions and Discharge)*, Leicestershire, Leicester and Rutland Records Office: T615 107.

CHAPTER 6

"Well, Mr Merrick, I'll Call You Joseph If I May"

I'll get my living by being exhibited about the country. Knowing Mr Sam Torr, Gladstone Vaults, Wharf Street, Leicester, went in for Novelties, I wrote to him, he came to see me, and soon arranged matters, recommending me to Mr Ellis, Bee Hive Inn, Nottingham.[1]

Joseph Merrick was fully aware that his unique physical appearance drew interest, as crowds would often gather around him when he walked the open streets of Leicester. Merrick was also business-minded enough to know that crowds would pay good money to see the unusual, especially the 'grotesque'. He was now at a stage in a young man's life where his future is either made or broken, there and then, by the choices he makes. Should he accept a laborious life in the workhouse, where even the simplest of tasks would in time become increasingly difficult? Or should he take a chance in the bigger world?

Joseph knew precisely what he had and that money would be offered to see it, so he made the fateful decision to embrace the positives and contact the world of showbusiness. And in Leicester, showbusiness came in the form of Mr Samuel Torr, music hall owner and entertainer.

After Joseph had written to Torr, a meeting was arranged for the pair to speak with each other at Leicester workhouse. Sensing

---

1   *The Autobiography of Joseph Carey Merrick*
    (See Appendix One).

that he may be able to do something with this unassuming yet spectacularly captivating young man from Leicester, Torr persuaded three other gentleman from the entertainment business to form a syndicate with the aim of exhibiting Joseph around Leicestershire, Nottinghamshire and the rest of the East Midlands.

These were the travelling showman George Hitchcock, aka Little George, fairground operator Sam Roper, aka The Professor, and John Ellis, who styled himself as the Caterer of Public Novelties. The three men made an application for Joseph's discharge from the workhouse, and so, after giving the guarantees required by the authorities, Sam Torr managed to obtain the release of Joseph Merrick.[2]

By the end of the summer of 1883, Sam Torr was the proprietor of the Gaiety Palace of Varieties in Leicester, a well known music hall, and was also the licensee of The Green Man at 78 Wharf Street,[3] which stood almost opposite the Gaiety Palace, on a street which ran parallel to Merrick's childhood home of Lee Street.

Torr was also a music hall entertainer in his own right. After performing at various venues in London, making his fortune in the process, he went to Leicester where his father had been a tailor,[4] and after first taking on The Green Man, decided to venture into music hall ownership. So, on Thursday, 30 August 1883, a party by private invitation only took place at the Gaiety Palace of Varieties to celebrate the forthcoming opening.[5] The hall was also known by the name less-showbusiness name of the Gladstone Hotel, as it included Gladstone Hall, a spacious bar also used for entertainment, which the *Leicester Chronicle* described as an "excellently appointed saloon – for the purpose of furnishing amusement to the inhabitants

---

2 *The True History of the Elephant Man* by Michael Howell and Peter Ford (Kindle Edition 2011). It is unclear what the guarantees which Torr gave to the workhouse authorities were, and one suspects they may not have been entirely honest. However, what is clear is that Torr was offering to take Merrick off the parochial budget, and that may have been a big deciding factor in favour of Merrick being discharged.

3 1881 Census.

4 *The True History of the Elephant Man* by Michael Howell and Peter Ford (Kindle Edition 2011).

5 *Leicester Chronicle*, 1 September 1883.

residing in the crowded neighbourhood."[6]

The report goes on to describe

> The Palace of Varieties has many claims to admiration, the furnishings and decoration of the stage, proscenium hall etc, being of the most complete and artistic nature, and nothing is lacking that would tend to commence the undertaking to the appreciation of the public.[7]

There was space in the Palace for two hundred people in the main hall, with a promenade gallery upstairs providing seating for another 200. In addition, there was a reserved area near the orchestra and Chairman's seat for up to fifty guests. The building's beautiful gilding and stencilling was completed by a local painter named George Green.

On the opening night, Mr Stevenson Esq of Nottingham welcomed the audience on behalf of Sam Torr. He stated that he hoped the conduct of the house under Torr would result in cardinal support of his efforts, and he asked the audience to drink to the health of Her Royal Highness Queen Victoria.

After Stevenson's speech, new owner Sam Torr himself made an appearance, where he thanked the audience, and promised a future of the best entertainment under the guidance of the new manager he had recently appointed, Mr R.J. Rick. Torr then went on to perform one of his best known songs, *On the Back of Daddy-O*,[8] for which he dressed in a life-size dummy of his 'father', within a wicker frame, and on whose back he would appear to sit while singing:

> Here I am, friends, how do you do
> They call me Sam the silly-o
> This is my Dad you see
> Happy, good old billy-o[9]

---

6 Ibid. Gladstone Street runs off Wharf Street, and the Gaiety Palace of Varieties was situated on the corner of those streets.

7 *Leicester Chronicle*, 1 September 1883.

8 Ibid.

9 *The True History of the Elephant Man* by Michael Howell and Peter Ford (Kindle Edition 2011).

The chorus would follow each verse, with Sam hurtling around the stage while recounting:

> Gee up, gee whoa, and we go
> Mind yourself old laddie-o
> Gee up, gee whoa, and away we go
> On the back of Daddy-o[10]

After the private launch of the Gaiety Palace came the grand public opening, and one of the most successful music hall performers of her time, the popular male impersonator Vesta Tilley was topping the bill.[11] The Gaiety Palace continued with its musical acts, offering performances from the likes of the Four Gees, who were described as 'a talented combination, and with their eccentricity and grotesqueness of their performance create considerable amusement'.[12]

Torr's new venture seems to have focused mainly on musical and variety acts, not freak shows, and there is no evidence that Joseph ever worked at the Gaiety Palace, with no pamphlets, posters or newspaper articles found advertising Joseph. Sadly, in just under two years the theatre failed, and Torr sold the establishment. His daughter, Clara, kept a diary during this period, and the family's upset at this moment in time is laid bare in one written entry, which states:

> One morning my dear mother came into me in terrible distress saying "Clara, everything will be sold in a few days and we shall be homeless, whatever will become of us?".[13]

However, far from living on the streets, in 1891, the Torrs had moved to 87 Clapham Road in Lambeth, south London, by which stage Clara had followed in her father's entertaining footsteps and become a comedian, soprano and dancer.[14]

10 Ibid
11 *Leicester Chronicle*, 9 December 1893.
12 *Leicester Chronicle*, 6 September 1884.
13 arthurlloyd.co.uk.
14 1891 Census.

The original Gaiety Palace of Varieties was demolished in 1892, with the intention of opening a new theatre by October 1893. However, it wasn't until that December that J.B. Waring, acting on behalf of Messrs Westbrook Brothers, applied to name the new venue as The Empire Theatre of Varieties. This was not favoured so, after lengthy discussions, it was finally agreed the new name would be The New Empire Theatre.[15]

Joseph's debut was at the Bee Hive public house owned by John Ellis on Beck Street in Nottingham, probably in the August of 1884. He was presented as 'The Elephant Man, Half Man and Half Elephant',[16] a showbusiness name which was to resonate around the globe and establish Joseph's iconic status in later years.

By the October of 1884 the Nottingham Goose Fair was well underway. Wombwell's Royal National Menagerie was in residence, complete with its zoological collection.[17] Although there is no evidence that Joseph was exhibited, it's entirely possible that he was. Alderman Gilpin of the Nottingham Town Council had already put restrictions in place to "stop showman exhibiting anything revolting to the public".[18]

By 1884, freak shows had reached their glory days. Menageries, circuses, ghost shows, exhibitions and waxworks conquered the showground landscape. The thrill-seeking public congregated at these annual events to not only enjoy the exciting fairground rides, but to also witness the peep shows, illusion booths and exhibitions of freaks. Famous showmen such as Lord George Sanger, Tom Norman and the renowned Bostock and Wombwell Menageries had all become household names.[19]

Unfortunately, the manner of show at which Joseph exhibited himself was self-limiting, because once seen he was not forgotten, with little point in paying to view him again. So, in the late autumn of

15 *Leicester Chronicle,* 9 December 1893.
16 *The Leicester Historian* Vol 3, No. 7 (1989).
17 *Nottingham Evening Post,* 1 October 1884.
18 *Nottingham Evening Post,* 6 October 1884.
19 National Fairground Archive (www.sheffield.ac.uk/nfa/index).

1884, once Joseph had exhausted his tour of the Midland towns, he was sent to London to meet Tom Norman, a flash young showman whose nickname 'The Silver King' had been acquired when he appeared at the circus and Fair held at the Royal Agricultural Hall[20] in London's Islington[21] in 1882.[22]

At that time, Tom was oblivious to the fact that the distinguished showman Phineas Taylor Barnum was one of the spectators watching him work, and when the pair met after the show, the great P.T. pointed to Tom's large silver Albert watch chain, which he always wore, and said "Silver King eh?" From that point onwards the young showman wore his new nickname with pride.[23]

Not much older himself than Joseph, Norman did not grow up in the travelling showman fraternity, and he certainly wasn't the drunken bully portrayed in David Lynch's 1980 film *The Elephant Man*. There is no evidence whatsoever to show that Norman beat or struck Joseph, and he certainly didn't squander the show's earnings on drink. As far back as 1882, two years before meeting Joseph Merrick, Tom Norman had signed a pledge with the Church of England Temperance Society, a society set up to encourage self-discipline through abstinence from drink,[24] and a photograph of him taken at more or less the same time reveals an enamel badge on his left lapel bearing the letters T.N.T.A.U, the Travellers' National Temperance Abstinence Union.[25] It seems the portrayal of Tom Norman, renamed 'Bytes' in the film and plays, was nothing more than artistic license to sell a sympathetic story to the public rather than any attempt to stick to the facts.

20 *The Penny Showman: Tom Norman, Silver King.* With additional writings by his son George Norman (1985).

21 www.victorianlondon.org/entertainment/agricultralhall.htm.

22 www.sheffield.ac.uk/nfa/researchandarticles/tomnorman.

23 *The Penny Showman: Tom Norman, Silver King.* With additional writings by his son George Norman (1985).

24 socialconcern.org.uk/our-history.

25 *The Penny Showman: Tom Norman, Silver King.* With additional writings by his son George Norman (1985).

In the published account of Tom Norman's memoirs, his son George adds how they encountered the modern version of artistic licence:

> The television people sent a camera crew from Birmingham which my brother Arthur and I met outside the shop in Whitechapel Road, where Tom Norman had exhibited the Elephant Man almost a century before. The 'head' man said how pleased he was with the interview, and that every minute of it would be shown. I had my doubts about that. As one of the camera crew, or may have been the driver, muttered in my ear, 'like hell he will'. He mentioned the name of a titled gentleman who had big interests in both the TV and in the film. 'They won't put that lot out – you said the wrong things'. He was right, the interview was never shown.[26]

George continued:

> The TV people didn't find it very profitable to come from Birmingham to hear the truth about Tom Norman and the Elephant Man, which made parts of their film just what it was - the product of a distorted imagination.

Tom Norman was born Thomas Noakes in the Manor House in Dallington, East Sussex, in 1860. At the age of fourteen he left home, surrendering his birth right as the oldest son, and changed his surname from Noakes to Norman. No one in his family have any idea why he did this but he never used the name Noakes again.

Tom had originally grown up in a family butchering business, after his father had inherited the Manor House in Dallington and everything else that came with it, including the farm, grazing fields, slaughterhouse and butcher shops. Tom left school at twelve, and on his horse Little Wonder would help deliver meat around the surrounding villages. On occasion Tom would get distracted and end up following the East Sussex hounds, who were out on a hunt. He got so engrossed in the hunt one day that he left a customer's order hanging on a tree, and was later made to walk his round whenever

26 *The Penny Showman: Tom Norman, Silver King.* With additional writings by his son George Norman (1985).

the hounds were out.

On leaving home he headed to London, where he worked in many different high class family trade establishments in salubrious areas. It was when working as a butcher's assistant on Chapel Street in Islington that Tom noticed that the shop next door, which had been empty, was now in use. A man was standing on a box on the footpath outside the shop bellowing and drawing a large crowd. This was Tom Norman's first encounter of a penny show. According to his memoirs, he held no interest in them at all and if it hadn't been for his supervisor asking if he wanted to see the show, he probably wouldn't have bothered.

The penny show being exhibited was Madam Electra, a young girl of seventeen who, according to the showman, was born deaf and dumb and full of electricity in all parts of her body. The showman would ask the audience to lend him copper coins, which he would then place into a glass of water. He would explain that the more coins, the better the demonstration. After he had collected a sizeable number of coins, the showman would go on to enlighten the audience that Madam Electra would now walk among them holding the water and money-filled glass, and all they have to do is take the money out. Perhaps not surprisingly, the majority of the audience would dare not risk putting their fingers in the glass to retrieve the coins. The showman then ended the show by exclaiming: "Am I to understand that you have made me a present of coins that remain in the glass?" and, before any of the audience could reply, the showman ended with "that concludes the performance on this occasion – please tell your friends about it".

Instead of telling his friends about it, Tom Norman approached the showman and was invited to become his assistant. After contemplation, Tom considered it easier than butchering and decided to give the life of a showman a try-out. The first exhibit he managed was the one he had first encountered, Madam Electra, who according to Tom always took the lion's share of the takings, stayed in good standard apartments, and, as Tom quotes in his memoirs,

...notwithstanding the fact that she was supposed to be deaf and dumb, had quite a lot to say, especially when it came to sharing up the takings.[27]

Tom, as assistant, got a small percentage, and slept in tents or on boards underneath the barrow.[28] However, the business was lucrative, as an American newspaper commented: "It is a bigger thing to be a freak then to marry a rich widow".[29]

It was on a Thursday in November 1884 that Tom Norman agreed to take over the management of Joseph Merrick, the Elephant Man. Joseph was escorted to London by syndicate member George Hitchcock.[30] If travelling from Leicester, the pair would have boarded a train at the Campbell Street station, which had opened in 1840.[31] Joseph and 'Little' George walked up London Road, a street well known to Joseph as he would have trudged the very same pavements to and from the workhouse. Just before reaching Conduit Street, the road which led to the House on the Hill, Joseph and George turned off and headed towards the ticket booking office, which was approachable through Campbell Street itself. In the booking office, first class travellers were separated from their much poorer acquaintances by a well-designed iron railing. The station and line was run by the Midland Counties Railway, whose offices engaged the upper floor above the booking offices and gaslit waiting and refreshment rooms.[32]

Upon their arrival at the station's one and only platform,[33] the

27 Biography of Tom Norman from *The Penny Showman: Tom Norman, Silver King*. With additional writings by his son George Norman (1985).

28 Ibid.

29 *Leicester Chronicle*, 2 January 1886.

30 *The Penny Showman: Tom Norman, Silver King*. With additional writings by his son George Norman (1985).

31 Campbell Street rail station stood very close to where Leicester's present day station is situated on London Road.

32 *The Midland Counties Railway*. Edited by P.S. Stevenson (1989).

33 Ibid.

pair waited for the afternoon train to London's St Pancras station,[34] which rolled into Leicester at 4.09pm and was due to arrive at St Pancras at 6.40pm.[35] If Joseph and Little George were travelling on the Great Eastern Railway, an invalid carriage could be requested. Although extremely expensive and only truly for the upper classes, the invalid carriage, specially designed for those with disabilities, was a first class coach fitted with couches and an ante-room for the attendants. The cost was a double first class fare to the invalid, and a single first class fare for the accompanying passengers.[36]

After arriving in London in the late afternoon,[37] Joseph was taken to meet Tom Norman. Dressed in a long black coat and a black felt hat, with a woollen muffler up to his eyes, he was introduced as 'Joe'.[38]

Tom Norman recalled in his memoirs that when he took a good look at Joseph he thought "Oh God, I can't use you". However, when looking into Joseph's eyes Tom could see pleading and suffering, and he felt great pity and sympathy. To put Joseph at ease, Tom shook the nervous young man from Leicester's hand, and said, "Well, Mr Merrick, I'll call you Joseph if I may."[39]

By this time Joseph's head measured thirty-six inches in circumference, with a large substance of flesh at the back, and his feet and legs were covered with thick lumpy skin.[40]

The property where Tom Norman exhibited Joseph Merrick was not, as Dr Frederick Treves describes, 'a vacant greengrocer which

---

34 *The Penny Showman: Tom Norman, Silver King.* With additional writings by his son George Norman (1985).

35 *Cook's Continental Time Tables & Tourist Handbook.* (2013 Edition. Originally published March 1873).

36 Ibid.

37 *The Penny Showman: Tom Norman, Silver King.* With additional writings by his son George Norman (1985).

38 Ibid.

39 Ibid.

40 *The Autobiography of Joseph Carey Merrick*
    (See Appendix One).

was up for let',[41] but a waxworks which for several years had been owned by a man named Cotton, from whom Tom had rented it.[42]

Money for rent wasn't always obtainable, because as well as exhibiting the 'novelties' you had to pay them as well, as well as take care of their board and lodgings. The 'novelties' on display grew very rich, partly due to competition from museums which ran up the price of the 'curiosities', until their salaries were larger than that of any professional performer, making more money without ever opening their mouths than most accomplished actor or actresses of their day.

Captain Costentenus, the original tattooed Greek, retired on his fortune and lived on a fine estate in his homeland, and Dudley Foster, a very small man known as 'Hop-o-my-thumb', made enough money to buy his father his own farm.[43] During the height of their popularity, these shows were a livelihood for the deformed and outcast members of the working poor, who would struggle to support themselves in what could be termed as normal society. Rather than ending up in the workhouse or local asylums, they remained independent of any welfare state relief in the 19th century.

Even though plenty of money could be earned, sometimes the profits were just not there, and sometimes ways and means had to be found in order to get a shop for free. The busiest thoroughfares were preferred, and many were scoured for an empty shop upon them. The property's agent would be spoken to, usually between the hours of 10 and 11 o'clock on a Saturday morning, and the following conversation would then take place:

> "Good morning Sir, I see that you have the letting of premises in .... Street or Road?"
>
> "Yes, that is so"
>
> "What might the terms be?"

---

41 *The Elephant Man and Other Reminiscences* by Sir Frederick Treves (1923).

42 *The Penny Showman: Tom Norman, Silver King.* With additional writings by his son George Norman (1985).

43 Ibid.

The conversation usually ended with Tom getting the keys to the premises, and he would wait for the agent to leave their place of work about 12 o'clock to go home, which was usually out of town. The shop would be in use from Saturday afternoon through to Sunday, and would pack up first thing Monday morning, upon which Tom would leave the key in an envelope with the following message, thus ensuring a virtually free stay:

> Dear Sir
>
> Herewith please find enclosed the key of number so & so street. I am sorry to inform you, that the premises are not suitable for the company's purpose.
>
> Yours etc etc....[44]

Everything for the show had to be portable and easy to assemble and dissemble. Once the agent had left, oil paintings were put in windows, sawdust spread on the floors, and to write on the windows, soap or whitener was used. Old enamel advertisements were laid on the flooring to save the floor from being burnt when a coke fire was lit in a bucket. So frequent were these shows in any busy thoroughfare that hardly anyone ever complained, and according to Tom the police 'were as good as gold for about a sixpence a night'.

Number 123 Whitechapel Road, in London's East End, was kept clean, tidy and warm by Tom's young assistant 'Little Jimmy', a lad of about 12-years-old who would sweep the shop every morning. Warmth came from a large installed gas ring, which was surrounded by bricks to keep in the heat. This also doubled up as a stove to heat food and drink. There were two small iron beds, one for Tom Norman himself, and the other for Joseph. Once Norman sent Little Jimmy out to buy new mattresses and blankets, which he put on Joseph's bed, and installed a curtain for Joseph's privacy. Even though it was 'rough and ready' comfort, Joseph confided in Norman, saying "I don't ever want to go back to that place", probably referring to the workhouse.[45]

44 *The Penny Showman: Tom Norman, Silver King.* With additional writings by his son George Norman (1985).

45 Ibid.

Once Joseph was settled, the show commenced on the following Monday at around midday. Tom had been left posters by Little George Hitchcock which described Joseph as 'Half Man, Half Elephant', which a garish illustration depicting him rampaging through the jungle, with the head of an elephant .

As well as the posters, the showman's banter had to lure the public in. Norman describes this mockery as 'the showman's licence'. Pointing to the illustrations, Norman would educate the passersby:

> The Elephant Man is not here to frighten you, but to enlighten you, but I would like to stress that ladies in a delicate state of Health are advised not to attend.[46]

Once an audience had assembled he would then continue:

> Ladies and Gentleman, in the absence of the lecturer with your indulgence I would like to introduce Mr Joseph Merrick, the Elephant Man. Before doing so I ask you please to prepare yourselves – Brace yourselves up to witness one who is probably the most remarkable human being ever to draw breath of life.[47]

As the show was about to begin, the audience would stand in anticipation, their curiosity already roused by the showman's banter. The curtains were pulled back and many would gasp in horror and shock, and some leave the show, but Tom would carry on:

> Ladies and Gentleman, I ask you please not to despise or condemn this man on account of his unusual appearance. Remember we do not make ourselves, and were you to cut or prick Joseph he would bleed, and that bleed or blood would be red, the same as yours or mine.[48]

Tom would tell the account of a terrible accident with circus elephants which befell Joseph's mother when six months pregnant, his sad pitiful life in the Leicester Workhouse, and how Joseph seized the moment of joining 'the showmen' to secure his release, pay his

---

46 *The Penny Showman: Tom Norman, Silver King.* With additional writings by his son George Norman (1985).

47 Ibid.

48 Ibid.

way and be independent financially, free from charity.[49]

It was Tom Norman's role, as Joseph's manager, to sell him to the public, and like many other showmen in the business, his job was to 'tell the tale'. A fellow showman and friend of Norman's, Jib Bennett, did exactly the same thing. He would put a big gag cloth outside his show announcing: "The man with TWO _____. No Ladies Admitted, Gentleman only", but as soon as the spectators had flowed into the auditorium, he surprised and possibly disappointed his customers as the man with two thumbs on one hand appeared.[50]

As well as the banter and the posters, Tom had also been left with about a thousand pamphlets to be sold at ½d each at the end of the show. They explained a brief history of Joseph's life, and all money received in the sales went straight to Joseph himself.[51]

Joseph may well have received this money from the sales of his pamphlets, but George Hitchcock, who had escorted him from Leicester, had to wait a little longer for his wages, as an article in the *London Evening Standard* reported:

> A man made an application for a summons for wages against the proprietors of the "Half Elephant Man" – Mr Bushby: What is that? – Warrant officer Ringer explained that the Applicant was speaking of a "show" which had recently been exhibited at Whitechapel - . The Applicant said that he had agreed with the proprietors of what was called the "Half Elephant Man" to look after the "show". He travelled with it from Leicester, and his duty was to see that the "Half Elephant" was properly looked after. The Applicant then stated that he could not obtain his full wages. – Mr Bushby said he could not entertain the case but the complainant must go to the County Court.[52]

About a week after Joseph's arrival, Tom awoke and, as Joseph hadn't fastened his curtains securely, noticed that he was sleeping sitting up with his knees supporting his chin. Joseph later explained he slept in that position because to lie down was too perilous; he

49 Ibid.
50 Ibid.
51 Ibid.
52 *London Evening Standard*, 14 January 1885.

might possibly awake with a broken neck.[53] On hearing this, Tom enlisted the help of friend named Joe Wintle to make a light yoke, which would be secured to Joseph's shoulders to support his head whilst laying down. Wintle's wife and their next door neighbour were basket weavers, and they made the basketware 'pillow' which would support Joseph's head. It was padded with lamb's wool, and within a few days Wintle had completed the yoke, and passed it to Joseph to use. Everybody seemed happy with the final result, but Joseph was soon to complain that it wasn't that comfortable.[54]

The mid- to late-Victorian era was the heyday of the modern freak show, but its history goes back further. In medieval Europe, monstrous births were interpreted as divine signs and omens, warning of impending danger, but by the 16th century this began to change and these unfortunate people were seen as objects of curiosity, and those with physical defects such as hunchbacks or dwarves were looked upon as court jesters or fools.

One well-known dwarf, Jeffrey, lived in the court of Queen Henrietta Maria, wife to Charles I. He was born in 1619 in Oakham, Rutland, and by the time he was eight years old was only 18 inches tall. He remained at this height until he was thirty, when, rather oddly, he grew another two feet. His father was employed by George Villiers, the Duke of Buckingham, and when Jeffrey was seven-years-old he was presented to the Duchess of Buckingham, who took him into service and dressed him in fine silk and satins. When Charles I and his Queen visited the Buckingham's estate in Burley, the Duke and Duchess hosted a banquet in their honour. Jeffrey was made to get inside a huge venison pie, which was placed on the table. As a trumpet was blown the pie was cut, and Jeffrey jumped out in a full suit of armour. Not long after the banquet, Jeffrey joined the court of Queen Henrietta Maria.[55]

By the 17th century, freak shows and curiosities were increasingly

---

53 *The Penny Showman: Tom Norman, Silver King.* With additional writings by his son George Norman (1985).

54 Ibid.

55 *Tales of Old Leicestershire* by Marian Pipe (1991).

seen across the country and the continent in taverns, market places and fairs.

By the mid-19th century these shows were an international institution, and as there was no legislation in Britain preventing the exhibition of human curiosities, medical professionals were free to visit shows and examine the deformed bodies on display.[56]

In fact, just after Tom Norman had the sleeping yoke made for Joseph, the show was starting to attract the attention of medical students from the London Hospital, which was situated directly opposite the shop on the Whitechapel Road.[57] At first the visits from medical students during their breaks were welcomed, attracting money and much-needed free advertisement, but after a few days they became a nuisance with their questions. They were holding up the business, and Tom reluctantly asked them to leave.

One eminent surgeon, Sir John Bland-Sutton, often visited the Mile End Road, especially on Saturday nights, to see dwarves, giants, fat women and other monstrosities at the freak shows. There was a freak museum at The Bell and Mackerel public house, near the London Hospital, and it was on one of these visits in 1884 that Bland-Sutton saw the Elephant Man, whom he described as "a poor fellow, deformed in head, face and limbs. His skin, thick and pendulous, hung in folds and resembled the hide of an elephant."[58]

Sometime in late November 1884, London Hospital's Dr Reginald Tuckett approached Tom Norman asking to meet Joseph. Tom writes in his memoirs that he liked Tuckett's appearance, and he straight away introduced him to Merrick. After the three of them had chatted, Dr Tuckett asked if a Dr Treves could also visit Joseph, but before the shop was open, so as not to obstruct business.

Norman later wrote:

> Had I only known at the time the trouble, antagonism and abuse that man [Treves] caused me, my answer would definitely had been quite

56 Ibid.
57 *The Penny Showman: Tom Norman, Silver King.* With additional writings by his son George Norman (1985).
58 *Lancashire Evening Post*, 1 May 1930.

different, and I would not have agreed to meet Mr Treves at that time, or any other.[59]

However, the Silver King did meet Dr Frederick Treves. One morning not long after Tuckett's visit, Tom was in a coffee house on the Whitechapel Road buying breakfast for himself and Joseph, when his young manager Little Jimmy sent out a whistle, and pointed Dr Treves in his direction.[60]

"Are you Tom, the showman?" asked Treves.

"That is my name Sir, unfortunately".

Norman always added the word 'unfortunately' to break the ice in a conversation. Usually when asked "Unfortunately, why?" Norman would answer, "I sometimes wish I was someone else".

Treves, according to Norman, ignored his light-hearted response, so Tom continued to order breakfast for Joseph and himself. He gave Treves at most 15 minutes with Joseph, explaining they both needed and wanted their breakfast.[61]

Not long after Treves' visit, Dr Tuckett enquired if Tom would be willing for Joseph to attend the hospital and appear before a group of medical people. Joseph agreed, believing more publicity could do no harm, and might do himself a bit of good. After his second or third visit, Joseph said he didn't want to go again. According to Norman, Joseph claimed he had no objection to being on show under the showman's stewardship, as he was presented in a decent manner and getting paid for it,

> But over there [referring to London Hospital] I was stripped naked, and felt like an animal at the cattle market.[62]

59 *The Penny Showman: Tom Norman, Silver King*. With additional writings by his son George Norman (1985).

60 Ibid. It must be noted that this account differs from the more brutal, sordid and well-known account of the meeting given by Treves. It is understandable that both men would wish to recall there events in such a way that their own image comes across as the more favourable.

61 *The Penny Showman: Tom Norman, Silver King*. With additional writings by his son George Norman (1985).

62 Ibid.

Treves, like Bland-Sutton, made a habit of scouting street exhibitions for pathological cases. An article in the *Guyoscope* in 1898 described the scientific obsession with sideshow acts, and reported that a senior physician on the staff of the London Hospital had attended P.T. Barnum's show in order to "inspect the Freaks in the scientific interest."[63]

Dr Treves repeated presentations of his medical specimens at meetings of the Pathological Society, almost mirroring the sensationalism of the penny shows. His subjects were repeatedly gruesome, and the medical 'sideshows' seemed to be very lucrative and competitive. In 1888 Bland-Sutton medically exhibited Lalloo, an Indian male who came into this world accompanied his parasitic twin, whom Bland-Sutton had seen at a show on Tottenham Court Road. In Bland-Sutton's memoirs he explained the difference between sideshow and the scientific, and claimed with pride that his anatomical demonstrations got the name of 'Bland-Sutton's entertainment'.[64]

About a week after Joseph had confessed to Tom Norman that he "felt like an animal at a cattle market", Tom was again asked to allow Joseph to go back over to the hospital, but this time the request was refused. This rejection was followed almost immediately by a personal visit from Treves, who claimed he had a few distinguished guests who would like to meet Joseph. Norman describes Treves as "almost desperate, afraid, I imagine, of 'losing face' among his colleagues."[65] Norman turned to Joseph to see if his business colleague would consider another visit, but Joseph, having a will of his own, refused, stating that Treves and his colleagues would only be able to view him as paying customers.[66]

According to Norman, Treves could hardly control his rage at being

---

63 *The Spectacle of Deformity: Freak Shows and Modern British Culture* by Nadja Durbach (Kindle Edition 2010).

64 Ibid.

65 *The Penny Showman: Tom Norman, Silver King*. With additional writings by his son George Norman (1985).

66 Ibid.

turned down, and it was from this moment which Norman believed Treves started a campaign of disparagement against him, Tom being convinced that Treves was instrumental in closing down the show, and through this, splitting he and Joseph up.

When the show was closed down a few days later, Tom sent Joseph to live with an elderly couple in Whitechapel for a few months, until the new travelling season began in 1885. Joseph had £50 in his pocket, money he had earned from freely displaying himself and selling pamphlets. He had always been keen to earn his own living and be independent of charity, according to Tom Norman.

One day a fellow showman came to see Joseph's show, and suggested they should work the 'nobbings', which was the act of going round the crowds with a hat collecting money, something Norman had never done before. However, upon hearing this, Norman claimed, Joseph immediately turned round and said "We are not beggars are we Thomas?"[67]

During the 1880s and 1890s, many penny shows and sideshows were being shut down, with showman receiving hefty fines, mainly due to the increase of people complaining of nuisance and noise.

In February 1889, Thomas Barry, a showman at 106-107 Whitechapel Road, was indicted at the Old Bailey[68] on the charge of "creating a nuisance by exhibiting figures illustrating a show and causing idle people to assemble and remain in the Queen's highway". PC28 JR, who was called as a witness, said the pictures which caused the most attention were those relating to the Whitechapel Murders by Jack the Ripper, with one of the pictures showing six women lying down, covered in blood and with their clothing disturbed. As many as 200 people had gathered for this show, for which Thomas Barry was fined £100.[69]

Two years later, Henry Davies of John's Place, Bedford Street in Stepney and Henry Roberts of Tyson Passage were summoned

67   *The Penny Showman: Tom Norman, Silver King.* With additional writings by his son George Norman (1985).

68   *London Daily News,* 26 February 1891.

69   *The Era,* 9 February 1889.

to Worship Street Police Court for causing an obstruction of the highway at the very same address at Barry had been caught, 106-107 Whitechapel Road. Evidence of the disturbance was given by one of the House Governors and nurses at the London Hospital, who had complained the show was disturbing patients and that the approach to the hospital had been obstructed.

Despite his show being closed down, Norman carried on with his career, continuing with the pattern of shows closing down, him being fined, and then opening up again elsewhere.

One of his shows was staged at 151 High Street in Shoreditch when he was summoned for wilfully obstructing a free passageway. It was Inspector Williams who saw large pictures and placards in the windows of a shop announcing a 'fat woman as the celebrated only Russian Giantess' and two midgets and ponies. The show was being announced by a man standing at the doorway, inviting people to walk up and come on in, and although cautioned, Tom Norman continued to open this show every evening.

This was not Norman's first conviction, and it seemed to have been a regular occurrence, as he had previous convictions going back four or five years.[70] In April 1891 he spent one month in Pentonville Prison after receiving 13 summonses to appear in front of magistrate Montagu Williams for causing an obstruction by using a tout to advertise his shows,[71] but Tom was not deterred. At one point he was fined £67 after receiving 32 summonses to appear at Worship Street Police Court. In his defence he stated he hadn't spoken outside the show, but this wasn't taken into account; he had caused an obstruction and was liable to a penalty.[72]

The legality of street performances was outlined in the *Police Code*, drawn up by the Director of the CID, Howard Vincent:

> Every person who, to the annoyance or obstruction of the inhabitants, exhibits any show or public entertainment in a thoroughfare, is liable

70 *Tamworth Herald*, 23 March 1891.

71 *The Era*, 2 May 1891.

72 *The Penny Showman: Tom Norman, Silver King*. With additional writings by his son George Norman (1985).

to a penalty, and may be apprehended if necessary, and the offence is committed within sight of the constable to whom complaint is made.[73]

Tom Norman, the Silver King, carried on with his showman career right up to his death in Croydon on 24 August 1930, a calling which took him all over the country in a career spanning almost 60 years. Even at the time of his death, his son, George Norman, revealed that his father was even then making plans to travel a large auction show around the country.[74]

Tom Norman was no saint, but the generosity and magnanimity he showed to his 'novelties, freaks, clients', and to his fellow showmen, as well as his relationship with the Temperance Association, reveal the unfairness done to his character by the erroneous versions of Tom's relationship with Joseph Merrick.

The following tribute to Tom Norman was published in the *World's Fair* newspaper:

> There are very few showmen who have not met the famous showman's auctioneer, "The Silver King". He has been a conspicuous and charismatic figure in our business for the past half a century and has conducted more showman's sales than any other auctioneer in the country. During his fifty years with us, he has endeared himself to all sections from the humblest to the highest. He was a charming personality with a commanding appearance that left a lifetime impression upon anyone that he met. All his life he has been a showman and as such he died.[75]

As for Joseph Merrick, he was back on the show circuit after his jaunt in Whitechapel, carrying £50 and a series of photographs which Dr Frederick Treves had had taken. One of the photographs had been used for promotional purposes, with a bit or artistic licence applied, as an artist had added a trunk to the front of Joseph's face to

---

73 *Sir Howard Vincent's Police Code, 1889* by Neil R.A. Bell and Adam Wood (2015).

74 www.sheffield.ac.uk/mfa/researchandarticles/tomnorman.

75 Ibid.

76 *The True History of the Elephant Man* by Michael Howell and Peter Ford (Kindle Edition 2011).

produce a leaflet called *The Autobiography of Joseph Carey Merrick*.[76]

It was now the early spring of 1885, and Joseph had joined 'Professor' Sam Roper's travelling circus.[77]

Life on the open road began once again.

---

77   Ibid.

CHAPTER 7

Looking For the Only Real Friend Joseph Ever Had

In the winter and early spring of 1885, Joseph had found himself on the road once more, travelling around the Midlands with Sam Roper, one of the four gentleman who had helped secure his discharge from the Leicester Union Workhouse.[1]

During his time with Sam, Joseph was lucky enough to be provided with his own caravan in which to travel, rest and sleep in, affording him some privacy.[2] Whilst working with Tom Norman in London he temporarily lived in the shops where he was being exhibited, but touring with Sam Roper and his circus meant the scenery changed constantly as they were travelling to numerous towns weekly, and sometimes daily. The chances of the attraction shutting down were lower outside of London, and Joseph's exhibition had less chance of becoming stale with the public.

The 'Burton' was the caravan of choice most showman used.[3] Waggons had characteristics relative to their place of build, with the Burton being identified with the Staffordshire town of Burton-on-Trent. The caravan was straight-sided, with the wheels projecting either side of the body to give maximum floor space for the user. In the roof was a skylight, and the walls were panelled with elaborately-

---

1   *The True History of the Elephant Man* by Michael Howell and Peter Ford (Kindle Edition 2011).

2   Ibid.

3   Ibid.

carved oak plaques fixed to each panel.[4]

The Burton caravan measured 10 ft x 10 ft 6", with a porch, two shuttered windows on either side and one at the rear. The front porch was fitted with a striped canvas awning, which was strutted from front corner pillars; however, this canopy had a tendency to deteriorate after a few years and was infrequently replaced. In the interior of the caravan was a stove, which was centrally placed between the two offside windows. And opposite to the stove was a chest of drawers with a table top, where Joseph would have kept his personal items, and above, a shallow glazed cupboard for tableware with small drawers beneath for cutlery. Although the caravan had two beds which filled the whole width of the van, Joseph obviously only used one, and the odour that followed him around probably meant that he didn't share his caravan. At the furthest end from door, the upper berth was 6 ft x 3 ft 4", with the lower berth a little narrower. If typical of the era, Joseph's windows would have had laced curtains which were bobble-fringed or lace-edged and looped back as drapes. The floor was lined with linoleum and skin rugs. As cooking was usually done outside over a wood fire, the caravan's stove was only used occasionally, for heating, making tea or preparing food in bad weather.[5]

During his time spent with Sam Roper, Joseph made friends with the young boys who worked in the boxing booth, Bertram Dooley and Harry Bramley. Bertram was the nephew of Sam Roper through marriage, and Harry Bramley's cousin. They were known as 'Sam Roper's boxing midgets':[6]

> About 300 persons assembled at the Corn Exchange, on Monday evening, to witness an assault at arms, promoted by Mr W. Hebberd of this town. Several noted 'pugs' were engaged and a capital performance was witnessed. The first bout was between Alex Munroe, 'the black' and Red Condon, both of whom have won prizes in the ring. These were followed by young Wilson, of Leicester, and Birchall,

---

4 Ibid.

5 *The English Gypsy Caravan* by C.H. Ward-Jackson & Denis E Harvey (1973).

6 Ibid.

some sharp exchanges being the result. Professor Roper's midgets (nine and ten years) were next introduced, and greatly pleased the onlookers. Others engaged included Alf Kilbridge, Richard Birch, Pat Condon (London) and Walter Hebberd (Northamptonshire).[7]

Bertram delighted in visiting Joseph in his caravan, where they would often sit and natter, undoubtedly parking themselves on the porch, with a wood fire burning, looking up at the night sky and enjoying conversations "on subjects that you would never really think a man in that condition would talk about".[8] Considering Frederick Treves wrote in his memoirs the Joseph's speech "almost unintelligible"[9] Bertram and Joseph would apparently discuss some "very upstage subjects".[10]

Bertram Dooley's son, William Dooley (who himself was in the entertainment industry going under the stage name of Benson Dulay), remembers his father saying that Joseph "was a bit on the religious side too..."[11]

As boxers, obviously strong, fit and active, Bertram and Harry took it upon themselves to become Joseph's unofficial bodyguards, warding off any unwelcome attention Joseph attracted.[12]

It was Sam Roper who had Joseph's 'theatrical' cloak made to hide his unusual shape, because local children from the towns they visited would often pursue Joseph outside the fairground and to his caravan.[13] On one occurrence, when the fair had been set up in Market Square in Northampton, Joseph was being harassed by the town hoodlums and the instigator tried to pull Joseph's cloak from around him, but Harry came to the rescue, and according to Bertram

---

7   *Northampton Mercury*, 5 April 1884.

8   *The True History of the Elephant Man* by Michael Howell and Peter Ford (Kindle Edition 2011).

9   *The Elephant Man and Other Reminiscences* by Sir Frederick Treves (1923).

10 *The True History of the Elephant Man* by Michael Howell and Peter Ford (Kindle Edition 2011).

11 Ibid.

12 Ibid.

13 Ibid.

Dooley "laid the boy out, completely out. He must have hit him hard, but he was a good boxer, was Harry. He was pretty broad, well-built chap, and could use them...".[14]

After some months had passed, Sam Roper began to grow nervous about the Elephant Man and the attention that followed him. He felt the show was under close scrutiny, and feared some kind of pending court case.[15] In the spring of 1885, a series of adverts appeared in the entertainment newspaper *The Era*, a weekly national newspaper which carried details about theatres, actors and music halls. One article dated 18 April 1885 suggests that Joseph had ended his contract with Sam Roper, and had gone back to Leicester with Sam Torr, who was probably acting as his agent. It seemed he was now looking for employment on the continent:

> The Greatest Monstrosity of the Age, the Elephant Man, is out of engagement. Would only show on the continent.
>
> Has shown with great success in England. For photos and terms apply to agent, Mr Sam Torr, Gaiety Palace, Leicester.[16]

As the weeks passed, it seems Sam Torr was getting impatient; more freak shows were shutting down and the Gaiety Palace on Wharf Street in Joseph's home town of Leicester was closing for the summer months.

A final advert appeared in *The Era* at the end of May 1885:

> Gaiety Palace of Varieties, Wharf Street, Leicester
> Proprietor, Mr Sam Torr
>
> NOTICE – In consequence of the Closing of this establishment for the Summer Months, all engagements from Saturday, May 30th instance, are cancelled.
>
> To foreign agents -- The Elephant Man, the greatest novelty on record, prefers the continent. Address, Sam Torr, as above.[17]

---

14 Ibid.
15 *The True History of the Elephant Man* by Michael Howell and Peter Ford (Kindle Edition 2011).
16 *The Era*, 18 April 1885.
17 *The Era*, 30 May 1885.

It wasn't long before Joseph's wish to tour abroad was granted. William Dooley, Bertram's son, remembers his father saying that "an Italian with name like 'Ferrari' proposed the tour." He was "an Italian born, but he was really the same as a cockney Italian, like the ice cream version".[18]

Bertram recalls Ferrari claiming "I will put him in a show like yours and I am going to the continent" and that was that, Joseph was gone: "He took the Elephant Man away from us."[19]

Famous showmen had already established themselves in Europe, which is probably why Sam Torr, Joseph Merrick and the syndicate who were looking after his interests were keen to launch his show on the continent.

From 1874, 'Lord' George Sanger presented fifteen seasons of his circus tent shows overseas. He claimed that his huge success was due to his variety of programmes presenting novelty shows, wild animals and mass entertainment for the general public. In 1871 Sanger had acquired one of the most prestigious circus venues on the continent, Astley's Amphitheatre in Paris, which he continued to run until 1893.[20]

Another prominent showman, Phineas Taylor Barnum, who had famously given the nickname 'Silver King' to Tom Norman, was also well established in Europe.[21]

Freak shows or human zoos seemed to have been flourishing during this era on the continent. Étienne Geoffroy Saint-Hilaire ran the 'Jardin d'Acclimatation', which drew audiences exceeding one million people, and between 1877 and 1912 at least thirty ethnological exhibitions were presented at the 'Jardin zoologique d'Acclimatation', including Inuit and Nubians.

---

18 *The True History of the Elephant Man* by Michael Howell and Peter Ford (Kindle Edition 2011).

19 Ibid.

20 National Fairground Archive (www.sheffield.ac.uk/info/researchandarticles/ Sanger).

21 National Fairground Archive (www.sheffield.ac.uk/info/researchandarticles/ Barnum).

Native Suriname were displayed in the International Colonial and Export exhibition in Amsterdam's Rijkmuseum in 1883, and when Paris staged the World Fair in 1878 and 1889, it presented the 'Negro Village', which was visited by twenty-eight million people. In its 1889 World Fair, Paris exhibited 400 indigenous people as the major attraction.[22]

However, Joseph show didn't last long at all on the continent, as the police in Europe were resistant to the exhibition of Joseph's deformities. The tour was a failure, and they were constantly moved from place to place.[23] It may have just been the way Joseph exhibited himself, as the one-man human exhibit who disgusted the public. The reception Joseph and his manager received in Brussels was dispiriting; the exhibition was forbidden and described as indecent and immoral.[24] Joseph and his then 'Italian' manager, probably realising that the continental show wasn't as profitable as they had hoped for, finally parted company.

According to Dr Frederick Treves,

> The impresario, having robbed Merrick of his paltry savings, gave him a ticket to London, saw him on a train and no doubt in parting condemned him to perdition.[25]

If the manager had taken Joseph's earnings, it was no doubt what he thought was his fee for escorting Joseph around the continent. Apart from Treves' very compressed account of Joseph's return to England, in which he claimed that his destination was Liverpool Street station,[26] there is only one other very short description of his return to London from the people who were with him at the time.

An English gentleman by the name of Mr Wardell Cardew was in

---

22 The Human Zoo: Science's Dirty Secret (www.Used116.org/ProfDev/AHTC/lessons/GoerssFel10/lessons/lesson3/TheHumanzoo.pdf).

23 *The True History of the Elephant Man* by Michael Howell and Peter Ford (Kindle Edition 2011).

24 *The Elephant Man and Other Reminiscences* by Sir Frederick Treves (1923).

25 Ibid.

26 Ibid.

Ostend, Belgium at the same time Joseph had been abandoned. After arriving back in England he spoke with William Hunter Grimston, the husband of the 19th century actress and later benefactor to Merrick, Madge Kendal, saying: "I have had the most awful case in my care in Ostend; would you care to see it?"

Madge would write in her autobiography:

> My husband saw M. Merrick at the London Hospital and on coming home I asked him, as usual, whether he has enjoyed himself there seeing the doctors and patients.
>
> "No" he replied. "I have not; I have seen the most fearful sight of my life".

Madge explained that she didn't want to hear any more about it, but William carried on:

> "The extraordinary thing is that out of the distorted frame came the most musical voice."[27]

Although later known by his stage name of W.H. Kendal, as a youth, William Grimston began to train for the medical profession and was frequently offered the opportunity of seeing interesting cases by Sir John Bland-Sutton,[28] the eminent surgeon described in the previous chapter as often visiting the Mile End Road to visit freak shows.

It has been suggested that, appalled by Joseph's appearance, the captain of the cross-channel ferry which Joseph intended to use on his return trip home from Ostend refused to allow him on board, so, on the advice of Mr Cardew, Joseph travelled to the Belgian port of Antwerp and boarded the regular packet service to Harwich, the North Sea port in Essex, which would take him on to the Great Eastern Railway and to his final destination at Liverpool Street station in London.[29]

If Joseph had been indeed refused passage from Ostend, one of the

27 *Dame Madge Kendal By Herself* by Madge Kendal (1933).

28 Ibid.

29 *The True History of the Elephant Man* by Michael Howell and Peter Ford (Kindle Edition 2011).

easiest routes to get back to England would have been the 59 mile journey down the west coastline of Belgium to Calais in France, and then a cross-channel steamer to Dover, rather than the longer 77 mile journey from Ostend to Antwerp.[30]

If we put to one side the suggestion by Treves in his memoirs that Joseph arrived at Liverpool Street station, and instead read a letter by F.C. Carr-Gomm, Chairman of the London Hospital, which was published in *The Times* of 4 December 1886, not long after Joseph arrived on their doorstep, the question of his arrival at the Hospital is raised:

> He therefore, though with much difficulty, made his way there, for at every station and landing place the curious crowd so thronged and dogged his steps that it was not an easy matter for him to get about. When he reached the London Hospital he had only the clothes in which he stood.[31]

Another letter written by Carr-Gomm, in April 1890, carries on the same theme:

> With great difficulty he succeeded somehow or other in getting to the door of the London Hospital.[32]

There is no mention in either letter of Joseph's arrival at Liverpool Street station, or Treves's description on his heroic rescue of Joseph Merrick, which dramatically reads:

> At Liverpool Street, he was rescued from the crowd by the police and taken into the third class waiting room. He sank to the floor in the darkest corner. The police were at a loss what to do with him.[33]

Treves goes on to say:

> His speech was so maimed that he might as well have spoken in Arabic. He had, however, something with him which he produced

---

30 Routes Ostend to Calais, Ostend to Antwerp on maps.google.com.

31 *Leicester Chronicle*, 11 December 1886.

32 *The Elephant Man and Other Reminiscences* by Sir Frederick Treves (1923).

33 Ibid.

with a ray of hope. It was my card.[34]

Dr Treves paints a very romantic description of Joseph's final liberation:

> He seemed pleased to see me, but he was nearly done. The journey and want of food had reduced him to the last stage of exhaustion. The police kindly helped him into a cab, and I drove him at once to the hospital. He appeared to be content. For he fell asleep almost as soon as he was seated and slept to the journey's end.[35]

But was this 'rescue' overly dramatised to sell his book? Two letters written by Treves in 1922 suggest he was having doubts about his manuscript. In a letter dated 2 September, Treves writes to a recipient he refers to as 'My dear Flower' that he is writing a book called *The Elephant Man and other Reminiscences*. Although he had written many books before this one, Frederick Treves informed the letter's recipient that "in the hands of a more competent writer, [it] would make very 'hot stuff' [sic]", but he does confess further on in the correspondence that "It has one merit – that every incident is true."[36]

In another letter to 'My Dear Flower' dated 9 October 1922, Treves writes that he has submitted the manuscript on *The Elephant Man...* and reveals that he is "full of horrible doubts about it", going on say:

> It is no use to brag that every incident in the book is true; for I am doubtful if these are the kind of truths the public want.[37]

Steamers from Calais to Dover at that time took as little as 65 minutes to cross the English Channel,[38] and from Dover, the London, Chatham and Dover Railway (LCDR) went straight to London

---

34 *The Elephant Man and Other Reminiscences* by Sir Frederick Treves (1923).
35 Ibid.
36 Series of letters written to 'My Dear Flower', held at the Leicestershire & Rutland Record Office (Ref: b. biography LB 13-M).
37 Ibid.
38 www.calais-port.fr/en/the-history/crosschannel-trafic/steamers/port-of-calais.

Victoria rail station.[39] The LCDR arrived in Dover in 1861, forming a link with the docks. Railway connections were allowed into the docks themselves the following year, and in 1864 the LCDR obtained permission to run their own steamers across the English Channel.[40]

The catamaran *Castalia* was built in 1874, formed by two half vessels connected by beams, but it was difficult to manoeuvre and caused damaged to the Dover pier on her maiden voyage. Only after three seasons, the *Castalia* was withdrawn on 22 July 1874.

Another catamaran, the *Express*, was built in 1878 and on being bought by the LCDR was renamed *Calais-Douvres*. She was 110 metres long and 30 metres wide. *Calais-Douvres* made the channel crossing in one hour and thirty minutes, but she became too slow and costly to run compared to new steamers, and was eventually decommissioned in 1887.

A new steamer, the *Invicta*, was built in 1882. She was 96 metres long and made of steel, with a bow at the front and rear and a rudder at both ends.[41] The LCDR's express train from London Victoria station to Paris, France used the *Invicta* as she was a quicker sea passage then their older catamaran, *Calais-Douvres*.[42] The *Invicta* had a 600-horse power engine which enabled a speed of eighteen knots, and on her maiden voyage she reached twenty-two knots making the crossing in sixty-five minutes.[43]

The improved crossing time was appreciated by *The Star*:

> *Invicta* hoped to bring the terrors of crossing from Dover to Calais within sixty minutes...

> Perhaps not five percent of the sum total of humanity are really on pleasant and friendly relations with a stormy sea, and the remaining ninety-five in every hundred will be only too glad to know that if

39 www.kentpost.co.uk/history.

40 www.simplonepc.co.uk/dover.html.

41 www.calais-port.fr/en/the-history/crosschannel-trafic/steamers/port-of-calais.

42 *London Evening Standard*, 20 April 1886.

43 www.calais-port.fr/en/the-history/crosschannel-trafic/steamers/port-of-calais.

business or pleasure compels them to make the shortest possible trip to France their sufferings are to be shortened, though it be a quarter of an hour. The boats are a great improvement upon those of the olden times, and given smooth seas the comfort and convenience of the passengers are admirably secured.[44]

Ferries crossed daily between the two ports of Calais and Dover, leaving Calais at 1.30pm and, including the train journey to London, one would have arrived at London Victoria rail station at 6.15pm.[45]

Even though the journey from Ostend to Calais was a lot shorter than the route from Ostend to Antwerp, there may have been another explanation as to why Joseph gravitated to the Port of Calais, a more personal reason than just ease of travel.

Thomas Cook, a former Baptist preacher who believed that most Victorian social problems were related to alcohol,[46] became regarded as the grandfather of modern day tourism and his name known throughout the world.

He also lived and worked in Leicester at precisely the same time Joseph was growing up there.

Cook was born in Melbourne in Derbyshire and trained as a woodturner and cabinet maker. In 1841 he moved to Market Harborough, the south Leicestershire market town, and gave up the woodworking business in favour of printing. He convinced his wife to "open her house for the accommodation of temperance travellers, who desired freedom from drinking practices in licensed hotels". When the Cooks moved to Leicester, his wife Marianne opened up her house once more, and in 1853 Thomas Cook opened the Temperance Hotel at what is now numbers 34-36 Granby Street. This was to be Thomas' home, tour office and print works, as well as a hotel.[47]

As well as being a local business entrepreneur extremely well known throughout Leicester, Thomas Cook and his family had long been associated with Archdeacon Lane Baptist Church, the same

---

44 *The Star*, 19 August 1886.

45 *Cook's Continental Timetable and Tourist's Handbook* (2013 edition)

46 www.thomascook.com/thomas-cook-history.

chapel where Joseph Merrick and his family also worshipped.[48]

Cook's daughter Annie taught Sunday School at Archdeacon Lane Baptist Church, as did Mary Jane Merrick, Joseph's mother. Annie Cook was born on 21 June 1845, and would have been about the same age as Mary Jane. She may possibly have taught Joseph at Sunday School, and from that moment the name Cook could have held a memory deep in his heart.

However, a terrible, tragic event struck the Cook family on Sunday, 7 November 1880 when Thomas Cook found his daughter drowned in the bath tub at the family home at Thorncroft, London Road. Annie would usually bring her father a cup of tea at 7.15am, but on this particular morning she had failed to do so, and feeling anxious her mother went to see what the matter was. On finding her bed unslept in, her father went straight to the bathroom and found Annie dead. She was laying on her right hand side, her face, head and body wholly submerged and her hands tightly clenched. At the inquest, held at Thorncroft, Thomas Cook said he noticed a strong smell of gas in the bathroom.[49] It was rumoured that Annie committed suicide because she wished to marry one of her father's employees, much to Thomas's disapproval.[50] However, the jury returned a verdict in accordance with the medical testimony,[51] that Annie drowned as a result of a temporary loss on consciousness caused by a fall in blood pressure.[52]

Her funeral took place on Friday, 12 November 1880 at the Leicester Cemetery on Welford Road. The teachers and pupils of the Archdeacon Lane Baptist Church Sunday School followed behind the cortege at the non-conformist chapel. The oak coffin was covered in a violet pall and the service was conducted by the Reverend W.

47 www.le.ac.uk/lahs/downlaods/cook.smpagesfromvolume xlix-3.pdf.

48 *Leicester Chronicle and Leicestershire Mercury*, 6 May 1882.

49 *Leicester Journal*, 12 November 1880.

50 www.findagrave.com/cgi-bin/fg.cgi?page=gr&GRid=138141867.

51 *Leicester Journal*, 12 November 1880.

52 www.findagrave.com/cgi-bin/fg.cgi?page=gr&GRid=138141867.

Bishop, preacher at Archdeacon Lane.[53] In memory to his daughter, Thomas Cook commissioned a Memorial Hall and Sunday School at Archdeacon Lane, adjacent to the Church.

The Memorial Hall and Sunday School was opened on Sunday, 30 April 1882. It was constructed of red brick, with Bath stone dressings covered with red tiles and slate. The doorway was a sunk panel bearing the inscription in raised letters" "Annie Elizabeth Cook – Memorial Hall and Sunday School Rooms".[54]

Thomas Cook regularly organised trips to the continent, and ran tours across the English Channel from the Port of Dover to the Port of Calais. The company was a regular advertiser in the local and national press, and one of the regular fixed day services in the summer months was Dover to Calais and Calais to Dover, with one advertisement detailing a journey beginning with a ferry departing Calais at 3.30pm, then catching the train from Dover and arriving at London Victoria train station at 7.30pm.[55]

While in Ostend Joseph could have glimpsed a notice for Thomas Cook Tours; recognising the name of someone may possibly have prompted him to go to Calais to seek the gentleman's help in returning to England.

The London, Chatham and Dover Railway picked up its ferry passengers at the Admiralty Pier in Dover harbour, and headed for its final destination of Victoria station in London. The closest station to Whitechapel on this rail journey was Holborn Viaduct, just two miles from the Whitechapel Road.

But was Joseph turning towards Dr Frederick Treves at the London Hospital, or had he intended to seek out Tom Norman, the Silver King - "the only real friend Joseph ever had" - whose last address known to Merrick was the shop at 123 Whitechapel Road?[56]

---

53 *Leicester Journal*, 12 November 1880.

54 *Leicester Chronicle and Leicestershire Mercury*, 6 May 1882.

55 *London Daily News*, 20 August 1880.

56 *The Penny Showman: Tom Norman, Silver King.* With additional writings by his son George Norman (1985).

The Old Clock Tower, Leicester, where Joseph Merrick sold his wares
© *Leicester, Leicestershire and Rutland Record Office*

Churchgate, Leicester, as seen from the site of No. 144,
where Joseph lived with his uncle Charles Barnabus Merrick
© *Leicester, Leicestershire and Rutland Record Office*

With Best Wishes

Charles Barnabus Merrick, Joseph's uncle,
with whom he lived at 144 Churchgate, Leicester, from 1877 to 1879
© *Michelle Merrick*

Joseph Merrick's father? The caption of this recently-discovered photograph of Archdeacon Lane Baptist Church, where the family worshipped, states: "With beard - Ebenezer Smith. At organ - J. Merrick."
© Leicester, Leicestershire and Rutland Record Office

Joseph's cousin Charles Henry Merrick, Charles Barnabus's eldest son, with his wife Sofia.
© Michelle Merrick

Joseph's cousin James Merrick with wife Margaret and children.
James was the son of Charles Barnes Merrick, transported to Tasmania
© Ken Stewart

Top: William Merrick
Bottom: Jim Merrick
Sons of James and Margaret Merrick
© Ken Stewart

Catherine and George Potterton,
Joseph's aunt and uncle on his mother's side.
George was Mary Jane's brother; Catherine was present at her death
© *Patricia Selby*

Joseph's cousins Catherine, Sarah. Mary and Lily Potterton (it is unknown which is which)
© Patricia Selby

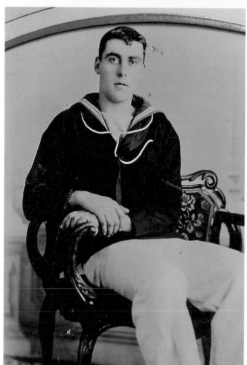

Joseph's cousin James Leonard Potterton
© Patricia Selby

Joseph's cousin John Thomas Potterton
© Patricia Selby

IN LOVING MEMORY
OF

JOHN POTTERTON.
WHO DEPARTED THIS LIFE
JUNE 4TH 1903
AGED 58 YEARS

ELIZABETH,
THE BELOVED WIFE OF
JOHN POTTERTON,
WHO DEPARTED THIS LIFE
DECEMBER 16TH 1877
AGED 39 YEARS

ANN POTTERTON

Mary Jane Potterton
Merrick
20 November 1836 – 19 May 1873
The loving mother of
Joseph Carey Merrick
also John, William and
Marion

The grave of Mary Jane Merrick, Joseph's mother,
with recent memorial stone incorrectly adding a third son 'John'
Author's collection

Communion register entry for Joseph Rockley and Mary Jane Merrick
© Leicester, Leicestershire and Rutland Record Office

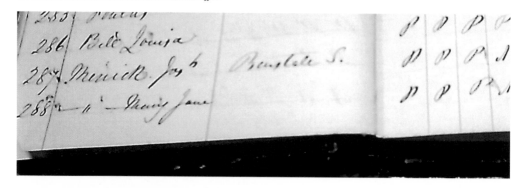

Middle: Leicester Union Workhouse
Bottom: Record of Joseph Merrick's admittance into the Workhouse
© Leicester, Leicestershire and Rutland Record Office

Record of Joseph Merrick's discharge from the Workhouse
© Leicester, Leicestershire and Rutland Record Office

The Gaiety Theatre on Wharf Street, Leicester
© Leicester, Leicestershire and Rutland Record Office

Tom Norman, the Silver King
Chronicle / Alamy Stock Photo

*Right: Former 123 Whitechapel Road,
where Joseph was first exhibited in London
© Marc Haynes, Darkest London*

*Entry recording Joseph Merrick's admission into the London Hospital
© Marc Haynes, Darkest London*

The entrance to Joseph's rooms at 'Bedstead Square' in August 2005 © Christian Jaud

The London Hospital

The steps leading to Joseph's rooms in August 2005
© Christian Jaud

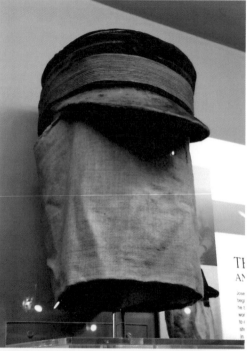

Joseph's cap and mask
© Adam Wood

Joseph's model of Mainz Cathedral
© Adam Wood

Dear Miss Maturin

Many thanks
indeed for the grouse, and
the book, you so kindly sent
me, the grouse were splendid
I saw Mr Treves on Sunday
He said I was to give his
best respects to you With much
Gratitude I am Yours Truly
Joseph Merrick
London Hospital
Whitechapel

The letter sent by Joseph to Mrs. Leila Maturin
© Leicester, Leicestershire and Rutland Record Office

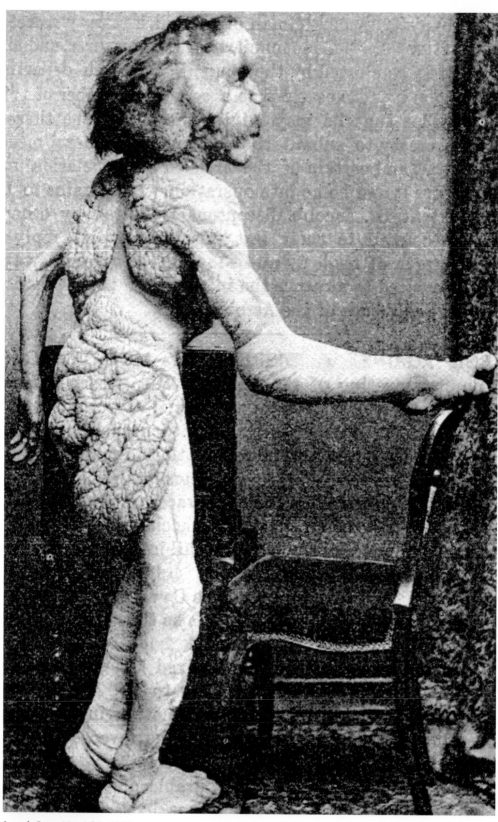

Joseph Carey Merrick in 1888

No.	Date of Burial	Name of Person Buried	Description, Avocation, and Personal Residence of Person Buried	Sex and Age	Parish in which the Death is registered	From what Parish removed			No. of Grave	Description of Interment	Consecrated or Unconsecrated Ground	By Parson—The Union	Ceremony performed by	Extract
219837	April 24th	Henry Marshall	N. E. Orphan	male	103 years	Bromley Middlesex	Bromley			20205		Consecrated	Chaplain	St Saviour's	
219838	April 24th	Elizabeth McKenna	N. E. Orphan	fem		Bromley Middlesex	Bromley			20205		Consecrated	Chaplain	St Saviour's	
219839	April 24th	Emma Burgess	Infirmary	fem	29	West Holborn Middlesex	Holborn			20205		Consecrated	Holborn	St Saviour's	
219840	April 24th	Ben Graham	Infirmary	male	54	West Holborn Middlesex	Holborn			20206		Consecrated	Holborn	St Saviour's	
219841	April 24th	Henry Field	Infirmary	male	30	West Holborn Middlesex	Holborn			20207		Consecrated	Holborn	St Saviour's	
219842	April 24th	Ann Cook	Holborn Union	fem		Holborn Middlesex	London			20208		Consecrated	Holborn	St Saviour's	
219843	April 24th	Eveline Barker	Holborn Union	fem	11	City Road Middlesex	London			20209		Consecrated	Holborn	St Saviour's	
219844	April 24th	Hannah Grace	Holborn Union	fem	15	Holborn St Middlesex	London			20210		Consecrated	Holborn	St Saviour's	
219845	April 24th	Thomas James Fox	Infirmary	male	52	Mile End Middlesex	Mile End			20211		Consecrated	Mile End	St Saviour's	
219846	April 24th	Joseph Merrick	London Hospital	male	28	St Philips house London	London			20212		Consecrated	Hospital	St Saviour's	
219847	April 24th	Charles Harwood	Common Fund City	male	42	St Philip City	London			20213		Consecrated	St Andrew	St Saviour's	
219848	April 24th	Eliza Batholin	St Philip City	fem	3	St Philip City	London			20214		Consecrated	St Andrew	St Saviour's	

219845	1890 April 24th	Thomas James Fox	Infirmary	male	52 Years
219846	1890 April 24th	**Joseph Merrick**	London Hospital	male	28 Years
219847	1890 April 24th	Charles Harwood	Common Fund City	male	42 Years
219848	1890 April 24th	Eliza Batholin	St Philip City	Fem	3 Years
219849	1890 April 24th	Janet Leslie	Bow Road	Fem	33

Burial entry for Joseph Merrick in the
City of London Cemetery records

The final resting place of Joseph Carey Merrick at the City of London Cemetery

CHAPTER 8

Merrick Must Not Again
Be Turned Out Into the World

Dover, in 1886, was in essence little different from the town of today - an extremely busy sea port whose close proximity to the Continent made it prior to the building of the Channel Tunnel Britain's main gateway to Europe, and visa versa.

One can envision a young, tired and possibly emotional Joseph Merrick leaning on the ship's taffrail as the harbour waters churned beneath, pondering what, exactly, the future held in store. One can also picture Joseph as he hobbled off the ferry, still using his stick and wearing the cloak given to him by Sam Roper just over one year ago, making his way to the southern section of Dover Priory railway platform, before boarding the train to complete the last part of his journey, a journey which would take Joseph back to London. As he shuffled towards the waiting train, he may have noted the tall, Italianate clock tower standing proudly at the Dover Priory station entrance,[1] not dissimilar to the Clock Tower in his home town of Leicester.

The train from Dover would take him directly into London, and alighting at Holborn Viaduct station would mean only a two-mile journey to his final destination of Whitechapel Road.

The question is, why was Joseph heading straight back to London? Was he hoping to get another train to take him back to Leicester, and back to the only family member he seemed to have trusted, his Uncle

1   doverhistorian.com/2013/09/12harbourstation.

Charles, or was Joseph hoping to find his friend Tom Norman?

By this time, Uncle Charles Merrick had moved the family across Leicester from 144 Churchgate to 248 Belgrave Gate. Joseph's elder two cousins, Charles Jr and Albert, were both working as assistant hairdressers, and his two younger cousins, Alice and John, were at school.

Joseph's own father, Joseph Sr, didn't want him all those years ago, and probably wouldn't have entertained his eldest child's presence now, as he and Joseph's stepmother Emma had welcomed three more children since Joseph had left their home: Cassandra (b. 1879), Dora (b. 1880) and Pauline (b. 1883). The family had moved house twice since Joseph had left Leicester, finally settling in Justice Street in the town.

Maybe Leicester wasn't the answer. A trip home may not have resulted in a cordial family reunion between father and son, although Uncle Charles, by all accounts, would have welcomed his nephew with open arms. But however a joyful such a reconciliation might have been, it should be remembered that the popularity of 'oddity' shows was declining in Leicester, so by returning to his hometown it was likely that Joseph would have most likely faced a laborious life of drudgery, hard graft and his nemesis, the workhouse.

Another option was Tom Norman, but where was he? Had he reopened in a shop near to where he and Joseph last worked together in Whitechapel?

In December 1886 Tom Norman was indeed still in London, working his shows once again, as an advertisement in *The Era* exclaimed:

> Wanted, to sell, extraordinary Living subject, wonderful freak of nature, horse never exhibited. Apply Tom Norman, National Panorama, York Street, Westminster.[2]

Was Joseph aware that his friend was still in 'the smoke'?

According to the letter by the Francis Carr-Gomm, Chairman of London Hospital's Committee, published in *The Times*, Joseph had

---

2   *The Era*, 18 December 1886.

encountered great difficulty in getting to the London Hospital.

The underground's Central Line, which runs through Holborn on its way to Liverpool Street station, wasn't opened until 1900, so apart from walking the two miles to Whitechapel the other options for Joseph were the omnibus or the recently-introduced horse-drawn tram.

The omnibus, pioneered in London in 1829, was introduced by the London coach builder George Shillibeer. It was initially drawn by three horses and could accommodate 22 persons sitting inside. Having three horses made manoeuvring around London's narrow streets problematic, so in the early 1830s a new omnibus was launched drawn by only two horses, enhancing its manageability. The first double-decker omnibus was put together in the late 1840s. The knifeboard bus had a single seat fitted lengthways on its roof. In the 1880s, when Joseph may have journeyed on the omnibus, a new design was presented, with the introduction of the garden seat, forward-facing seats and a curved staircase at the rear to make boarding simpler, and these horse-drawn buses remained untouched throughout most of the nineteenth century.

In 1870 horse-drawn trams were introduced on steel rails. They were able to transport more travellers using the same number of horses, which meant tram fares were cheaper than the omnibus, and journey times slightly faster, going at 6mph rather than the usual 4mph.[3]

Starting at Notting Hill, the first tram of the day, the dark green 'Bayswater' departed at 7.42am and ran every few minutes until 10.00pm.[4] The tram went via Elgin Crescent, Kensington Park Road, Archer Street, Westbourne Grove, Bishops Road, Eastbourne Terrace, Edgware Road, Marble Arch, Oxford Street and Oxford Circus, before arriving at Holborn Viaduct station to pick up more passengers. It would then carry on up Newgate Street, Cheapside, Cornhill, Leadenhall Street and Aldgate before finally arriving in Whitechapel.

3   www.ltmcollection.org/resources.
4   www.victorianlondon.org/dickens/om6.png.

The alternative tram which passed via Holborn Viaduct departed from Notting Hill ran every 15 minutes until 11.10pm, and instead of a final destination of Whitechapel it carried on to Mile End Road.[5]

Though we shall never know the true reason why Joseph returned to the East End area of London, one explanation could be as follows.

Getting off the tram at its stop in Whitechapel, 123 Whitechapel Road, where Joseph spent his time with Tom Norman and Little Jimmy, would have been in sight. As Joseph staggered nearer and nearer to the shop, his hopes of finding his friend where undoubtedly dwindling. The shop was no longer what he remembered, and was now in use by Ebenezer Shepherd, a Glass and China dealer.[6]

Not knowing what to do, Joseph turned round and recognised the only other place that looked familiar to him. The London Hospital, where he had been stripped naked and made to feel like an animal at a cattle market,[7] was now directly in front of him. It may have been at this point that Joseph reached inside his pocket and pulled out the card which Dr Frederick Treves had given him more than eighteen months previously.

When Joseph arrived at the Hospital's doors and stumbled into the Receiving Room on 24 June 1886,[8] his only possessions were the clothes in which he stood. A bare hall painted the colour of stone, the Receiving Room held rows of benches, with a framed printed notice upon the wall giving instructions on how to revive a victim of drowning. On each side of the Receiving Room were two dressing rooms, one for women and one for men, and it was in these rooms that the house surgeon worked, examining their patients before either treating or referring them on to the doctors.

All that Joseph could conceivably do was hand over Dr Treves' card to the Receiving Room nurse and wait. In the male dressing room, where Joseph perhaps waited for the surgeon, was a large sink, and

5   Ibid.

6   Electoral registers 1832-1965

7   *The Penny Showman: Tom Norman, Silver King.* With additional writings by his son George Norman (1985).

8   *London Hospital Admissions Register.*

on the ledge above it a large number of pewter porringers. One side of the room was a cupboard containing dressings, gags, manacles and emetics, and in the centre of the room were a table and another hard chair.

Fortuitously, Frederick Treves was in the building when Joseph arrived, and whatever conversation passed between them, Joseph was given nourishment and a temporary bed on the Isolation Ward in the attic rooms of the London Hospital.[9]

Frederick Treves was born in 1853 at 8 Cornhill, Dorchester, in the county of Devon. When his father died in 1867, his mother moved the family to London, and it is here Frederick Treves became a student at Merchant Taylor's School in the City of London before training as a doctor at the London Hospital.[10]

He married Anne Mason on 8 February 1877 at the Holy Trinity Church in Sydenham, south east London, a ceremony overseen by the Reverend H. Stevens.[11] The union bore two daughters, Enid Margery (b. 1878) and Hetty Marion (b. 1882).[12] The marriage may have come under close scrutiny in 1880, as Treves was named in an adultery case concerning a married woman, the events of which were alleged to have occurred just a couple of years prior to his wedding:

> The petitioner, Sylvester Richmond prayed, for the dissolution of marriage with his wife Agnes Bruce Richmond by reason of adultery with the respondent and co-respondents William Fowle and Frederick Treves. The respondent and co-respondent filed answers in denial of the charge and the respondent further made a counter charge of cruelty against her husband who denied the accusation.[13]

Sylvester Richmond, a practising doctor in Northallerton, Yorkshire, married Agnes Bruce in 1866 in Scotland. Six years into

---

9   *The Elephant Man and Other Reminiscences* by Sir Frederick Treves (1923).

10   www.dorsetlife.co.uk/2014/12/just-who-was.sirfredericktreves.

11   *Sussex Agricultural Express*, 13 February 1877.

12   1891 Census.

13   *Yorkshire Gazette*, 28 February 1880.

their marriage, Agnes started to drink, and over the next two years she was frequently seen in a state of intoxication. In 1877, under her own consent, Agnes went to stay with a Mrs Theobald who kept an establishment for the treatment of dypsomaniacs in Leicester. She returned home on three occasions, supposedly cured, but ended up being forced to return to Mrs Theobald's.

During her stay in Leicester, her husband corresponded with her on affectionate terms, but in October 1878 he wrote explaining that he believed her return to their North Allerton family home would be destructive to his prospects, and so he could not allow her to share his home. Mrs Theobald, the owner of the Leicester establishment, endeavoured to dissuade Dr Richmond, and assured him that his wife was fully reformed, adding in her letter that it was impossible for Agnes to remain at the institution in Leicester beyond the following June. On receipt of the letter from Mrs Theobald, Dr Richmond's sister, who had the care of the household, told him of certain communications she had had with the servants in relation to his wife's conduct with Frederick Treves and William Fowle.

Treves had been Dr Richmond's assistant between 12 August 1875 and 22 March 1876, and although Richmond had never observed any familiarities between Treves and his wife, two witnesses came forward to support the accusations. Margaret Fox, who had been a cook in Mrs Richmond's service, declared that she saw endearments pass between her mistress and Treves on the very day he first entered the house on 12 August 1875, and the following day she saw through the surgery keyhole the act of which the parties were accused. The other witness, a man named Hutton, said on one occasion he had followed Treves and Mrs Richmond along a footpath into a certain field at about nine o'clock at night, and mentioned circumstances from which the jury were asked to infer guilt.

When Treves spoke to defend himself, he stated he was engaged to be married when he became Dr Richmond's assistant in August 1875, and that the cause of his leaving in March instead of May the following year was to read for certain examinations which he had to pass in London. Treves admitted that it was quite possible he and

Mrs Richmond might have been alone together in the harness room adjoining the coach house, as he occasionally went down to the stables to meet Dr Richmond on returning from afternoon visits. He denied that he and Mrs Richmond had been guilty of adultery either there or elsewhere.[14]

Throughout his career, Dr Frederick Treves gave many lectures on papers and examinations.

In 1882, he gave an address at the Town Hall in Kensington, London, on 'The Dress of the Period'. He seemed quite concerned with the eccentricities of present-day fashions and its effects on the body. He started the lecture explaining the reason for clothes, stating that the primary object of dressing was to cover the body and maintain an equable temperature.

He pointed out that in the low evening dress, the neck, arms and upper part of the chest and back were left bare, while the lower extremities comprised an accumulated mass of raiment that would clothe a dozen children, and the unnatural thin waist achieved by using a corset was hideous. He demonstrated how, by the compression of the lower ribs and the stomach, the liver and lungs were displaced and their free necessary action thus prevented, quoting medical evidence of the many serious and often fatal consequences.

Treves wasn't too concerned with the outer manipulation of the body. He continued his speech by pointing out that

> The deformed feet of the Chinese women, the flattened heads, perforated nostrils and distended lips of the savage tribe were less senseless freaks of fashion, for they only injured but one part of the body and not the vital part.

To demonstrate his hypothesis Treves had brought with him diagrams from works on physiology and fashion plates, a life size cast of Thorwaldsen's Venus, a skeleton, a costume a la mode, and a figure on which an adaptation of a Greek dress was shown as a

---

14 *Yorkshire Gazette*, 28 February 1880.

suggested improvement on the present style of dress.[15]

On 9 April 1884, at a conference at the Royal College of Surgeons, he was bestowed the Jacksonian Prize for his essay on 'The Pathology, Diagnosis and Treatment of Obstruction of the Intestine', completed in December, 1883.[16]

Two years later, having now rekindled his acquaintance with Joseph, Treves may have seen this as a opportunity to exhibit this unusual medical specimen, rather than show fashion plates, life-size casts and skeletons.

Did Treves offer Joseph a bed in return for him agreeing to be paraded again in front of the medical fraternity? Treves certainly admitted in his memoirs that he had "been guilty of an irregularity in admitting Joseph... as the hospital was not a refuge or a home for incurables".[17] As far as Treves was concerned, Joseph was a chronic case, not requiring active treatment, and those cases were not dealt with at the London Hospital.

If Joseph was to continue his stay at the London Hospital, he needed the support of the Hospital Committee, so Treves wrote to Francis Carr-Gomm seeking approval for his actions. Carr-Gomm supported Treves, and agreed that "Merrick must not again be turned out into the world".[18]

The Chairman wrote a letter to *The Times* in December 1886 describing the events of Joseph's life, and asking for money for his support. The letter was published in local papers around the country, including those in Joseph's hometown, the *Leicester Chronicle and Leicestershire Mercury*:

> "The Elephant Man"
>
> The chairman of the London hospital wrote a letter to the Times of Saturday in order to bring to public notice the pathetic case of Joseph Merrick, a young man and native of Leicester, who is now in a little room off one of the attic wards of the London Hospital. He has

15 *St James Gazette*, 27 February 1882.

16 *Aberdeen Evening Express*, 11 April 1884.

17 *The Elephant Man and Other Reminiscences* by Sir Frederick Treves (1923).

18 Ibid.

been called "The Elephant Man" on account of his terrible deformity, which renders only one arm available to work. The poor fellow was exhibited at a recent fair in Leicester.

The letter proceeds as follows: - Some 18 months ago Mr Treves, one of the surgeons of the London Hospital, saw him as he was exhibited in a room off the Whitechapel Road. The poor fellow was then covered by an old curtain, endeavouring to warm himself over a brick which was heated by a lamp. As soon as sufficient number of pennies had been collected by the manager at the door, poor Merrick threw off his curtain and exhibited himself in all his deformity. He said the manager went halves in the net proceeds of this exhibition, until at last the police stopped the exhibition of his deformities as against public decency. Unable to earn his livelihood but exhibiting himself any longer in England, he was taken in hand by an Austrian, who acted as his manager. Merrick managed in this way to save a sum of nearly £50, but the police there too kept him moving on, so that his life was miserable and a haunted one. ~One day however, when the Austrian saw that the exhibition was pretty well played out, he decamped with poor Merrick's hardly saved capital of £50, and left him alone and absolutely destitute in a foreign country. Fortunately, however, he had something to pawn, by which he raised sufficient money to pay his passage back to England, for he felt that the only friend he had in the world was Mr Treves, of the London Hospital. He therefore, though with much difficulty, made his way there, for at every station and landing place the curious crowd so thronged him and dogged his steps that it was not an easy matter for him to get about. When he reached the London Hospital he had only the clothes in which he stood. He had been taken in by our hospital, though there is unfortunately no hope of his cure, and the question now arises what is to be done with him in the future. He has the greatest horror of the workhouse, nor is it possible indeed, to send him into any place where he could not insure privacy, since his appearance is such that all shrink from him. The Royal Hospital for Incurables and the British Home for Incurables both decline to take him in, even if sufficient funds were forthcoming to pay for him. The police rightly prevent his being personally exhibited again; he cannot go out into the streets as he is everywhere so mobbed that existence is impossible; he cannot, injustice to others , be put in the general ward of a workhouse, and from such, even if possible, he shrinks with the greatest horror; he ought not to be detained in our hospital (where he is occupying a private ward, and being treated with the greatest kindness – he says he has never before known in his life what quiet and rest were), since his case is incurable, and not suited, therefore, to our overcrowded general hospital; the incurable hospitals refuse to take him even if we paid for him in full, and the difficult question therefore remains what is to be done for him. Terrible though his appearance is, so terrible indeed that women and nervous persons fly in terror from the sight of him, and that he is debarred from seeking to earn his livelihood in any ordinary way, yet he is superior in intelligence, and can read and write, is quiet, gentle, not to say even refined in his mind. He occupies his time in the hospital by making with his one available hand little cardboard models, which he sends to the matron, doctor, and those who have been kind to him. Through all the miserable vicissitudes of his life he has carried about a painting of his mother to show that she was a decent and presentable person, and as a memorial of the only one who was kind to him in life until he came under the kind care of the nursing staff of the London Hospital and the surgeon who has befriended him. It is a case of singular affliction brought about through no fault of himself; he can but hope for quiet and privacy during a life which Mr Treves assures me is not likely to be long. Can any of your readers suggest to me some fitting place where he can be received? And then I feel sure that, when that is found, charitable people will come forward and enable me to provide him with such accommodation. In the meantime, though it is not the proper place for such an incurable case, the little room under the roof of our hospital and out of Cotton Ward supplies him with all he wants. The Master of the Temple on Advent Sunday preached an eloquent sermon on the subject of our Master's answer to the question "Who did sin, this man or his parents, that he was born blind?" showing how one of the Creator's objects in permitting men to be born to a life of hopeless and miserable disability was that the works of God should be manifested in evoking the sympathy and kindly aid of those on whom such a heavy cross is not laid. Some 76,000 patients a year pass through the doors of our hospital, but I have never before been authorised to invite public attention to any particular case, so it may well be believed that this case is exceptional.

Any communication about this should be addressed either to the chairman or to the secretary at the London Hospital.[19]

---

19 *Leicester Chronicle and Leicestershire Mercury*, 11 December 1886.

The sermon which Carr-Gomm refers to was preached by Dr Charles John Vaughan, and was taken from the Gospel according to John, Chapter nine, Verse two. It has been questioned whether the choice of text was coincidental, or whether he selected that specific reading because he knew of Joseph's anguish.

Charles Vaughan's thoughts could have been applied to Joseph's state of affairs by Carr-Gomm, who himself was a barrister of the Inner Temple.[20] It may have been likely that Dr Vaughan took a personal interest in Joseph, as he was born and spent his childhood in Leicester, where his father and grandfather had served successively as vicars throughout a great part of the 19th century in the parish church of St Martin's, now known as Leicester Cathedral.

Within a week of Carr-Gomm's letter being published the money came flooding in, and according to Treves' reminiscences,

> Enough money was forthcoming to maintain Merrick for life without any charge on the hospital funds.[21]

On Tuesday, 7 December 1886, a meeting of the House Committee at the London Hospital made Joseph's situation the first item on their itinerary. As Chairman, Carr-Gomm summarised the steps already taken, and assessed the background and circumstances that resulted in the appeal in *The Times*. Carr-Gomm also specified that a significant number of letters had been received, containing considerable amounts of money. One hundred pounds had been sent, and a Mr Singer had proposed to donate fifty pounds annually for Joseph if he continued to reside at the London Hospital. The House Committee considered his case, and decided to let Joseph remain.[22]

Money was also raised by the actress Madge Kendal, who wrote in her memoirs:

20 *The True History of the Elephant Man* by Michael Howell and Peter Ford (Kindle Edition 2011).

21 *The Elephant Man and Other Reminiscences* by Sir Frederick Treves (1923).

22 *The True History of the Elephant Man* by Michael Howell and Peter Ford (Kindle Edition 2011).

I did raise the money and no one knew anything about my association with the case until the money was obtained and Merrick was duly installed in two rooms, one furnished as a bed-sitting-room and the other as a bathroom.[23]

In January 1887, Carr-Gomm wrote a letter of thanks to *The Times* and its readership, outlining the success of his first appeal to help the London Hospital secure a permanent home for Joseph Merrick. Again, this letter filtered through to the local papers, and once again the *Leicester Chronicle* picked up on the story:

"The Elephant Man"

Mr F.C. Carr-Gomm, chairman of the London Hospital, writes as follows to the times:

In a letter which you were kind enough to insert some weeks back about Joseph Merrick, who had formerly been exhibited under the name of "The Elephant Man", I asked whether anyone could suggest a fitting home where he could be received, adding that I felt sure when such a home was found charitable people would come forward and enable me to place him therein. The letter interested many, and I received numerous kind answers from all parts of the country and had my appeal been directly for money I am convinced abundance would have speedily been sent to me. The practical result of the correspondence is that no home is to be found so suitable to his needs as the hospital, and we now feel ourselves justified in keeping him with us; and although a general hospital supported by voluntary contributions is strictly for curative purposes, where each occupied bed represents an outlay little short of £70 per annum, our committee have decided under the peculiar circumstances to set apart a small room where the poor fellow not only secures that privacy which is so essential to his comfort, but also is supplied with all essential to his comfort, but also supplied with all that can possibly alleviate his sad condition, such as baths, good nursing and medical supervision. This is in accordance with the wishes expressed by most of the contributors, and Merrick himself, naturally enough, much prefers remaining where he has found so much sympathy and comfort. His generous supporters will be glad to hear of our decision, and Merrick had desired me to convey to them his most grateful

---

23 *Dame Madge Kendal By Herself* by Madge Kendal (1933).

thanks, and to say that he is deeply sensible of their kindness and that he has never had so happy and peaceful Christmas time as he has had now. He is newly clothed and well supplied with books and papers, while the kind care of the sisters and nurses, with visits from the Chaplain and others, relieves the monotony of his existence. One lady has most thoughtfully engaged to provide for his being taught basket-weaving, to give him some definite occupation, and I hope at once to start this work. If he leaves, and he is of course a free agent, I shall now be able to provide for his being properly taken care of by an uncle at Leicester, who is too poor a man to take him in unless means were given to him, but there can be no question that he is far better off with us than he could possibly be outside, and this is his own feeling. As I have not thought it necessary to publish any list, but I have received and hold in trust sufficient to enable me to provide for the poor fellow's comfort for some four or five years to come, and if more should then be required I will ask for it. As many have desired to know particulars of this unique case, I would add that some details are given with illustrations in the British Medical Journal of the 11th ultimo. One of our objectives, however is to prevent his deformity being made anything of a show, except for purely scientific purposes, and the hospital officials have instructions to secure for him as far as possible immunity from the gaze of the curious.[24]

In December 1886, Joseph Merrick had taken up permanent residence in his own basement flat in the East Wing of the London Hospital, known as Bedstead Square. And due to the generosity and compassion shown by others for his plight, life was never to be the same again for the Elephant Man.

24 *Leicester Chronicle*, 8 January 1887.

CHAPTER 9

The Elephant House

The Grocers' Wing of London Hospital was opened on 7 March 1876 by Her Majesty Queen Victoria accompanied by her daughter Princess Beatrice, and the event was quite a spectacle for those living in the East End of London. A procession of four carriages left Buckingham Palace at 11.20am, passing along the Thames Embankment, Queen Victoria Street, Leadenhall Street, Aldgate and then on to Whitechapel Road. The route was lined with troops from Blackfriars bridge, and a guard of honour was mounted by the Grenadier Guards at the entrance of the hospital.[1]

The Grocers' Wing, named after the donations which were provided by the Grocers' Company of the City of London, was located at the back of the hospital. And it was between this new wing and the high walls of the East Wing that the myriad of buildings opened up into a courtyard, which was utilised, so hospital legend has it, as the space where the beds from the hospital were cleaned and painted, and was therefore colloquially known as 'Bedstead Square'.

On one side of the square stood flats which were commonly used by nurses. One particular flat, which could only be reached by a flight of concrete steps leading down to a small wooden door, became home to Joseph Merrick. The comfort sought had finally been gained.[2]

Behind the door were two small rooms, and it was due to the diligent hard work of the hospital's Chief Engineer, Mr William Taylor, that Joseph enjoyed a little bit of luxury in this small dwelling.

1   *Morning Post*, 8 March 1876.

Daylight streamed through the glass panels set into the wooden door and the narrow deep-set sash windows. Running past these window was a little alleyway, which lead to the concrete steps taking visitors to street level.[3]

Inside stood a table with chairs, a small fireplace with a mantelpiece, and an armchair specially built for the new resident. Joseph's bed, which was in the same room, was also specially contracted by the hospital works' department. It was a couch type bed; custom carved to receive Joseph's anomalous physique, and luxuriously covered in leather. Inside the living room-cum-bedroom was an inner door which led to the bathroom, which William Taylor had assembled under the strict instruction by Frederick Treves that no mirrors were permitted.

An unfortunate incident had occurred before Joseph was relocated to Bedstead Square, when he was residing in the attic rooms in the Isolation Ward. A nurse was instructed to take him up some nourishment but unfortunately, she hadn't been informed as to the extent of Joseph's deformities. As she walked into the room and saw him propped up with pillows, she promptly abandoned the tray and fled screaming. According to Treves, Joseph didn't even notice the disturbance. In all probability, because this sort of reaction had occurred throughout life he saw it as the norm.[4]

In 1887, the London Hospital on Whitechapel Road was the largest hospital in Great Britain and treated about 8,000 in-patients a year,[5] chiefly men, women and children from the streets, factories and docks of one of the largest slum areas in the land.

A former nurse described life at the London Hospital to the *London Daily News*:

> The people of the East end have no horror of the hospital such as exists in most country places: some, indeed, will seek by every

---

2   *The True History of the Elephant Man* by Michael Howell and Peter Ford (Kindle Edition 2011).

3   ibid.

4   *The Elephant Man and Other Reminiscences* by Sir Frederick Treves (1923).

subterfuge to get taken into its quiet wards for a time. One man, who in spite of applications of magnesium and electricity, refused to walk for no discoverable reason, had finally been carried out and left on the pavement till cold and hunger recalled the use of his limbs, and he slunk away in the darkness...

A woman insisted that she had swallowed her false teeth, and calmly underwent many operations, though no traces of the teeth were ever found; the surgeons, indeed were nearly sure they had never been swallowed.[6]

Although some may have contrived to get into the hospital, many grumbled once in there. One regular complaint was having to sleep in a room with the windows constantly open, another to eat the plain food that was provided while the nurses whisked around with brooms and dusters, which does not sound very hygienic.

The House Physician did his rounds with his attendant students each morning, staying only a few minutes by each bed unless a case was particularly noteworthy, when, if time permitted, he would linger just a little more than half an hour. At noon dinner was served, and the sustenance provided varied depending on the condition of the patient. In the surgical ward the meals consisted of meat, vegetables and beer, followed by a plain pudding. In the medical wards a banquet of beef tea, fish or mutton chops.

After dinner the physicians and surgeons would conduct their rounds again and, once completed, the patients were ready to receive their visitors. At four o'clock tea was served, when the patients could congregate around the fire to exchange in conversation or play games. Finally, at eight o'clock in the evening, provisions for the night began and those patients who had been allowed to stay up were escorted back to their beds, gas lights dimmed and the curtains of each bed drawn. It was at this point that the day nurses would leave for their supper and the night nurses took over.[7]

Bedstead Square was the home Joseph could call his own, although he did request on occasion to Treves that, if he was to move again,

5   *London Daily News*, 21 May 1887.

6   Ibid.

could he go to an asylum for the blind, or alternatively a lighthouse, which could offer him peace and seclusion. He was enthralled by the idea that he could exist surrounded by people who could not see him[8]

However, Bedstead Square did offer Joseph safety and security in a world which could be cruel and violent, although in Treves' own reminiscences he recalls that occasionally a snooping porter or ward maid would open Joseph's door to let inquisitive acquaintances peep in.[9] Once Joseph was settled in his new residence, Treves stopped by to visit him every day, and he also urged his house surgeons to do the same.

Dr Wilfred Grenfell, one of the surgeons at London Hospital, wrote that Joseph

> used to talk freely of how he would look in a huge bottle of alcohol – an end to which in his imagination he was fated to come. He was of a very cheerful disposition and pathetically proud of his left side which was normal.[10]

Was Joseph's comment an indication that he was aware he was going to become a medical specimen after his death?

In due course, because of the numerous visits and callers Joseph's rooms in Bedstead Square became colloquially known as 'the Elephant House'.[11]

In his new residence, Joseph became acquainted with most of the individuals who daily hustled and bustled about the place, and he familiarised himself with people's movements. None of these regulars took any more than a friendly interest in him. William Taylor, the Chief Engineer who had helped construct Joseph's rooms, one day introduced him to his son Charles, a young lad of about seventeen years of age. The new friendship quickly grew, and

7   Ibid.
8   *The Elephant Man and Other Reminiscences* by Sir Frederick Treves (1923).
9   Ibid.
10 *A Labrador Doctor* by Sir Wilfred Thomason Grenfell (1929).
11 Ibid.

Charles would call in on Joseph frequently, bringing along with him his violin to play private recitals for Joseph's amusement.[12]

Along with Nurse Emma Ireland, who ran Blizzard Ward, a small group of volunteer nurses were there to take care of Joseph and tend to him during his recovery from severe bronchitis and malnutrition brought on during his time on the continent[13] and journey back to England in 1886.

Joseph still felt isolated, however, and didn't feel as if he was regarded as an equal to everybody else, especially by the female nursing staff. Treves recounts in his reminiscences that the nurses were just doing the duty which they were employed to do, and that their service to Joseph was purely official.[14]

It was this distant professionalism which isolated Joseph and, despite regular attendance, left him feeling lonely. To counter this, Treves asked a young female acquaintance of his, "a young pretty widow", if she would visit Joseph in his rooms. The young widow agreed, and so met Joseph with a smile, wishing him good morning and shaking him by the hand.[15]

The young widow was Mrs Leila Maturin, the widow of Dr Leslie Maturin who had died in 1884.[16] The impact this meeting had on Joseph was not what Treves had envisaged, because as Joseph relinquished Leila's hand he bent his head on his knees and wept until Treves thought that he would "never rest".[17] Joseph later disclosed to Treves that Leila Maturin was the first lady who had ever smiled at him,[18] apart from his mother of, course, but Treves painted a very cold view of Joseph's memories of his mother and his early life in Leicester:

12 *The True History of the Elephant Man* by Michael Howell and Peter Ford (Kindle Edition 2011).

13 *Measured by Soul: The Life of Joseph Carey Merrick (also known as 'The Elephant Man')* by Jeanette Sitton and Mae Siuwai Stroshane (2012).

14 *The Elephant Man and Other Reminiscences* by Sir Frederick Treves (1923).

15 Ibid.

16 *London Evening Standard*, 21 November 1884.

17 *The True History of the Elephant Man* by Michael Howell and Peter Ford (Kindle Edition 2011).

> Of his early days I could learn but little... He was very loath to
> talk about the past. It was a nightmare, the shudder of which was
> still upon him. He was born, he believed, in or about Leicester. Of
> his father he knew absolutely nothing. Of his mother he had some
> memory. It was very faint and had, I think, been elaborated in his
> mind into something definite.[19]

It may well have been the case that Joseph didn't want to divulge
his past and talk about his mother, preferring to keep these things
private.

In his memoirs, Treves goes on to suggest that Joseph had
transposed the loving mother figure often featured in the tales
he'd read onto his own mother, or in his own words, "one of those
comfortable lullaby singing persons who are so loveable."

Treves considered that somewhere in Joseph's subconscious there
was a dim recollection of some maternal individual who had been
compassionate to him at some point, and he adhered to this concept,
which made it real in his mind:

> It was a favourite belief of his, his mother was beautiful. The fiction
> was, I am aware, one of his own making, but it was a great joy to
> him. His mother lovely as she may have been, basely deserted him
> when he was small, so small that his earliest clear memories were
> the workhouse to which he had been taken. Worthless and inhuman
> as this mother was, he spoke of her with pride and even with
> reverence.[20]

And once, Joseph spoke of being puzzled at his appearance, saying"
"It is very strange, for, you see, mother was so beautiful."[21]

Treves claimed that Joseph's personality changed after he had met
Leila Maturin. He gained self-confidence, and started to become the
object of much personal attention. How this interest came about
Treves doesn't divulge, but according to the doctor's memoirs
Joseph greeted a succession of callers, and everyone who was

18 Ibid.
19 *The Elephant Man and Other Reminiscences* by Sir Frederick Treves (1923).
20 Ibid.
21 Ibid.

anyone wanted to call upon him. Treves recalled that "he must have been visited by almost every lady of note in the social world."[22]

Joseph welcomed his visitors with a shake of his hand and a smile, and he was conversant with the elite in London's polite society. He accepted gifts, ornaments and pictures, and was presented with numerous books. Joseph never asked for anything material, nor ventured upon the kindness of his callers, but was respectful and overwhelmingly grateful. He had left behind his shyness, and took pleasure in his door being pushed open, welcoming the populace looking in on him.[23]

Was this part of a much larger plan on Treves' side? Was Joseph an experiment to see if 'a freak', who was more used to penny show exhibits, could be accepted into London's high society? Treves and other medical professionals did have a reputation for combing exhibitions for their pathological cases; was this just another type of 'side show', except for the amusement of the aristocratic and well-to-do?

Not long into Joseph's residency at Bedstead Square, his old friend Tom Norman received a note brought to him by Jack Simmons, a porter at the London Hospital. Tom went to drop in on Joseph at the hospital but was refused admission.[24] He didn't make any additional endeavours to see Joseph, but a few weeks later Simmons, who by this stage had departed the hospital, sought out Norman at his premises in East Dock Road before returning home to Ireland. According to Norman's memoirs, after the long chat he'd had with Simmons he took a statement from the former porter. This testimonial was not published in the reminiscences, but the following additional note written by Norman's son George explains why:

> I do not wish to publish this statement in which Mr Simmons (whose duties often caused him to enter Joseph's room) stated that on more than one occasion Joseph was heard to ask "Why can't I go back to

22 *The Elephant Man and Other Reminiscences* by Sir Frederick Treves (1923).

23 Ibid.

24 *The Penny Showman: Tom Norman, Silver King.* With additional writings by his son George Norman (1985).

Mr Norman?". The statement gave almost a day to day account of Joseph's life in his little room, and how he was constantly seen and examined by a stream of surgeons, doctors and Dr Treeve's [sic] friends. However, as this statement was written by Mr Norman and signed by Mr Simmons with no witness I doubt if it would give much credibility.[25]

If Joseph was able to evoke the memory of the visit made by the Prince and Princess of Wales to Leicester in May 1882, when they opened the town's Abbey Park while he was still an inmate at the Leicester Union workhouse, then he certainly wouldn't forget the royal visit to his new home five years later.

On 21 May 1887, the London Hospital was honoured by a visit from the Prince and Princess of Wales, who were there to inaugurate two new buildings, the nursing home, which provided much-needed accommodation for the large nursing staff, and the new medical college building which provided a new home for the oldest, and one of the largest, medical schools in the country at that time.[26]

The *Morning Post* described the events and celebrations of the day:

Cheering crowds lined the thoroughfares, flags hung across the broad roadway, mounted police were riding about and the strains of volunteer bands were heard. A guard of honour at the hospital door was furnished by the 2nd Tower Hamlets Rifle Volunteers.[27]

Just behind Joseph's rooms, in the hospital gardens, where he was known to take nightly walks, the band of the 3rd Queen's Royal West Surrey Volunteers performed a programme of music for the enjoyment of the many visitors invited to witness the opening of these new buildings. Treves recollects in his memoirs that Joseph would express himself by beating time upon a pillow to some tune that was ringing in his head, and perhaps he was doing exactly that on this special day.

The Prince and Princess of Wales were accompanied by the three

---

25 Ibid.

26 *Morning Post*, 23 May 1887.

27 Ibid.

young Princesses - Louise, the Princess Royal, Princess Victoria of Wales and Princess Maud - and were received by the Duke of Cambridge, who was the President of the Hospital, the Vice President, the Treasurer, and the Chairman, Mr Francis Carr-Gomm. The Royal entourage first visited the Queen Victoria Ward, a children's ward opened by Her Majesty Queen Victoria in 1876. Alexandra, the Princess of Wales, was bestowed with gifts of flowers as she walked and talked amongst the patients. After visiting the male Gloucester accident ward, the Royal party were directed into the dining room of the nurses' home, and after a hymn and the prayer of the day spoken by the Bishop of Bedford, the Princess of Wales declared the nurses' home open.

Prince Edward, Princess Alexandra of Wales and their three young daughters were also present for the principal ceremony, which was held in the library of the new medical college, and were received by Carr-Gomm along with a member of the College Board. The Duke of Cambridge, as President of the London Hospital, read a long address to their Royal Highnesses, tracing the history of the hospital up to where they were now, in 1887.[28]

The *Morning Post* detailed the Prince's reply:

Your Royal Highnesses and Gentlemen – we thank you for your address and can assure you that we have much pleasure in coming here to-day to open the nursing home and the college buildings of this important institution. The Hospital which is the largest civil one in the United Kingdom, which contains nearly 800 beds, and which supplied last year medical and surgical attendance to 80,000 out-patients, may almost be regarded in the light of a national institution – (cheers) and as every description of cases, except those of an infectious or incurable nature is admitted, such a hospital cannot fail to be of inestimable value to the population of over a million persons residing in its vicinity, and especially to the labouring classes, who are so extensively employed in the neighbouring railways and docks. But it has other and additional claims on public sympathy and assistance – first with an annual expenditure of nearly £50,000 it is mainly supported by voluntary subscriptions; secondly it has

28 *Morning Post*, 23 May 1887.

undertaken the difficult task of improving the system of nursing and providing a higher class of nurses, with better discipline and superior training and instruction. To effect these objects house accommodation was essential, and instead of closely packed dormitories the new home provides separate rooms, a cheerful dining hall and other advantages all tending to brighten the lives of the inmates while securing the necessary rest and quiet. The new library and buildings which I am now about to declare open, belong to a college over 100 years old, which was the first in the metropolis at which a comprehensive curriculum was established, and being attached to the largest hospital in the country, situated in the midst of a populous artisan neighbourhood in London, it offers greater facilities for the acquirement of medical and surgical knowledge than perhaps any other college of a scientific character. I understand that amongst the important duties which the students perform in the hospital are those of dressers, clinical clerks, maternity pupils & c [sic] and that from their numbers the resident medical officers are selected after they have become qualified practitioners. The Princess of Wales and I most earnestly pray that every blessing may attend the labours and efforts of those who are working among the sufferers of the London Hospital, and you may rest assured that we shall ever take the warmest interest in the welfare and prosperity of your noble institution (loud cheers).[29]

Shortly before Prince Edward and Princess Alexandra made their way to the nursing home and the medical college, the Prince paid a special visit to

a very singular inmate of the hospital, one whom Nature has treated with perhaps unequalled cruelty – the so called 'Elephant Man'. Perfectly rational, this unfortunate being so repulsive in appearance, owing to physical characteristic hinted at in that appellation, that he cannot, it is said be successfully exhibited. After an unhappy career the poor man has found a refuge in the London Hospital, where – not being a proper subject for hospital relief – he is sustained by means of a fund specially contributed for his support.[30]

It has since been written that it was actually Alexandra, Princess of Wales, who visited Joseph on that day, and that she had entered

29 Ibid.

the room with relaxed grace, smiled and taken the introduction with perfect serenity, shaking him by the hand and sat beside his chair so that she may talk to him.[31]

Whichever member of the Royal family visited Joseph first, Prince Edward certainly was no stranger to alternative attractions, as Tom Norman wrote of his own meeting with the Prince:

> I may here state that during the next season's travelling, I found myself at Ascot in time for the races (all the fun of the fair was allowed there then) and I had Dick Baker's Petrified Girl as the attraction...

> It was during the big day that a gentleman approached me and said that a few friends and himself would like to meet Miss Eliza Jenkins, but did not dare to be seen going into the show by the front entrance, and had I a back door? "Yes" I said "if you want to see her so bad, go round to the back and get under the canvas". This they did, four of them in number, each in high silk hat lifting up the canvas, and more or less crawling on all fours.[32]

Tom makes it clear that they had not been in the show long when they began calling for him to come inside and fetch out Eliza. After answering their appeals, he went in and told them not to get too excited as he wasn't dependent on their few coppers for his living, but the men continued with their demands until Tom fetched her out.

> One of them said "Come on showman, let's have a look at her", which I did. I told them the usual tale where upon they burst out laughing.

Tom remembers one of the men turning to the other and saying, "Why he's a bigger damn liar then you are."

Norman ends his memory of the event by stating:

> He threw me half a sovereign, and the four of them retired the same way that they entered, on all fours under the canvas. One of the party

30 *London Daily News*, 23 May 1887.

31 *The True History of the Elephant Man* by Michael Howell and Peter Ford (Kindle Edition 2011).

32 *The Penny Showman: Tom Norman, Silver King.* With additional writings by his son George Norman (1985).

being none other than the Prince of Wales (later King Edward VII). Of course it was the oil painting and the no females notice that did it.[33]

Among many of the gifts Joseph was to receive was a silver watch presented to him by the Duke of Cambridge, President of the London Hospital, possibly on the day of the Royal visit.[34] The following day, the Duke paid a visit to his mother, the Princess Augusta, Duchess of Cambridge, as recorded in the journal of her Lady-in-Waiting, Lady Geraldine Somerset:

May 22nd 1887

At 3 came the Duke. He gave H.R.H. an account... of the Princess of Wales... at the London Hospital, tearing up her bouquet, to give a flower of it to each sick child & each sick woman. Of their having seen the Elephant-man, poor creature – a sad spectacle! Enormous, with two great bosses on the forehead really like an elephant's head & protruding face like a snout, one enormous hand like the foot of an elephant, the other, the left hand, extraordinary. Exceptionally small! He can never go out, he is mobbed so & lives therefore a prisoner; he is less disgusting to see than might be, because he is a gentle, kindly man, poor thing![35]

During Joseph's time at the London Hospital, the Princess of Wales paid numerous visits and sent him handwritten Christmas cards and letters every year. She also sent a signed photograph of herself. Treves recorded that Joseph was so overwhelmed with the picture he deemed it sacrosanct, and would hardly allow Treves to touch it. Joseph would often shed tears over it, and had it framed and put up in his room.

Joseph wrote to the Princess, and as Treves explained in his reminiscences,

I allowed the letter to be dispatched unedited. It began 'My dear Princess' and ended 'Yours very sincerely'.

---

33 Ibid.

34 *The True History of the Elephant Man* by Michael Howell and Peter Ford (Kindle Edition 2011).

35 Ibid.

Although Dr Treves believed Joseph's letter unorthodox in its content, he judged that it was "expressed in terms any courtier would have envied."[36]

Princess Alexandra's attentiveness towards Joseph resulted in an increase in other renowned visitors. The Prince of Wales never erased Joseph from his mind either, and from time to time a gift of game meats would appear on Joseph's table following a shoot on the Royal estates.[37]

Dr John Bland-Sutton puts in plain words the effect Joseph Merrick had on the Princess's friends, when he claimed that:

> It became a cult among the personal friends of the Princess, to visit the Elephant man in the London Hospital.[38]

The Elephant House was indeed open, and Joseph Merrick, the humble lad from the backstreets of Leicester, was enjoying every minute of his new found fame.

36 *The Elephant Man and Other Reminiscences* by Sir Frederick Treves (1923).

37 Ibid.

38 *The True History of the Elephant Man* by Michael Howell and Peter Ford (Kindle Edition 2011).

CHAPTER 10

Do You Think the Poor Man is Still in the Dungeon?

His mantel-piece and table became so covered with photographs of handsome ladies, with dainty knickknacks and pretty trifles that they may have almost befitted the apartment of an Adonis-like actor or famous tenor.[1]

Madge Kendal, one of the most famous theatrical actresses of her age, played an extraordinary role in Joseph's life, although she never met him in person. They were, however, prominent letter writers, and often exchange correspondence and gifts to one another.

Kendal recalls in her memoirs that she and her husband

Always considered it a great privilege to be allowed to soothe his [Joseph's] suffering...

He was most appreciative of everything I had done for him and expressed his gratitude in several letters to me.[2]

Later, after Joseph's death, Madge bestowed the correspondence and gifts she had received from Joseph to the London Hospital so that they might be well looked after with any other vestiges connected to him. Unfortunately, when Madge made enquiries regarding the letters at the London Hospital when writing her autobiography in 1933, she was informed that they no longer existed. However, one much-loved item which she deposited at the Hospital does still

1   *The Elephant Man and Other Reminiscences* by Sir Frederick Treves (1923).
2   *Dame Madge Kendal By Herself* by Madge Kendal (1933).

exist – a model of Gothic church which Joseph had made and later presented to her as a gift.[3]

The model is of St Martin's Mainz Cathedral in Germany,[4] and is still on display at the London Hospital museum. A Romanesque architectural style cathedral, Joseph's reproduction of this magnificent place of worship was made from a cardboard kit. Although the origins of the kit are unknown, Joseph probably put together the meticulous model with the support of nurses, a remarkable achievement for a gentleman who only had one functioning hand and, even with assistance, it shows that Joseph was an extremely productive and a creative young man.

On one occasion, Joseph put pen to paper and wrote to Kendal expressing his wish to learn basket work. On reading this, Madge arranged for Joseph to be taught the craft, and he sent her the first basket he ever created.[5]

An 1888 article in the *Pall Mall Gazette* makes it clear just how intricate the skill of basket weaving is, with a description of how a typical gardener's basket, known as a swill, was made:

> Quantities of hazel sticks and blocks of oak are boiled in water, filling the room with a delightful odour that adds a charm to its picturesque effect. The hazel sticks are bound into an oval ring, the oak split into ties or thin laths, one of which is bent to a semi- circular shape, and its ends secured to the opposite sides of one of the hazel wood rings; this forms the basis of the basket. All that now remains is to weave in the other laths until the swill is finished.[6]

Although Madge Kendal did not go and see Joseph, and doesn't offer any explanation in her memoirs as to why she could not, she did send photographs of herself, photographs which would later be commented on by the by-now Edward VII when they both attended Sir William Purdie Treloar's charity fete at the Chelsea hospital in

3   *Dame Madge Kendal By Herself* by Madge Kendal (1933).
4   Thought to be Mainz Cathedral.
5   *Dame Madge Kendal By Herself* by Madge Kendal (1933).
6   *Pall Mall Gazette*, 20 October 1888.

1909, the King remarking:

> I think, Mrs Kendal, you must have given your best photographs to James [sic] Merrick.[7]

That 1909 fete which Madge Kendal was involved in was in aid of the Alton Cripples' Home and College in Hampshire.[8] This institution, initially the Princess Louise Hospital, was founded in 1901 by public subscription for the sick and wounded soldiers returning from the Boer War. It was Sir William Purdie Treloar who, during his office as Lord Mayor of London, raised £10,000 in his mayoral cripples' fund, and re-established the Alton site for use as a hospital for the care and treatment of children up to the age of twelve who were suffering from tuberculosis of the bones and joints[9] - a disease which may have caused the problem in Joseph's hip.

Kendal also commented on Joseph's love of music, and she presented him one of the early gramophones which was worked by hand.[10]

His passion for the arts was highlighted again when he told Frederick Treves of another aspiration of his, a desire to visit the theatre, a wish which soon came to pass.[11]

Neither Treves nor Madge Kendal divulge which show Joseph went to see, or when, but the description of ballet dancers, ogres, kings and queens in Treves' memoirs matches the narrative of the pantomime *Puss in Boots*, which was running at the Drury Lane Theatre in December 1887.[12]

Getting to the theatre was not a problem; a private carriage could easily be arranged but the biggest issue was how to ensure such a conspicuous individual as Joseph Merrick could arrive at a very public performance without being observed, possibly triggering an

---

7   *Dame Madge Kendal By Herself* by Madge Kendal (1933).

8   *Shoreditch Observer*, 5 June 1909.

9   www.childrenshomes.org.uk/altontreloar.

10   *Dame Madge Kendal By Herself* by Madge Kendal (1933).

11   *The Elephant Man and Other Reminiscences* by Sir Frederick Treves (1923).

12   *Pall Mall Gazette*, 27 December 1887.

unpleasant situation.

Frederick Treves praised the efforts of Joseph's illustrious benefactor for providing the solution, stating:

> The whole matter was most ingeniously carried through by that kindest of women and ablest of actresses – Mrs Kendal.[13]

Kendal reached out to the philanthropic Baroness Burdett-Coutts, who held a private box at the Drury Lane Theatre. Although happy to oblige, the Baroness asked whether Madge herself would be answerable for what might happen to any woman who might set eyes on Joseph.[14]

Kendal assured the Baroness that preparations would be made so that no one would see him either coming or going, or indeed while he was in the theatre box during the performance. The procedure to get Joseph into the theatre was executed with precision:

> Merrick was brought up in a carriage with drawn blinds and was allowed to make use of the royal entrance so as to reach the box by a private stair. I had begged three of the hospital sisters to don evening dress and to sit in the front row in order to dress the box, on the one hand, and to form a screen for Merrick on the other.[15]

Treves and Merrick sat in the back of the box, which was kept in shadow, and the doctor confirmed that "No one saw a figure, more monstrous than any on stage, mount the staircase or cross the corridor."[16]

The first circle, comprised exclusively for private boxes, was draped in scarlet cloth trimmed with gold, and the front of the boxes were laced with a bold trellis of gilt moulding with suspended festoons of flowers, also in gilt.[17]

---

13 *The Elephant Man and Other Reminiscences* by Sir Frederick Treves (1923).

14 *Dame Madge Kendal By Herself* by Madge Kendal (1933).

15 *The Elephant Man and Other Reminiscences* by Sir Frederick Treves (1923).

16 Ibid.

17 *Illustrated London News*, 16 October 1847; www.arthurlloyd.co.uk/drurylane. htm.

The pantomime was advertised in many newspapers, including the *St James's Gazette*:

PUSS IN BOOTS

FOUR HOURS FUN AND FROLIC
A FEAST OF SPLENDOUR
FULL OF FUN
THE BEST OF EVERYTHING
ORDINARY PRICES
THE HOME OF PANTOMIME

AUGUSTUS HARRIS, in announcing

His Ninth Drury Lane Pantomime, begs to call attention to the fact that year by year they have surpassed one another, and that

It his intention to endeavour again this Christmas to offer a production unrivalled in the annals of the traditional Home of pantomime.

No trouble or expense will be spared to please every section of the public, and whist a delicious and funny spectacular extravaganza

Will unfold a new version of the old, quaint and fanciful story of PUSS IN BOOTS, it will appeal no less to the practised and

Enlightened playgoer than to the unsophisticated, and more impressionable spectator of more tender years. All that is charming and

Delightful to the lover of pretty sparkling music, gorgeous and graceful dresses, grand and poetic scenery, will, as heretofore, be lavished

With an unsparing hand. The company has been most carefully selected, with the hope of presenting the best and funniest yet gathered together

At this theatre.

PUSS IN BOOTS

Miss Wadman
Miss Letty Lind
Miss Jenny Dawson
Miss Marie Williams
Miss Leslie Bell
& c., & c

PUSS IN BOOTS

HARRY NICOLLS
HERBERT CAMPBELL
CHARLES LAURIE Jun
LIONEL RIGNOLD
CHARLES DANBY
GRIFFITHS BROS & c., & c[18]

At the same time *Puss in Boots* was being performed at the Drury Lane Theatre, Madge Kendal was starring with her husband in *Lady Clancarty* at the St James's Theatre in King Street.[19]

Joseph was in awe of the pantomime. He watched with wonder and amazement, Treves recalling:

> The spectacle left him speechless, so that if he were spoken to he took no heed. He often seemed to be panting for breath.[20]

Although Joseph would have no doubt been enthralled with even the simplest of performances, reviews of the pantomime give the impression that even the most seasoned theatre-goer would have been impressed:

> 'Puss in Boots' is the most splendid pantomime that has ever been seen on the stage of Drury Lane. The stage was full of knights and their attendants in glittering armour of gold and silver, whose evolutions cause the stage to flash with brilliant light, while gorgeous banners, rich velvets, glorious plushes [sic], beautiful brocades, and lovely faces complete the picture.[21]

Although the grandeur and display mesmerised Joseph, Treves believes it was the ballet which he enjoyed the most.[22] The dancers were the child ballet troupe of Madame Katti Lanner, an Austrian dancer, choreographer and ballet mistress,[23] whose work caught the

18 *St James's Gazette*, 21 December 1887.
19 Ibid.
20 *The Elephant Man and Other Reminiscences by Sir Frederick Treves* (1923).
21 *Pall Mall Gazette*, 27 December 1887.
22 *The Elephant Man and Other Reminiscences* by Sir Frederick Treves (1923).
23 www.oxfordreference.com/view/10.1093/oi/authority.20110803100051211.

eye of the *Pall Mall Gazette*:

> Each little girl has a little doll and each little doll has a little cradle. The little girls sing their little dolls to sleep in a pretty lullaby, dance a few simple steps and sing a few soft bars.[24]

Treves revealed that Joseph didn't like the ogres or giants:

> The Giant Ogre's stronghold is a fearful looking dwelling, and the inhabitants of this strange country are all over twenty feet high.[25]

The funny men didn't impress Joseph at all, who seemed to have had little sympathy with the frolics of the clown. However, one piece of slapstick did impress:

> He was pleased when the policeman was smacked in the face, knocked down and generally rendered undignified.[26]

In the weeks that followed the visit to the theatre, Treves felt that Joseph had interpreted the pantomime as real life, and everything he had absorbed during the performance was to him a reality. Joseph would ask Treves questions such as "I wonder what the prince did after we left?" and "Do you think the poor man is still in the dungeon?"[27]

It is hard to imagine Joseph as a fanciful romantic with no perception of adult life. He was a man who had experienced extremely difficult circumstances, hawking the streets of Leicester, living in a workhouse, travelling in his own 'freak show', making his own decisions, travelling abroad. So to be described as "a being with the brain of a man, the fancies of a youth and the imagination of a child", as he was in Frederick Treves' memoirs, does seem unmerited.

After years of abuse and self-reliance, was Joseph now regressing back to his childhood fantasies? Although his new life gave the impression he was well cared for, having a home he could call his

---

24 *Pall Mall Gazette*, 27 December 1887.
25 Ibid.
26 *The Elephant Man and Other Reminiscences* by Sir Frederick Treves (1923).
27 Ibid.

own and receiving visitors who were genuinely pleased to meet him, one can't help questioning whether Joseph was truly happy. Was he suffering from stress and anxiety? He was still subjected to Dr Treves' examinations and investigations, and the last known photograph taken of Joseph, in 1888, was a medical one.[28]

According to psychoanalyst Anna Freud,[29] when anxiety occurs the mind first responds by problem solving, and tries to find rational ways of escaping the situation.[30] Joseph tried the rational approach by writing to Tom Norman. And although Tom writes in his memoirs he did try to visit but he was refused entry, Joseph probably wasn't aware of this, most likely Joseph believing that Tom had abandoned him.

As his rational approach to the situation was not successful, this, according to Anna Freud is when the defence mechanisms are triggered. These mechanisms often appear unconsciously and have a tendency to misrepresent, alter and fabricate reality. In twisting reality, there is an adjustment in perception which allows for a lessening of anxiety with a parallel decline in felt tension.

One of the defence mechanisms Anna Freud puts forward is regression: reverting to acting as a child.[31] Was Joseph unconsciously regressing back to a time in his childhood when he felt safe and secure?

There is another suggestion of Joseph's regression in Treves' memoirs, when he wrote:

> He had all the invention of an imaginative boy or girl, the same love
> of make believe, the same instinct of dressing up and of personating
> heroic and impressive characters.[32]

---

28 *The True History of the Elephant Man* by Michael Howell and Peter Ford (Kindle Edition 2011).

29 Daughter of Sigmund Freud, the neurologist and founder of psychoanalysis.

30 *The Ego and the Mechanisms of Defence by Anna Freud* (1937). Accessed via changingminds.org/explanations/behaviors/coping/defense_mechanisms. htm.

31 Ibid.

32 *The Elephant Man and Other Reminiscences* by Sir Frederick Treves (1923).

Treves went on to describe an event one Christmas when he enquired what Joseph would like to receive as a Christmas gift. Somewhat bashfully, Joseph requested a dressing bag with silver fittings.[33] He had spotted an advertisement for a case which had taken his fancy, and kept it aside. These gentlemen's dressing bags were regularly advertised. One such bag, a travelling dressing bag of Moroccan leather, silver fittings was advertised at £5 5s to £50, and could be purchased at Rodrigues' of 42 Piccadilly in London's West End.[34]

Just as Joseph had asked, Treves purchased the travelling bag. The case came with silver fittings, silver-backed brushes and a comb, ivory-handled razors, a toothbrush, silver cigarette case, silver shoe horn and a hat brush, but as Treves explained:

> He could not use the silver backed brushes and the comb because he had no hair to brush. The ivory handled razors were useless because he could not shave. The deformity of his mouth rendered an ordinary toothbrush of no avail, and his monstrous lips could not hold a cigarette the cigarette case was a mockery. The silver shoe horn would be of no service in the putting on of his ungainly slippers, while the hat brush was quite unsuited to the peaked cap with its visor.[35]

Regardless of the fact that Joseph was unable to use many of these items, they still gave him much pleasure. He would lay them out daily upon his dressing table with proud precision. Treves filled the cigarette case with cigarettes, and now Joseph was ready to be the "Don Juan who he had so often read", the hero, the lover the young man walking in the gardens with his one true love:

> Just as a small girl with a tinsel cornet and a window curtain for a train will realise the conception of a countess on her way to court, so Merrick loved to imagine himself a dandy and a young man about the town. Mentally, no doubt, he had frequently dressed up for the part.

---

33 Ibid.
34 *Morning Post*, 18 June 1887.
35 *The Elephant Man and Other Reminiscences* by Sir Frederick Treves (1923).

> He could make believe with great effect, but he wanted something to render his fancied character more realistic.[36]

Amid all this fantasy life, Joseph still had a healthy obsession for learning and expanding his knowledge of the world. He was curious and anxious to view the inside of 'a real house'. Although Joseph hadn't lived in the poorest parts of Leicester, he certainly hadn't lived in the richest areas either, and even as a hawker he wouldn't have got close to the doorstep of some of the plusher houses.

By this time, around 1888, Joseph's family in Leicester were living in the more respectable neighbourhood of Belgrave Village, Justice Street, just on the outskirts of the town. They had moved away from the Wharf Street area some seven years earlier. In 1889 some properties in Justice Street were advertised for rent with six bedrooms, and described as clean with a large garden.[37] Horse-drawn trams finally linked the village of Belgrave to Leicester town centre, costing 2d and running from the Belgrave to the Clock Tower.[38]

Justice Street, where Joseph Sr spent the last years of his life, no longer exists. Like many old residential areas, the houses were demolished and new modern buildings replaced the Victorian terraces.[39]

Back in London, to satisfy Joseph's ambition Treves took him to his own house on Wimpole Street. Although the street attracted many of London's high society, and during the 1820s doctors had begun opening their own practices in the district,[40] Treves' house was not the huge mansion which Joseph may have read about, and Treves

---

36 Ibid.

37 *Leicester Daily Mercury*, 19 March 1889.

38 www.visitleicester.info/things-to-see-anddo/heritage/historicvillages/belgrave-village.

39 Justice Street is now Mortoft Road, off Claremont Street, to the northern end of the Loughborough Road area of Leicester.

40 One of Dr Treves' neighbours was nursing pioneer Ethel Manson, who spearheaded the campaign for nurses to receive better training and for the state registration of nurses.

explained that it was a "modest dwelling of the Jane Austen type", which Joseph could relate to, having read the author's *Emma*.[41]

There was one more burning ambition to which Joseph aspired; he yearned to return to the countryside he once visited in early September 1887, to see the green grass and the rolling hills, to see birds and animals and walk along deserted footpaths with sweet smelling flowers... and a chance to escape the horrors of 1888 enfolding on his doorstep.[42]

41 *The Elephant Man and Other Reminiscences* by Sir Frederick Treves (1923).
42 Ibid.

CHAPTER 11

Merrick Had Such Nice Brown Eyes

The estate of Fawsley Park in the idyllic Northamptonshire countryside had been a Royal Manor since the 17th century, when prominent lawyer Richard Knightley, Member of Parliament and Teller of the Exchequer to King Henry V, acquired the estate in 1416 from Geoffrey Somerton.[1] By the late 1880s the estate was under the guardianship of Rainald III, Baronet of Fawsley, and his wife Lady Louisa. And it was Lady Louisa Knightley who offered an opportunity for Joseph to escape the relative imprisonment of the London Hospital, and the claustrophobic city itself, by inviting him to stay on the grounds of Fawsley Park. It was a journey, as documented in Lady Louisa's diary's, that Joseph made at least three times between 1887 and 1889.[2]

Once Lady Knightley opened her estate up to Joseph for the first time in 1887, Frederick Treves had the dilemma of how to get Joseph from London to Northamptonshire. Joseph's appearance still drew interest from those not privy to his condition, so to shield him from the curious on the London and North Western Railways, the party sat in a carriage with the blinds drawn, the usual way by which Joseph moved around the capital. The transport authorities kindly ran a second class carriage into a siding and Joseph was chauffeured on board unnoticed. The carriage was then attached to the main

1   www.thehistoryofparliamentonline.org/volume/1386-1421/member/ knightly-richard-1442

2   *Biography of Joseph Carey Merrick* (Record Office of Leicestershire, Leicester and Rutland: Ref: B. Biography LB=13M local studies).

train, and Joseph's expedition to the Rose of the Shires commenced.[3]

As the crow flies, the nearest train station to Fawsley Hall is Long Buckby, which opened in 1881, serviced by London and North Western Railways.

Once the train pulled out of London's Euston station Joseph may well have raised his blinds and enjoyed the countryside passing swiftly by, although Charles Dickens once wrote complaining that the speed and noise made the journey impossible to enjoy:

> Away, with a shriek, and a roar, and a rattle, from the town, burrowing among the dwellings of men and making the streets hum, flashing out into the meadows for a moment, mining in through the damp earth, booming on in darkness and heavy air, bursting out again into the sunny day so bright and wide; away, with a shriek, and a roar, and a rattle, through the fields, through the woods, through the corn, through the hay, through the chalk, through the mould, through the clay, through the rock, among objects close at hand and almost in the grasp, ever flying from the traveller, and a deceitful distance ever moving slowly within him: like as in the track of the remorseless monster, Death![4]

The train would have cut its way through the English countryside at a speed of around thirty miles per hour, and the journey from London to Long Buckby taking about three hours. With no toilet facilities nor dining cars, 'comfort stops' were the only means of breaking up a journey. However, with these stops lasting just ten minutes or so, Joseph's mobility problems meant it is highly unlikely he moved out of his carriage once settled.

The first entry in Lady Louisa's diary mentioning Joseph is dated, Friday 9 September 1887, when he was staying with the Bird family, who were known to Lady Louisa:

> Mother and I went to Badby where two sad cases – poor old Powell dying of cancer in the face – and young Billingham of consumption. Then on to Haycocks Hill where Joseph Merrick, the 'elephant man' about whom there has been so much in the papers, has boarded out

---

3   *The Elephant Man and Other Reminiscences* by Sir Frederick Treves (1923).

4   *A Cyclopedia of the Best Thoughts of Charles Dickens* by Charles Dickens (1873).

for some weeks with the Birds. I think it is impossible to imagine three more melancholy things – they haunt me; one can only pray – and remember that Jesus lived and died for them. Merrick has such nice brown eyes! I looked straight into them – but he is very awful to behold. Croquet with my darling afterwards.[5]

Another entry was made on Saturday, 29 October:

Wednesday I went again to see poor Merrick at Haycocks Hill and thence to Daventry to distribute prizes at a work show.[6]

Although not located on the Fawsley Park estate, Haycocks Hill Farm was just less than two miles from the Hall,[7] and situated just outside the village of Badby. Famous for its bluebells in Badby Wood, which blanket the ground between May and June, Badby is said to be one of the most picturesque villages in the country.[8]

The farm was worked by Rachel Bird, a widow of six years when Joseph came to stay in the autumn of 1887.[9]

On his way from Long Buckby station to Haycocks Hill Farm, the route of just under ten miles would have taken Joseph through the village of Badby, through the open country side of Northamptonshire, and he would no doubt have been in pure wonderment when he caught sight of the ironstone cottages, thatched roofs, village greens and orchards.[10]

In the September of 1887, when Joseph was residing at Haycocks Hill Farm, there was a great fete held at Fawsley Park organised by the Knightley Habitation of the Primrose League.[11] The League had

---

5   *Biography of Joseph Carey Merrick* (Record Office of Leicestershire, Leicester and Rutland: Ref: B. Biography LB=13M local studies).

6   Ibid.

7   historicengland.org.uk/listing/the-list/list-entry/1001033.

8   www.rightsofwaynorthamptonshire.org.uk.

9   1881 Census.

10 www.rightsofwaynorthamptonshire.org.uk

11 *Supplement to the Northampton Mercury*, 1 October 1887. The Primrose League was set up in November 1883 as the Primrose Tory League by Sir Henry Drummond Wolf and Lord Randolph Churchill, father of Sir Winston Churchill. The 'Tory' part was soon dropped. Information from primrose-league. leadhoster.com/history.html.

been opened to women in 1885, and soon formed a separate branch called Ladies Grand Council. Two of the female associates were Lady Louisa Knightley[12] and Lady Dorothy Nevill, the grand-daughter of Robert Walpole.

The fete was held in fine weather, with entertainment provided by Signor Trevori, a ventriloquist and Punch and Judy proprietor. The main purpose of the fete, however, was to attract attention to the Primrose League. The speeches, which were mainly political, were heard by about 500 people attending the event, some of whom would have almost certainly been the Bird family.[13] The working classes of the nearby villages were given a day's pay to attend the fete, and according to a letter published in the *Northampton Mercury* by someone who was obviously not a supporter of the League, the only reason why the working man was invited was "to go there and don the badge and swell the number":

> These incidents show how far the Primrose League are prepared to go in order to get hold of somebody wearing a workman's garb and hard up for a day's pay.[14]

Lady Dorothy had also opened her estate up to Joseph Merrick, but on the condition that he did not leave the cottage until after dark.[15] Whether Joseph did visit is not chronicled, but venturing outside only after dark seems a bit purposeless as the reason for holidaying in a country estate was so Joseph could venture out in daylight without being disturbed.

Joseph returned to his home in Bedstead Square sometime before Christmas 1887, when as we have read he went to the pantomime. That Christmas may have been the first time that he received

---

12 Lady Louisa Knightley was extremely politically active, becoming a Primrose Dame in 1885 and establishing the Knightley Primrose Habitation the same year. She was also a suffragette sympathiser, and always felt her lack of vote was an injustice. See *Conservative Suffragists: The Women's Vote and the Tory Party* by Mitzi Auchterlonie (2007).

13 *Supplement to the Northampton Mercury*, 1 October 1887.

14 *Northampton Mercury*, 26 November 1887.

15 *Dame Madge Kendal By Herself* by Madge Kendal (1933).

Christmas cards and gifts from his new acquaintances, not only from the nurses and staff at the London Hospital, but also from the visitors he had received, including the Princess Alexandra.

In the weeks leading up to Christmas Day the hospital staff organised decorations and gifts were donated from the public. In the early hours of Christmas morning a choir made up of the nursing sisters and nurses progressed from ward to ward singing carols. All through the morning, Father Christmas, helped by an assorted troupe of fairies, shared out gifts to every patient. Joseph, of course, received his gentleman's silver travel bag from Frederick Treves.

At midday, a turkey was carved by the resident doctors in the atrium of each ward, and Christmas lunch was brought to an end with a plum pudding. After lunch had settled, the festivities continued with amateur shows in the wards performed by the resident staff, with Punch and Judy shows for the children, and in the evening, when the hospital had fallen into darkness and all the patients safely in bed, Christmas dances were held for the ward maids, with a midnight supper for the 'scrubbers'.[16]

The Christmas festivities of 1887 were long forgotten when a series of brutal murders plagued Whitechapel, mere yards away from the Hospital where Joseph was living. The Whitechapel murders file contains reports involving a total of eleven women between 1888 to 1891. The first case in the file is that of Emma Elizabeth Smith.[17]

Smith, a 45-year-old widow who lodged at 18 George Street, Spitalfields, was brutally assaulted while on her way home on the Bank Holiday Monday of 2 April 1888.[18]

Although she eventually staggered back to her lodgings, she had suffered terrible injuries and was taken to the London Hospital, where she died on 6 April. The Hospital authorities informed Wynne

---

16 *The True History of the Elephant Man* by Michael Howell and Peter Ford (Kindle Edition 2011).

17 *Capturing Jack the Ripper: In the Boots of a Bobby in Victorian England* by Neil R.A. Bell (2014).

18 *Morning Post*, 6 April 1888.

Baxter, the East Middlesex coroner, of the death,[19] with the inquest being widely reported:

Mr Wynne Baxter held an inquiry yesterday morning at the London Hospital into the terrible death of an unfortunate named Emma E Smith, who was assaulted in the most brutal manner early Tuesday morning last in the neighbourhood of Osborn Street, Whitechapel, by several men. The first witness, Mary Russell, the deputy keeper of a lodging house in George Street, Spitalfields, deposed to the statement made by the deceased on the way to the London Hospital, to which she was taken between four and five o'clock on Tuesday morning. The deceased told her she had been shockingly maltreated by a number of men and robbed of all the money she had. He face was bleeding, and her ear cut. She did not describe the men, but said one was a young man of about nineteen. She also pointed out where the outrage occurred, as they passed the spot, which was near the cocoa factory (Taylor's).

The house surgeon on duty, Dr Hellier, described the internal injuries which had been caused, and which must have been inflicted by a blunt instrument. It had even penetrated the peritoneum, producing peritonitis, which was undoubtedly the cause of death, in his opinion. The woman appeared to know what she was about but she had probably had some drink. Her statement to the surgeon as to the circumstances was similar to that already given in evidence. He had made a post-mortem examination and described the organs as generally normal. He had no doubt that death was caused by the injuries to the perineum, the abdomen, and the peritoneum. Great force must have been used. The injuries had set up peritonitis, which resulted in death on the following day after admission. Another woman gave evidence that she had last seen Emma Smith between twelve and one on Tuesday morning, talking to a man in a black dress, wearing a white neckerchief. It was near Farrant Street, Burdett Road. She was hurrying away from the neighbourhood as she herself had been struck in the mouth a few minutes before by some young men. She did not believe that the man talking to Smith was one of them. The quarter was a fearfully rough one. Just before Christmas last she had been injured by men under circumstances of a similar nature, and was a fortnight in the infirmary.

19 Ibid.

> Mr Chief Inspector West, H Division, said he had made inquiries of all the constables on duty on the night of the 2nd and 3rd April in the Whitechapel Road, the place indicated.
>
> The jury returned a verdict of 'Wilful murder against some person or persons unknown.'[20]

It is of no surprise that in recent years Joseph Merrick has made it to the list of Jack the Ripper suspects. A lone figure, dressed in a black theatrical cloak, wearing a hood and shuffling along in the darkness in the hospital grounds, would under normal circumstances cause panic and shock to any passer-by, but Joseph was undoubtedly well known by all the night staff to wander around the grounds at night.

A doctor at the hospital at this time, Dr Wilfred Grenfell, would write:

> Only at night could the man venture out of doors, and it was no unusual thing in the dusk of night fall to meet him walking up and down in the little court yard.[21]

Joseph always carried a picture of his mother as an *aide-memoire* of the only female who had displayed him any love. He had experienced the appalling reactions from women who found him repulsive. According to the theory of 'Merrick as Ripper', Joseph fostered a bitter abhorrence of women and had easy access to surgical instruments in the hospital, providing both the means and the motive to carry out the repugnant attacks.[22] This is, of course, a preposterous idea considering Joseph's physical condition.

Even Frederick Treves has been put forward as a suspect, on account of his anatomical knowledge and the fact that he once criticised the women attending the wounded in the Boer War as "a plague of women."[23]

Both theories that either Joseph Merrick or Frederick Treves may have been the notorious Jack the Ripper have been quite rightly

20 *Lloyd's Weekly Newspaper*, 8 April 1888.
21 *A Labrador Doctor* by Sir Wilfred Thomason Grenfell (1929).
22 *Jack the Ripper: the Celebrity Suspects* by Mike Holgate (Kindle Edition 2013).
23 Ibid.

condemned by Ripperologists around the globe.

To escape the horrors of Whitechapel, in the autumn of 1888 Joseph once more went to the Northamptonshire countryside, this time to Redhill Farm to stay with the Goldbys near the village of Chipping Warden,[24] just off the Fawsley Park estate.[25]

When arriving at the cottage, Joseph was greeted with a welcome he had encountered many times before:

> He duly arrived at the cottage, but the housewife (like the nurse at the hospital) had not been made clearly aware of the unfortunate man's appearance. Thus it happened that when Merrick presented himself his hostess, throwing her apron over her head, fled, gasping, to the fields. She affirmed that such a guest was beyond her powers of endurance, for, when she saw him, she was 'that took' as to be in danger of permanently 'all of a tremble'.[26]

This 'all of a tremble' state didn't last long, for on Wednesday, 19 September 1888, Lady Louisa Knightley recorded in her diary:

> Mother and I went to a pleasant enough garden party at Edgecott, and I visited poor Merrick by the way – and found him very comfortable and the Goldbys quite reconciled to him.[27]

A year later, Joseph returned to Redhill Farm, and one final entry in Lady Louisa's diary, made on Thursday, 5 September 1889 records:

> Went on the way to see poor Merrick who is at Redhill Farm again.[28]

On this particular holiday, Joseph made the acquaintance of a young farmhand by the name of Walter Steel. A youthful boy of twelve years of age, Walter was born in the neighbouring village of Byfield,[29] just three miles from Redhill Farm were Joseph was

---

24 *Biography of Joseph Carey Merrick* (Record Office of Leicestershire, Leicester and Rutland: Ref: B. Biography LB=13M local studies).

25 historicengland.org.uk/listing/the-list/list-entry/1001033.

26 *The Elephant Man and Other Reminiscences* by Sir Frederick Treves (1923).

27 *Biography of Joseph Carey Merrick* (Record Office of Leicestershire, Leicester and Rutland: Ref: B. Biography LB=13M local studies).

28 Ibid.

29 1881 Census.

staying. Steel called on Joseph daily to chat and collect any letters which he had written and take them to post,[30] including some to Dr Treves, full of enchanting and passionate interpretations of his escapades. Joseph expressed his bewilderment at the strange birds he had seen, how he had startled a hare, had made friends with a fierce dog and watched a trout darting in the stream. Joseph also sent Treves wild flowers he had picked, which to him seemed valuable and priceless.[31]

Walter Steel, like Bertram Dooley and Harry Bramley, the boxing midgets at Sam Roper's Circus, was enthralled by Joseph's thought-provoking conversation, and sensed he was a well-educated man:

> Mr Merrick, composed a great many letters, and would sit out of sight in the woods to write them.[32]

Walter also remembered that Joseph spoke of the pleasure he took in the natural world, and that he read a great deal of poetry.[33] This was evident in the way he ended his autobiography, with a poem by the popular 18th century writer Isaac Watts:

> Was I so tall, could reach the pole,
> Or grasp the Ocean with a span
> I would be measured by the soul
> The mind's the standard of the man[34]

By 7 October 1889, Joseph was back in London. On that date he had composed a letter to Mrs Maturin, the 'young pretty widow' whom Frederick Treves had introduced him to not long after he moved into Bedstead Square.

The letter, postmarked London Oct 7 89, is beautifully written,

30 *The True History of the Elephant Man* by Michael Howell and Peter Ford (Kindle Edition 2011).

31 *The Elephant Man and Other Reminiscences* by Sir Frederick Treves (1923).

32 Ibid.

33 Ibid.

34 *The Autobiography of Joseph Carey Merrick* (See Appendix One).

addressed to Miss L. Maturin at Sunderland House, Islay, N.B West Coast of Scotland. In the letter, Joseph thanks her profusely for the recent gifts she had sent:

> Dear Miss Maturin
>
> Many thanks indeed for my grouse and the book you so kindly sent me the grouse were splendid I saw Mr Treves on Sunday He said I was to give his best respects to you. With much gratitude I am yours truly
>
> Joseph Merrick, London Hospital, Whitechapel.[35]

It is sad to note that just six months after writing this letter Joseph Merrick was dead. The expectation of such an event was always present, however that did not lessen the shock.

35 *Biography of Joseph Carey Merrick* (Record Office of Leicestershire, Leicester and Rutland: Ref: B. Biography LB=13M local studies).

CHAPTER 12

It Was Clear That His Health Was Waning

Joseph returned back to a cold, wet, foggy London in the October of 1889,[1] back to his rooms in Bedstead Square seemingly much improved in health, and pleased to be home and to be among his books.[2]

The shop at 123 Whitechapel Road which he had shared with Tom Norman while doing his show five years earlier was now a pawnbrokers run by James Boddington.[3]

The penny shows and exhibition of novelties seemed to be closing down across the country due to the growing distaste in such entertainment, In November 1889, for example, the Islington Vestry suppressed the showing of fat women and monstrosities of nature at its cattle show.[4]

Despite this, in that same month the 'Greatest Show on Earth' was about to hit London, as P.T. Barnum, the great American showman who gave Tom Norman his title of the Silver King, was hosting a huge extravaganza at London Olympia in the November of 1889.

The arena had three circus rings, each 44 feet in diameter, and between the rings stood three platforms, allowing acts to be

---

1 www.metoffice.gov.uk/learning/library/archive-hidden-treasures/monthly-weather-report-1880s.

2 *The Elephant Man and Other Reminiscences* by Sir Frederick Treves (1923).

3 *Lloyd's Weekly Newspaper,* 3 November 1889.

4 *Lloyd's Weekly Newspaper,* 24 November 1889.

performed simultaneously with the equestrian feats in the circus, with five performances therefore running concurrently. A large annexe was built off Olympia to hold the menagerie of exotic animals such as lions, tigers, hippopotamus, elks, camels and an army of elephants. A skeleton of a huge jumbo elephant, and its stuffed hide, was placed near the north entrance. The sideshows of 'freaks and monstrosities' were arranged in the outer circle, an area devoted to smokers.[5]

The *Illustrated London News* realised that certain members of society were still fascinated in such shows, and reported:

> Freaks will be attractive from morning until night, because there is something in the human race that is strangely attracted by monstrosities. Women and men are alike influenced by this potent fascination...

> We shall have all society talking of the skeleton dude, the Aztecs, the armless youth, the legless man, the comely giant, the obese giantess, the squeaking pocket dwarf who would go into General Tom Thumb's pocket.

> There never has been a time when the English people have ignored freaks. They go periodically wild about them.[6]

Only a few weeks after opening of 'The Greatest Show on Earth', the fun of the fair was met by tragedy. On Tuesday, 3 December 1889, George Stevens, an elephant keeper at the show, was killed by one of his elephants. The animal which caused the man's death had been part of the circus for about eight years and, according to Anthony Bailey, part-proprietor of Barnum's exhibition, it had never shown any viciousness or vindictiveness and was considered very docile.[7]

According to the inquest held by Coroner Dr Thomas Diplock, George Stevens had been crushed by the elephant. A larger elephant had a smaller elephant up against the post; and all the keepers were told that if the elephants were frisky or vicious to wait until they

5 *The Era*, 9 November 1889.

6 *Illustrated London News*, 16 November 1889.

7 *London Evening Standard*, 7 December 1889.

had settled down. About midday on the Tuesday, George Conklin, another circus employee heard Stevens shouting "Take him away!" Conklin swiftly took a broom, and calling the elephant by its name – Mandarin - walked it away to its stall. When the smaller elephant moved away from the post, Conklin then spotted Stevens sitting against the wall in a crouching position, his head bent forward. He was dead. There were no marks or injuries on his body, but blood coming from his mouth. From the position which Stevens was found, the coroner judged that Stevens had been crushed by the smaller elephant.[8]

After a season of approximately four months, Barnum's 'Greatest Show on Earth' departed London's Albert Dock on 20 February 1890 on the steamer *Furnessia*, heading back to America. The company comprised three hundred horses, seventeen elephants, fifteen camels, fifty ponies and zebras, forty-six cages of assorted animals and five hundred performers. Staying behind for a further two to three weeks was P.T. Barnum himself.[9]

Coincidently, during those same four months, a killer was sweeping its way through Europe. By the end of 1889 and into 1890, a pandemic of the Russian flu had swiftly crept across the continent, infecting four million people and causing the deaths of 27,000.[10]

The newspapers kept their Victorian readers well informed with the latest developments of the deadly disease. In the early days of January 1890, the *St James's Gazette* reported:

> The Epidemic of influenza continues to spread both in London and the provinces. On the continent, too, the epidemic continues to rage, and in New York it is causing a great increase in the death rate. A further serious development of the epidemic is reported within the metropolitan area. The Hospital staffs have seen more patients then they have been able conveniently to deal with: and the physicians

---

8   *London Evening Standard*, 7 December 1889.

9   *St James's Gazette*, 20 February 1890.

10   *The Great Dread: Cultural and Psychological Impacts and Responses to the Russian Influenza in the United Kingdom. 1889-1893* by Mark Honigsbaum. Accessed via shm.oxfordjournals.org/content/23/2/299.html.

and surgeons attached to the respective establishments are finding the strain of the past few days a very severe one.[11]

in early January 1890, the Outpatient's department of the Westminster Hospital treated 65 cases of influenza in just one day, and at the London Hospital, where Joseph Merrick was living, some 500 patients were seen for influenza-related illnesses on 8 January alone.[12]

Although Joseph returned to London from his Northamptonshire holiday refreshed and seemingly in good health, it was clear that by the end of 1889 his health was failing. His daily routine was becoming increasingly difficult, the attacks of bronchitis were recurrent and his heart was significantly weaker; the growth which had been removed from his mouth at the Leicester Union Infirmary back in 1882 had begun to spread once more, obstructing his speech and eating,[13] and the size of Joseph's head had increased to such an extent that he could only just hold it up.[14]

He found it essential to rest and preserve his strength, making it his routine to stay in bed until the middle of the day. During the afternoons, Joseph spent his time reading and writing, and his evenings were spent walking in gardens of the hospital. However, it was clear that his health was declining rapidly.[15]

Joseph had gained much from the spiritual instruction he received from Chaplain of the London Hospital, the Reverend Tristan Valentine,[16] and he was encouraged to attend mass by taking his Holy communion in the vestry of the chapel. There, Joseph could hear and take part by reading the appropriate psalms and appointed collect

11 *St James's Gazette*, 9 January 1890.

12 Ibid.

13 *The True History of the Elephant Man* by Michael Howell and Peter Ford (Kindle Edition 2011).

14 *Measured by Soul: The Life of Joseph Carey Merrick (also known as 'The Elephant Man')* by Jeanette Sitton and Mae Siuwai Stroshane (2012).

15 *The True History of the Elephant Man* by Michael Howell and Peter Ford (Kindle Edition 2011).

16 *Measured by Soul: The Life of Joseph Carey Merrick (also known as 'The Elephant Man')* by Jeanette Sitton and Mae Siuwai Stroshane (2012).

of the day in his prayer book. Joseph had already been privately confirmed into the Church of England back in the early years of his stay at Bedstead Square by Dr William Walsham How,[17] the then suffragan Bishop of East London.[18]

And so, on Easter Sunday, 6 April 1890, Joseph attended the chapel services at the London Hospital twice and took his Holy communion in the morning.[19]

It was to be his last.

---

17 *The Elephant Man and Other Reminiscences* by Sir Frederick Treves (1923).

18 www.hymary.org/person/How-William.

19 *The Elephant Man and Other Reminiscences* by Sir Frederick Treves (1923).

CHAPTER 13

Perhaps That's What He Wanted

Four days after Easter, on the evening of 10 April 1890, Joseph may have enjoyed a last evening walk in the gardens of the hospital, taking in the evening scents of the sun-kissed sweet pea and admiring the delicate peonies in captivating hues of white, creams, pinks and reds[1] as he saw his last sunset on that chilly but dry spring evening.[2]

The following morning, Miss Emma Ireland, the nursing sister of Blizzard Ward at the London Hospital who had known Joseph since his arrival four years earlier, dropped in to see how he was that morning, and noted that Joseph was in his 'usual health'.[3]

It had been ten years since Joseph had left his Uncle Charles' home in Churchgate, Leicester, and took the mile-long walk up to the Leicester Union Workhouse, and six years since he had written to Sam Torr, the proprietor of the Gaiety Theatre on the corner of Leicester's Gladstone Street to suggest he exhibit himself, forever changing his life.

Joseph had travelled the country, moved to London and met Tom Norman, the Silver King himself, possibly the only real friend Joseph had ever known. He had travelled the continent, met royalty, visited the theatre and spent holidays near great country estates, but now Joseph's health was drastically failing.

1   These are seasonal flowers for April which may have been flowering in the hospital grounds.

2   www.metoffice.gov.uk/media/pdf/a/g/Apr.1880pdf.

3   Inquest testimony of Nurse Emma Ireland in the *Morning Post*, 16 April 1890.

As the ward maid brought Joseph his lunch at the usual time of 1.30pm, she left quickly so that he could eat at his leisure. The next part of Joseph's daily routine was a 3 o'clock visit from one of the hospital's house surgeons, and so it was that Dr Sidney Hodges arrived on Joseph's doorstep to make his customary visit.[4]

As soon as he walked into the room, Dr Hodges instantly knew something was amiss, as Joseph was lying across his bed, his lunch sitting precisely where the ward maid had left it, untouched. Realising instantly that Joseph was dead and that there was nothing he could do, Hodges didn't touch the body but instead called at once for a more senior college, Dr Evelyn Ashe.

Upon Dr Ashe's arrival, the pair jointly examined Joseph, with Ashe noting that there were no marks upon his body indicating violence. The doctors concluded that Joseph had died of asphyxiation owing to the weight of his head pressing upon his windpipe. As Joseph was found stretched out across the bed, it indicated that he was awake and trying to get up when he suffered some catastrophic physical event, and subsequently fell backwards.[5]

The news soon filtered into the media and around the country. Just one day after Joseph's death the story was picked up in his hometown of Leicester, as the *Leicester Daily Mercury* reported:

DEATH OF THE "ELEPHANT MAN"

The "Elephant Man" who obtained considerable notoriety about four years ago, was on Friday found dead in his bed at the London Hospital. The unfortunate creature was terribly afflicted, apparently with some form of leprosy or elephantiasis, and was shown about the country till his sad case attracted the attention of the authorities of the London Hospital, and they offered him asylum within their walls. The man was provided with a small room of his own, and was sent on holiday to an out of the way cottage on Dartmoor. The man was apparently quite well on Friday morning, and the exact cause of death is not yet known. His name was Joseph Merrick and it is

---

4   *Treves and The Elephant Man.* Compiled by Jonathan Evans, Archivist, The London Hospital (2003).

5   Ibid.

understood he was a native of Leicester. He was exhibited more than once at the fair.[6]

It's impossible to know whether Joseph's father, Joseph Rockley Merrick, or any other members of his family read the story in the *Leicester Daily Mercury*, but with a daily circulation of over 10,000,[7] it is more than probable that one of them did. However, it was his uncle, Charles Barnabus Merrick, upon notification from the Coroner's Office, who made the journey from Leicester to London to formally identify his nephew's body.[8]

Four days after Joseph's passing, on Tuesday, 15 April 1890 an inquest was held into his death at the London Hospital. Coroner Wynne Baxter heard evidence,[9] and the following morning the *Leicester Daily Mercury* carried a full report headed "Death of the Elephant Man, the Inquest":

> The inquest on the body of Joseph Merrick better known as the "Elephant Man" was held this morning at the London Hospital by Mr Wynne Baxter, coroner for East London.
>
> Charles Merrick, 144 Churchgate, Leicester, a hairdresser, identified that body as that of his nephew. Deceased was 29 years of age, and had followed no occupation. From birth he had been deformed, but got much worse of late. He had been in the hospital five years. His parents were in no way afflicted, and the father, an engine driver, is alive now.
>
> Mr Evelyn Oliver Ashe, house surgeon, deposed that he was called to deceased at 3.30pm on Friday and found him dead. It was expected he would die suddenly. There were no marks of violence and the death was quite natural. The man had great overgrowth of the skin and bone, but did not complain of anything. Witness believed that the exact cause of death was asphyxia, the back of the head being greatly deformed, and while the patient was taking a natural sleep the weight of the head overcame him, and so suffocated him.

6   *Leicester Daily Mercury*, 12 April 1890.

7   www.kairos-press.co.uk/pdf/mercury.pdf.

8   *Treves and The Elephant Man*. Compiled by Jonathan Evans, Archivist, The London Hospital (2003).

9   *Leicester Daily Mercury*, 15 April 1890.

The Coroner: the man has been sent around the shows as a curiosity, and when death took place I decided as a matter of prudence to hold an inquest

Mr Hodges, another house surgeon, stated that on Friday last he went to visit the deceased, and found him laying across the bed dead. He was in a ward specially set apart for him. Witnesses did not touch him.

Nurse Ireland, of the Blizzard wards, said the diseased was in her charge. She saw him Friday morning, when he appeared in his usual health. His mid-day meal was taken in to him, but he did not touch it.

The Coroner, in summing up said there could be no doubt death was quite in accordance with the theory put forward by the doctor. – the jury accepted this view, and ruled a verdict to the effect that death was due to suffocation from the weight of the head pressing on the wind pipe.[10]

On exactly the same day as the inquest, the House Committee of the London Hospital used its usual Tuesday meeting to discuss Joseph's death and the question of what should be done with his body. It was agreed that the skeleton should be set up in the college museum after the funeral service had been held in the chapel, and the body handed over to Dr Treves, who was the licensed anatomist of the college.[11] Therefore, following the funeral service Joseph's remains were conveyed to the Hospital Medical College.[12]

It was assumed Joseph had anticipated to be preserved after his death, with his remains being made available for medical education and research.[13]

In the penultimate passage of the inquest report there is an extremely thought-provoking declaration:

---

10 *Leicester Daily Mercury*, 15 April 1890.

11 Minutes of the London Hospital House Committee, 15 April 1890. Published in *The True History of the Elephant Man* by Michael Howell and Peter Ford (Kindle Edition 2011).

12 *Treves and The Elephant Man*. Compiled by Jonathan Evans, Archivist, The London Hospital (2003).

13 www.leicestermercury.co.uk/petition-launched-to-bring-home-the-remains-of-joseph-merrick-the-elephant-man/story-29422346-detail/story.html.

> We understand that the committee of the London Hospital refused not only to permit a necropsy on the body of the Elephant man, but also declined to allow his body to be preserved.[14]

Instead, Joseph's bones were bleached twice and re-articulated for private display in the medical college,[15] with the rest of his remains transferred to the Episcopal Chapel at the City of London Cemetery and Crematorium where he would have been blessed by a priest followed by his internment in consecrated ground but in an unmarked common grave in the City of London Cemetery and Crematorium.

The description of Joseph Merrick's death in the official inquest differs to that given by Frederick Treves in his memoirs, who gave a theatrical description of Joseph's death:

> He was laying on his back as if asleep, and evidently died suddenly and without a struggle, since not even the coverlet of the bed was disturbed. The method of his death was peculiar. So large and so heavy was his head that he could not sleep lying down. When he assumed the recumbent position the massive skull was inclined to drop backwards, with the result he experienced no little distress.[16]

Treves goes on to describe how Joseph sat up in bed to sleep, just as Tom Norman had witnessed back in 1884. According to Treves, Joseph wished he could lie down to sleep in a 'normal' position, and his romanticised account of the death suggests that's exactly what Joseph intended to do:

> The pillow was soft, and the head, when placed on it, must have fallen backwards and caused dislocation of the neck. Thus it came about that his death was due to the desire that had dominated his life – the pathetic but hopeless desire to be 'like other people'.[17]

---

14 'Death of the Elephant Man'. Report in the *British Medical Journal*, Vol. 1, 16 April 1890, pp.916 – 17. Published in *The True History of the Elephant Man* by Michael Howell and Peter Ford (Kindle Edition 2011).

15 *QED: The True Story of Joseph Merrick*. BBC documentary, 1997.

16 *The Elephant Man and Other Reminiscences* by Sir Frederick Treves (1923).

17 Ibid.

Although Treves' description, written in his memoirs more than thirty years after the event, holds a different view from that the inquest, it could be that he was remembering the position in which he saw Joseph after Drs Hodges and Ashe had first examined the body. It would be more than reasonable to assume Hodges and Ashe had laid out Joseph on his bed, with his head on his pillow, to make the body more presentable for Treves to examine.

Treves had the challenging task of dissecting and anatomising Joseph's body. He oversaw the taking of plaster casts of the head and extremities, and the preservation of skin samples. Regrettably the skin samples were abandoned during the Second World War, when staff in the hospital were evacuated to Cambridge and the jars containing them dried out. Due to bomb damage in the area, dry rot set in and spread through the fixtures and fittings in the building and the decay affected the specimens. As a result, all the samples were burnt as renovations began.[18]

Also during the War, pre-1907 London Hospital documents, including Joseph Merrick's post mortem report, had been removed to a safe place underground due to the risk of bombing. However, this secret location consequently took a direct hit during the Blitz and was destroyed.[19]

On 16 April 1890, the day after the inquest, a letter appeared in *The Times* and subsequently in newspapers around the country, including the *Leicester Daily Mercury*. Written by Mr Carr-Gomm, the letter recounts Joseph's impoverished life before he made his way to the London Hospital.

It was printed directly under a report of the inquest in *The Times*, a bid by Francis Carr-Gomm to present to the world the full details of Joseph's existence in the London Hospital:

THE LAST YEARS OF THE "ELEPHANT MAN"

Mr F.C. Carr-Gomm writes to the Times from the Home Committee-room, London Hospital, regarding the case of Joseph Merrick a native

18 *The Elephant Man and Other Reminiscences* by Sir Frederick Treves (1923).

19 *The True History of the Elephant Man* by Michael Howell and Peter Ford (Kindle Edition 2011).

of Leicester, known from his terrible afflictions as the "Elephant Man". His death was recorded in our last issue. Mr Gomm says of the extraordinary case: - It was one of singular and exceptional misfortune; his physical deformities were of so appalling a character that he was debarred from earning his livelihood in any other way than by being exhibited to the gaze of the curious. This having been rightly interfered with by the police of this country, he was taken abroad by an Austrian adventurer, and exhibited at different places on the continent; but one day his exhibitor, after stealing all the savings poor Merrick had carefully hoarded, decamped, leaving him destitute, friendless and powerless in a foreign country. With great difficulty he succeeded somehow or other in getting to the door of the London Hospital, where through the kindness of one of our surgeons, he was sheltered for a time. The difficulty then arose as to his future; no incurable hospital would take him in, he had a horror of the workhouse, and no place where privacy was unattainable was to be thought of, while the rules and necessities of our general hospital forbade the fund and space, which are set apart solely for cure and healing, being utilised for the maintenance of a chronic case like this, however abnormal. In this dilemma, while deterred by common humanity from evicting him again into the open street, I wrote to you, and from that moment all difficulty vanished; the sympathy of many was aroused, although no other fitting refuge offered, a sufficient sum was placed at my disposal, apart from the funds of the hospital, to maintain him for what did not promise to be a prolonged life. As an exceptional case the committee agreed to allow him to remain in the hospital upon the annual payment of a sum equivalent to the average cost of an occupied bed. Here, therefore, poor Merrick was enabled to pass the three and half remaining years of his life in privacy and comfort. The authorities of the hospital, the medical staff, the chaplains, the sisters and nurses united to alleviate as far as possible the misery of his existence, and he learnt to speak of his rooms at the hospital as his own. There he received kindly visits from many, among them the highest in the land, and his life was not without various interests and diversions; he was a great reader and well supplied with books; through the kindness of a lady, one of the brightest ornaments of the theatrical profession, he was taught basket making, and on more than one occasion he was taken to the play, which he witnessed from the seclusion of a private box. He benefitted much from the religious instruction of our Chaplain, and Dr Walsham How, then Bishop of Bedford, privately confirmed him, and he was able by sitting in the vestry to hear and take part in the chapel services. The present chaplain tells me that on this Easter day, only five days before his death, Merrick was twice thus attending the chapel services, and in the morning partook of the Holy Communion; and in the last conversation he had with him, Merrick had expressed his feeling of deep gratitude for all that had been done for him here, and bringing him to this place. Each year he much enjoyed a six week outing in a quiet country cottage, but was always glad on his return to find himself once more "at home". In spite of all this indulgence he was quiet and unassuming, very grateful for all that was done for him and conformed himself readily to have the restrictions which were necessary. I have given these details, thinking that those who sent money to me for his support would like to know how their charity was applied. Last Friday afternoon, though apparently in his usual health, he quietly passed away in his sleep. I have in my hands a small balance of money which has been sent to me from time to time for his support, and this I now propose, after paying certain gratuities, to hand over to the general funds of the hospital. This course, I believe, will be consonant with the wishes of the contributors.[20]

Carr-Gomm ends the letter by thanking *The Times* for inserting his original letter requesting help and assistance back in 1886:

It was the courtesy of The Times in inserting my letter in 1886 that procured for this afflicted man a comfortable protection during the last years of a previously wretched existence, and I desire to take this opportunity of thankfully acknowledging it.

I am, sir, your obedient servant
F.C CARR-GOMM
House Committee Room, London Hospital, April 15[21]

Among those who took a personal interest in the news was Lady Louisa Knightley of Fawsley Park, who wrote in her journal:

I see in today's paper that poor Merrick, the 'Elephant Man', is dead, passed quickly away in his sleep. It is a merciful way of going out of what to him has been a very sad world, though he has received

20 *Leicester Daily Mercury*, 17 April 1890.

21 *The Elephant Man and Other Reminiscences* by Sir Frederick Treves (1923).

22 *The True History of the Elephant Man* by Michael Howell and Peter Ford (Kindle Edition 2011).

a great deal of kindness in it. Thank God – he was not unprepared. Now! He is safe and at rest.[22]

Dame Madge Kendal, another of Joseph's great benefactors, wrote in her autobiography that:

My husband and I always considered it a great privilege to be allowed to soothe his suffering.[23]

The man who first bought Joseph to the London Hospital, the contradiction who is Dr Frederick Treves, wrote of his patient and friend:

As a specimen of humanity, Merrick was ignoble and repulsive; but the spirit of Merrick, if it could be seen in the form of the living, would assume the figure of an upstanding and heroic man, smooth browed and clean of limb, and with eyes that flashed undaunted courage.[24]

Tom Norman, Joseph's former manager who was probably the person he had been closest to in adulthood, wrote:

Despite all Dr Treves' statements about Joseph Merrick being happy and contented in his 'haven of refuge' it is my belief that Joseph, whose only wish was to be free and independent, felt as if he were a prisoner and living on charity, and was keenly conscious of the indignity of having to appear undressed before a never-ending stream of doctors, surgeons and Dr Treves' friends - on the night, probably in a 'what the Hell' frame of mind, quite conscious of the risk, lay full length on the bed and never woke up. Perhaps that's what he wanted. The question is – who really 'exploited' poor Joseph? I, the showman, got the abuse. Dr Treves, the eminent surgeon (who you must admit was also a showman, but on a rather higher social scale) received the publicity and praise.[25]

23 *Madge Kendal by Herself* by Madge Kendal (1933).

24 *The Elephant Man and Other Reminiscences* by Sir Frederick Treves (1923).

25 *The Penny Showman: Tom Norman, Silver King.* With additional writings by his son George Norman (1985).

JOSEPH CAREY MERRICK

5 August 1862, Lee Street, Leicester

–

11 April 1890, Bedstead Square, London Hospital, Whitechapel

'One who is probably the most remarkable
human being to ever draw breath of life.'

- Tom Norman

Afterword

In 1923, the same year he passed away, the by-now Sir Frederick Treves published a book entitled *The Elephant Man and Other Reminiscences*. The first chapter gave a detailed account of Joseph Merrick's life at the London Hospital and his existence before arriving on their doorstep in 1886. This version of Joseph's life has been the foundation for books, plays and a film.

Joseph never wholly revealed to Frederick Treves the details of his early life in Leicester, in fact he never did as far as we know divulge anything about his childhood to anybody, apart from what is written in his autobiography. Consequently nothing has ever been written about his upbringing which can be taken as firm fact.

George Norman, the son of the Tom 'Silver King' Norman, published his father's reminiscences in 1985 and included further chapters on showmanship. The book detailed Joseph's short stay with Norman in Whitechapel in 1884.

This book totally refutes Treves' account of Joseph's life in the freak shows, as does, Michael Howell's and Peter Ford's *The True History of the Elephant Man* from 1980. Howell and Ford brought to light a large amount of new information about Merrick. They contradicted some of the imprecisions in Treves' interpretation of Joseph's early life in Leicester, showing that his mother did not abandon him, and that Joseph consciously chose to exhibit himself to make a living.

In 1971, Ashley Montagu, an English anthropologist and humanist published *The Elephant Man: A Study in Human Dignity* which drew on Treves's book and delved into Merrick's character.

With the publication and success of Treves' and Montagu's books,

Joseph Merrick's life story became the foundation of several award-winning and incredibly popular theatrical works.

In 1979, *The Elephant Man*, by American playwright Bernard Pomerance was staged, winning the Tony Award.[1] The character based on Merrick was played by Philip Anglim, and later by David Bowie.[2] In 1980, a film also titled *The Elephant Man* was released, receiving eight Academy Award nominations. It was directed by David Lynch, with Merrick played by John Hurt and featuring Anthony Hopkins as Frederick Treves. In 1982, Philip Anglim played Joseph Merrick again in the US television ABC broadcast of Pomerance's play.[3] Merrick also appears in two episodes of the second season of the BBC historical crime drama *Ripper Street,* portrayed by actor Joseph Drake. He also made an appearance in the 2002 Hollywood film *From Hell*, played by Anthony Parker.

In 1992, *Articulating the Elephant Man* written by Peter W Graham and Fritz H. Oehlschlaeger was published. The book investigates how the phenomenon of the Elephant Man has been created and recreated over the decades.

As well as major productions, and awarding winning films and plays, smaller fringe productions have appeared revealing their own interpretations on Joseph's life.

Thomas Gibbons's *Exhibition: Scenes from the Life of John Merrick* from 1977 is a one-act play with four scenes and only two characters, Joseph Merrick and Dr Frederick Treves. It is in essence a succession of monologues and conversations between the two, with many of the lines taken from Treves' reminiscences.

Roy Faudree's play *Elephant Man*, when performed by New York's Performing Garage in 1978, was described as a melodrama but was more akin to a pantomime. It offered "topical satirical social criticism entwined with slapstick comedy."[4] Another play about

---

1   *Daily News,* 1 June 1979.

2   *The Montreal Gazette,* 11 July 1980.

3   *The Telegraph,* 28 March 1981.

4   *Articulating The Elephant Man: Joseph Merrick and His Interpreters* by Peter W. Graham and Fritz H. Oehlschlaeger (1992).

Joseph Merrick, written in 1978 by William Turner, employed the unusual approach of using Princess Alexandra rather than Treves to be Merrick's voice.[5]

A more recent fringe production by Lucky Dog Theatre Productions, *Mr Merrick, The Elephant Man*, written by Philip Hutchinson, who played Dr Frederick Treves with Tony Carpenter as Joseph Merrick. The production is based on Joseph's life and relationship with Treves and the London Hospital. Although the play has only two actors, other characters such as Tom Norman and Nurse Ireland are projected onto a screen and interact with Merrick and Treves. The play was performed at Leicester's Guildhall in April 2016.

In 1987 it was reported that the late pop star Michael Jackson had put in an offer to the London Hospital Medical College to buy Joseph Merrick's bones. The singer had repeatedly stated he was determined to acquire the skeleton for his private museum, which included deformed skulls, skeletons, a library of medical books on strange diseases.[6]

Michael Jackson was not the only celebrity interested in Joseph Merrick. In 2013, the American actor Johnny Depp invited writer Brian Hiatt to the office of his Los Angeles based production company for an interview with *Rolling Stone*. Hiatt described sitting in the office facing a set of double doors that opened into a museum with all sorts of memorabilia:

> We're facing double doors open to the adjoining room, which serves as a sort of museum: There's a Pirates of the Caribbean pinball machine with Depp's face on it, and for no particular reason, a life-size replica of the Elephant Man's skeleton, behind glass. Between the skeleton and the pinball machine is a headless mannequin, clad in the original black-leather-and-metal outfit Depp wore as the tragic, mechanical man-boy title character in 1990's Edward Scissorhands.[7]

In a 2011 interview in *Vanity Fair*, Johnny Depp explains how he

5   Ibid.
6   *The Free-lance Star*, 18 June 1987.
7   *Rolling Stone*, 18 June 2013.

had made an appointment at the London Hospital Museum to see Joseph's skeleton. He doesn't indicate whether he saw the actual remains but he does describe the museum and seeing the plaster mask and his hat and veil:[8]

> And right on the wall next to him is this gorgeous poem that he wrote about himself and about his life: "Dragging this vile body / Round the years / I am not what first appears / A senseless freak / Devoid of hope or tears." This guy was deep, and so, so gifted.[9]

Joseph's condition has been linked with many diseases and illnesses, from maternal impression when his mother was supposedly startled by an elephant in 1862 when six months pregnant, to a type of leprosy or elephantiasis,[10] neurofibromatosis (a genetic disorder that produces deformities of the bones and skin as well as swellings around the nerves),[11] or the modern diagnoses such as Proteus syndrome, a rare genetic disorder first described by Wilderman at el in 1983.[12]

Proteus syndrome is a rare condition with an incidence of less than 1 in one million people worldwide. Only a few hundred affected individuals have been reported in medical literature. Characterized by overgrowth of the bones, skin and other tissues, organs and tissues affected by the disease grow out of proportion to the rest of the body. The overgrowth is usually asymmetric, which means it affects the right and left sides of the body differently. New born babies with Proteus syndrome display few, if any, signs of the condition. Overgrowth becomes apparent between the ages of 6 and 18 months, and becomes more severe with age.

8   *Vanity Fair*, January 2011.

9   Ibid.

10 *Leicester Daily Mercury*, 12 April 1890.

11 *Treves and The Elephant Man*. Compiled by Jonathan Evans, Archivist, The London Hospital (2003).

12 Ibid.

In people with Proteus syndrome, the pattern of overgrowth varies greatly but can affect almost any part of the body. Bones in the limbs, skull, and spine are often affected. The condition can also cause a variety of skin growths, particularly a thick, raised and deeply-grooved lesion known as a cerebriform connective tissue nevus. This type of skin growth usually occurs on the soles of the feet and is hardly ever seen in conditions other than Proteus syndrome. Blood vessels and fat can also grow abnormally in Proteus syndrome.

In a letter to *Biologist* magazine in June 2001, Paul Spiring, a chartered biologist and physicist, speculated that Merrick suffered from a combination of Neurofibromatosis type 1 (NF-1) and Proteus syndrome.[13] The possibility that Merrick suffered from both of these conditions formed the basis for a 2003 documentary entitled *The Curse of the Elephant Man* which was produced for the Discovery Health Channel by Natural History New Zealand.[14]

Genealogical research for the documentary led to an appeal in 2002 to trace Merrick's maternal family line, with the result that a Leicester resident named Patricia Selby was discovered to be the granddaughter of Merrick's uncle George Potterton.

A research team took DNA samples from Patricia in an unsuccessful attempt to diagnose Merrick's condition.[15] During 2003, the film-makers commissioned further tests using DNA extracted from samples of Joseph's hair, found embedded in the cast used to create his death mask, and also from the root of one of his teeth and bone from the inside of his skull.

However, the results proved inconclusive and at the time of writing the precise cause of Joseph Merrick's medical condition remains unknown.[16] Because Proteus syndrome is caused by AKT1 gene mutations that occur during early development, the disorder is not

---

13 'The Improbable "Elephant Man"', by Paul Spiring in *Biologist* (June 2001).

14 uk.linkedin.com/in/paulrspiring.

15 "Elephant Man's Descendant Found", *BBC News*, 20 November 2002.

16 "Elephant Man Mystery Unravelled", *BBC News*, 21 July 2003; "Science Uncovers Handsome Side Of The Elephant Man", *The Daily Telegraph*, 22 July 2003; "Unlocking the Secrets of the Elephant Man", *BBC News*; 29 August 2013.

inherited and does not run in families.

Within the last twenty years, the dermatologist Dr John Harper has suggested that Joseph Merrick suffered from an extreme case of neurofibromatosis that perhaps should be separately defined as having its own name, 'Merricks Disease'.[17]

Joseph Merrick's home town of Leicester remembers him with a black granite plaque installed by the group The Friends of Joseph Carey Merrick at Moat Community College, in the Highfields district. The college occupies the site of the Leicester Union Workhouse, but is sadly inaccessible to the general public.

Whatever illness Joseph did suffer from, it should not define him as a human being. He suffered greatly with his ailments, and yes, life's hardships were never far away.

Nevertheless, his family's love, especially from his mother and Uncle Charles, coupled with a low middle-class childhood saw him in good stead when compared to other Victorian Leicester families in dire need.

An education brought forth an inquisitive mind and an inspired man in the arts and crafts, and a business acumen which saw him turn his disadvantage to a great advantage. Those who met Joseph Carey Merrick face to face saw beyond his deformities, and instantly took to him... and that is a high testament to no other but the man himself.

17 *QED: The True Story of the Elephant Man*. BBC documentary, 1997; *Treves and The Elephant Man*. Compiled by Jonathan Evans, Archivist, The London Hospital (2003).

The Autobiography of Joseph Carey Merrick

I first saw the light on the 5th of August, 1860, I was born in Lee Street, Wharf Street, Leicester. The deformity which I am now exhibiting was caused by my mother being frightened by an Elephant; my mother was going along the street when a procession of Animals were passing by, there was a terrible crush of people to see them, and unfortunately she was pushed under the Elephant's feet, which frightened her very much; this occurring during a time of pregnancy was the cause of my deformity.

The measurement round my head is 36 inches, there is a large substance of flesh at the back as large as a breakfast cup, the other part in a manner of speaking is like hills and valleys, all lumped together, while the face is such a sight that no one could describe it. The right hand is almost the size and shape of an Elephant's foreleg, measuring 12 inches round the wrist and 5 inches round one of the fingers; the other hand and arm is no larger than that of a girl ten years of age, although it is well proportioned. My feet and legs are covered with thick lumpy skin, also my body, like that of an Elephant, and almost the same colour, in fact, no one would believe until they saw it, that such a thing could exist. It was not perceived much at birth, but began to develop itself when at the age of 5 years.

I went to school like other children until I was about 11 or 12 years of age, when the greatest misfortune of my life occurred, namely – the death of my mother, peace to her, she was a good mother to me;

after she died my father broke up his home and went to lodgings; unfortunately for me he married his landlady; henceforth I never had one moment's comfort, she having children of her own, and I not being so handsome as they, together with my deformity, she was the means of making my life a perfect misery; lame and deformed as I was, I ran, or rather walked away from home two or three times, but suppose father had some spark of parental feeling left, so he induced me to return home again. The best friend I had in those days was my father's brother, Mr Merrick, Hair Dresser, Church Gate, Leicester.

When about 13 years old, nothing would satisfy my stepmother until she got me out to work; I obtained employment at Messrs Freeman's, Cigar Manufacturers, and worked there about two years, but my right hand got too heavy for making cigars, so I had to leave them.

I was sent about the town to see if I could procure work, but being lame and deformed no one would employ me; when I went home for my meals, my step-mother used to say I had not been to seek for work. I was taunted and sneered at so that I would not go home to my meals, and used to stay in the streets with an hungry belly rather than return for anything to eat, what few half-meals I did have, I was taunted with the remark –'That's more than you have earned."

Being unable to get employment my father got me a pedlar's license to hawk the town, but being deformed, people would not come to the door to buy my wares. In consequence of my ill luck my life was again made a misery to me, so that I again ran away and went hawking on my own account, but my deformity had grown to such an extent, so that I could not move about the town without having a crowd of people gather round me. I then went into the infirmary at Leicester, where I remained for two or three years, when I had to undergo an operation on my face, having three or four ounces of flesh cut away; so thought I, I'll get my living by being exhibited about the country. Knowing Mr Sam Torr, Gladstone Vaults, Wharf Street, Leicester, went in for Novelties, I wrote to him, he came to see me, and soon arranged matters, recommending me to Mr Ellis, Beehive Inn, Nottingham, from whom I received the greatest kindness and attention.

In making my first appearance before the public, who have treated me well –in fact I may say I am as comfortable now as I was uncomfortable before. I must now bid my kind readers adieu.

> Was I so tall, could reach the pole,
>   Or grasp the ocean with a span;
> I would be measured by the soul,
>   The mind's the standard of the man

An Abstract from
'A Case of Congenital Deformity'

Frederick Treves, 'A Case of Congenital Deformity',
Transactions of the Pathological Society of London
Vol. XXXVI, 1885, pp.494-8

The Elephant Man is short, and lame through old disease of the left hip-joint. The deformity concerns the integuments and the bones. The subcutaneous tissue is greatly increased in amount in certain regions, with the result that the integument is raised prominently above the surrounding skin. This tissue is very loose, so that it can be raised from the deeper parts in great folds.

In the right pectoral region, at the posterior aspect of the right axilla, and over the back, the affected skin forms heavy and remarkable pendulous flaps. The skin is also subject to papillomatous growths, represented in some parts, as in the right clavicular region, by a mere roughening of the integument. Over the right side of the chest, the front of the abdomen, the back of the neck, and the right popliteal space, the growth is small; on the other hand great masses of papillomata cover the back and the gluteal region.

The eyelids, the ears, the entire left arm, nearly the whole of the front of the abdomen, the right and the left thigh, the left leg and the back of the right leg, are free from disease.

The deformities of the osseous system are yet more remarkable. The cranial bones are deformed and overgrown, so that the circumference of the patient's head equals that of his waist. This deformity is better shown by the engravings than by any verbal description. Bony exostoses spring from the frontal bone, the posterior part of the parietals, and the occipital. Irregular elevations lie between these bosses, and all these deformities are very unsymmetrical.

The right superior maxillary bone is greatly and irregularly enlarged. The right side of the hard palate and the right upper teeth occupy a lower level than the corresponding parts of the left side. The nose is turned to the left and the lips are very prominent. The mouth cannot be shut.

All the bones of the right upper extremity, excepting the clavicle and scapula, and the bones of both feet, are enormously hypertrophied, without exostoses. The patient prefers to sleep in a sitting posture with the head resting upon the knees. The deformity is in no way allied to elephantiasis.

The following was added by Joseph Merrick himself:

I should like to say a few words of thanks to all those that came forward with help and sympathy after my case was made known by Mr Carr Gomm in the public press. I have much to thank Mr Carr Gomm for, in letting me stay here, till something definite was done concerning me, as the London Hospital is not a place where patients are kept permanently, although the Committee have made arrangements for me to do so. I must also greatly thank the Hon. Mrs Wellesley, Mrs Kendal, and Lady Dorothy Nevill who have been very kind to me, and lastly my kind doctor, Mr Treves, whose visits I greatly prize, as many more in the hospital do, besides me. He is both friend and doctor to me. I have a nice bright room, made cheerful with flowers, books, and pictures. I am very comfortable, and I may say as happy as my condition will allow me to be.

'Tis true my form is something odd, but blaming me is blaming God;
Could I create myself anew I would not fail in pleasing you.
"If I could reach from pole to pole
  Or grasp the ocean with a span,
I would be measured by the soul;
  The mind's the standard of the man".

Wombwell's Menagerie Itinerary 1800-1862

1 October 1800	George Wombwell marries Mary Simm at St. Giles- in-the-Fields, London
1804	First record of Menagerie at Little Compton Street, London
September 1807	Bartholomew Fair, London
September 1808	St James' Fair, Bristol
September 1809	St James' Fair, Bristol
5 November 1809	Snake bite
5 September 1810	Escape of a Tiger at Piccadilly, London
1810	Bartholomew Fair, London
1813	Bartholomew Fair, London
1815	St James' Fair, Bristol
21 December 1816	Norwich Castle Ditches
13 June 1818	Northampton Broughton Green
12 December 1818	Norfolk Castle Hill
2 January 1819	Norfolk Castle Hill: Addition of Zebra
28 July 1825	Warwick Factory Yard
31 December 1825	Norwich
1827	Bartholomew Fair, London
1828	Bartholomew Fair, London
1829	Bartholomew Fair, London
23 October 1830	Northampton Market Square
19 November 1830	St. Andrew's Hill, Cambridge

1830	Bartholomew Fair, London
16 September 1831	Bristol: Night watchman loses arm to 'Wallace' the Lion
1831	Bartholomew Fair, London
1831	Camberwell Fair, London
1832	Bartholomew Fair, London
1833	Bartholomew Fair, London
24 February 1834	Northampton: Escape of Lions – four die (later reported as a hoax)
26 February 1834	Castle Hill: Kangaroo wakes old woman
1834	Bartholomew Fair, London
1 November 1834	Windsor Castle: Four cubs viewed by Her Majesty
1835	Bartholomew Fair, London
3 December 1835	Salford, Manchester: Lion and three cubs die
1836	Bartholomew Fair, London
18 November 1836	St. Andrews Hill, Cambridge: Four Lion cubs born
27 November 1837	Somerset: Boy savaged by Lion
1838	Bartholomew Fair, London
15 February 1839	Hull Myton Gate
28 March 1839	Commercial Road, London: Letter from George Wombwell about death of lions
14 October 1839	Nottingham: Four Lion cubs born
1839	Bartholomew Fair, London
1840	Bartholomew Fair, London
21 November 1840	Hastings: Caravan overturns and keeper savaged
11 February 1841	Woolwich, London: Boy savaged by lion
27 February 1841	Midsummer Green, Cambridge
28 May 1841	Ashburn: Four lion cubs born
11 October 1841	Carlisle: Giraffe Dies
1841	Bartholomew Fair, London
19 March 1842	Mident Fair, Staffordshire: Keeper savaged by tiger
25 March 1842	Mident Fair, Staffordshire: Keeper dies
27 October 1842	Windsor Castle: Six young cats viewed by Her Majesty

1842	Bartholomew Fair, London
24 February 1842	Devonport: Leopard chocks to death
11 November 1843	Midsummer Green, Cambridge
10 January 1846	Norwich: Four lion – tiger cubs born
20 March 1847	Stamford: Lion queen injured
29 October 1847	Windsor Castle: Royal Patronage
1 January 1848	Bolton Market Place
12 June 1848	Stafford: William Wombwell savaged by lioness
26 June 1848	Coventry
17 June 1848	Walsall
13 October 1848	Hull: A hoax report on an escaped lion
1848	Bartholomew Fair, London
10 March 1849	March, Cambridge
26 March 1849	March, Cambridge: Boy savaged by bear
12/15 June 1849	Coventry: William Wombwell killed by an elephant
11/15 January 1850	Chatham: Ellen Blight killed by tiger
23 February 1850	Midsummer Green, Cambridge
6 November 1850	Durham: Boy savaged by lion
1850	Bartholomew Fair, London
17/27 November 1850	North Allerton: Death of George Wombwell
1 December 1850	Highgate Cemetery: Funeral of George Wombwell
15 September 1851	Oxford
29 November 1851	Chatham: Lion attack
1 May 1852	Norwich
2 May 1852	Clare
3 May 1852	Haverhill
4/5 May 1852	Saffron Walden
May 6/8 1852	Midsummer Green, Cambridge
1852	Ely
28 October 1854	Windsor Castle: Royal Command
10 March 1855	Ely
24 March 1855	March
20 April 1855	Knott Hill: Elephant hurts keeper

20 April 1855	Hackney
2 May 1855	Devon
7 November 1856	Midsummer Green, Cambridge
7 March 1857	March
14 March 1857	Wisbeach
3 November 1857	West Bromwich
29 November 1858	St Ives
30 November 1858	Over
1 December 1858	Cottenham
2/6 December 1858	Butt Green, Cambridge
1859	Chatteris
5 April 1859	Holywell
18/23 February 1861	Lynn Nart
May 1862	Leicester
23 June 1862	Coventry
October 1862	Leicester

Itinerary compiled and researched by
Richard Mackinder, relation of the Wombwell family.

APPENDIX FOUR
Charles Barnes Merrick

By Ken Stewart

Charles Barnes Merrick was baptised on 4th April 1824 at St James, Clerkenwell, in London, the son of Barnabas Merrick and Ann (nee Bowden).

When his father married for the third time and settled in Leicester, Charles was left in London to fend for himself. He does not seem to have been installed into an apprenticeship, as later records show he was not a turner like his father. He may have been apprenticed to a bootmaker, as his later life showed he was quite skillful in that occupation, but that bootmaking trade may have been learned in Australia.

Charles Barnes Merrick is first seen in London records at the Old Bailey:

> CHARLES MERRICK was indicted for stealing, on the 5th of March, 6lbs. weight of pork, value 3s., the goods of Jane Wing.
>
> JANE WING . I live in John's-row, St. Luke's—I am a widow, and keep a pork-shop. On the 10th of March, I had two bellies of pork, one on each side of my window—I saw them safe a minute before one of them was taken—I merely walked into my room from the shop, when a little girl called me, and told me something—I ran to the door, and a witness brought back the prisoner, and the pork, which was one of the bellies I had in my shop.
>
> GEORGE STOCKSLEY . I am a butcher, and live in Bath-street, opposite John's-row. I saw the prisoner and three others come down John's-

215

row—they stopped near my shop—the prisoner then went and took the pork out of the prosecutrix's window—one of the other boys took it from him as soon as he had taken it out of the window—they came towards my shop—I took the prisoner, and the other boy threw down the pork—one of the other boys picked it up, but they were pursued, and he dropped it again —a man took it up, and gave it to me, and I took it back—the other boys escaped.

Prisoner's Defence: I saw two boys go and take the pork—they began to run, and this man took me—I am innocent.

SENTENCE: GUILTY.

*Aged 16.— Transported for Seven Years.—Convict Ship.

Charles was firstly detained in Parkhurst Prison, but immediately ran foul of the prison authorities when he attempted to steal the £15. For this he received an additional sentence of 3 months. This sentence was apparently added to his 7 years' transportation.

Charles was transported on the *Runnymede*, departing London on 20th December 1839 and arrived in Tasmania on 28th March 1840, after a voyage of 99 days. A physical description on arrival was as follows: 4 ft 11 inches tall in his bare feet, brown hair, clean shaven, hazel eyes, fresh complexion with freckles, a long visage with small mouth, nose and chin. His 4 ft 11 inches as a 17-year-old was very small, but probably just a sign of those lean times.

During his early years of servitude he had a few run-ins with the authorities:

2 September 1841 - Misconduct making away with some tobacco. Three days of solitary confinement.

9 January 1843 - Absconding from Newtown Station. Three months' hard labour, the first and last 30 days of which to be passed in solitary confinement.

2 January 1843 - Insubordination, no sentence stated.

19 April 1843 - Absconding, to be kept to hard labour 3 months, the first and last months in solitary confinement.

6 November 1843 - Disorderly Conduct, 10 days' solitary confinement and then kept to his station.

He served out his remaining sentence in Tasmania with just these few sessions of hard labour and solitary confinement. These were not overtly the actions of a criminal, more those of a restless lad growing up away from home, but enough to keep him under the scrutiny of the authorities.

He was eventually awarded a Free Certificate on 4th July 1846, having served 7 years and 3 months of his sentence. He was a free man in Tasmania for the Convict Muster of October 1846.

Fifteen months after getting his Free Certificate, Charles left Launceston on 22nd October 1847 aboard the *Thomas Lord*, heading to Sydney. The *Thomas Lord* was a 72-tonne schooner carrying flour from Launceston to New South Wales, and on that trip carried eight passengers, landing in Port Jackson on 28th October 1847.

After spending some time in NSW, Charles moved to Victoria and took up residence in Cumberland Street, Geelong, in about 1854.

On 20th July 1857, at the age of 28, Charles married Mary Ahern. The ceremony took place in the house of the Reverend Alfred Scales on Virginia Street in Geelong, a the Minister of the Independent Denomination.

Mary Ahern was a 23-year-old spinster from Youghal, County Cork, Ireland, daughter to James Ahern, a baker, and Elizabeth Lee. Mary was born in Youghal around 1834 and arrived in Victoria close to May 1857, aged 22, having worked for a Mrs Graham of Mercers Hill in Geelong for three months from 30th January 1857.

Mary had been in Australia very few months before she was married. Her address was also Cumberland Street at the time of the marriage, and although Mary could write her name, but Charles signed the register with a mark.

The couple had six children: David (b. 1858), Charles (b. 1859), James (b. 13 May 1861), Ann Martha (b. 1863), Mary (b. c.1864, died very young) and William Edward (b. 1865).

Mary Ahern died in childbirth, along with the stillborn child, on 27th October 1867, leaving four boys and a surviving girl all under twelve years of age.

Charles Merrick remarried quite soon after, in 1868, to Bridget Cunningham, the thirty-year-old daughter of an Irish farmer,

Thomas Cunningham, and his wife Bridget O'Connell of County Clare, Ireland.

Charles had a further three children with Bridget Cunningham, all sons: Thomas (b. 1869), Michael (b. 1871) and George (b. 1873).

Charles Merrick worked as a bootmaker for many years in his workplace at 248/250 Elizabeth Street. He had the same postal address from 1865 until he died on 9th July 1878.

He was lucky not to lose the lot in a massive firestorm on 15th May 1868, which destroyed a lot of property around him, as reported in Melbourne's *Illustrated Australian News for Home Readers* of 20 June 1868:

> GREAT CONFLAGRATION IN ELIZABETH STREET:
> (between Franklyn Street and A' Beckett Street).
>
> About ten o'clock on the night of the 15th ult, a fire broke out at the Albion sawmills and timber yard, owned by Halstead & Kerr, corner of Elizabeth & A' Beckett Streets. The fire brigades were quickly on the spot, but for several hours their efforts to subdue the flames were perfectly futile.
>
> Mr Hoad's official report of the injury caused by the fire .... No. 248, C. Merrick, boot and shoe maker: Stock damaged by removal. Insured for £100.
>
> The evidence adduced did not tend in any degree to solve the mystery as to how the conflagration arose. ...The jury returned an open verdict, but expressed an opinion that the fire occurred accidentally.

In 1878, Charles' eldest son David, then aged 20, took over as the family breadwinner, operating as a bootmaker at Sydney Road in Brunswick. He was soon joined by his brother Charles.

Bridget died at 31 Wilson Street, Brunswick, on 10th October 1905, where the youngest son George was living. At this time James, the third son, was living nearby at 41 Wilson Street, and William, the fourth son, was at 57 Wilson Street.

Eldest son David Merrick appears continuously in the Melbourne Post Office Directories as a bootmaker for 42 years between 1879 and 1911.

Charles Merrick Jr does not appear in the directories, however in the 1899 Electoral Roll he is listed as a bootmaker of 382 Burnley Street, one of the earlier addresses of his brother David.

From 1895 until 1904 the EBC Boot Company operated from various street numbers, but mainly at 378/380 Burnley Street. This would have been a partnership of David and Charles, who both lived along Burnley Street.

The third child of Charles and Mary Ahern was James Merrick, my grandmother's father. His story continues below.

The fourth son of Charles and Mary, William Edward Merrick, was living in 57 Wilson Street, Brunswick, according to the 1899 Electoral Roll, and was like brother James practicing as a potter.

The youngest of the family, George is listed as a labourer of 31 Wilson Street, Brunswick, in 1899.

James Merrick was a 21-year-old potter of Richmond when he married Margaret O'Mahoney, daughter to Thaddeus O'Mahoney and Jane Stafford, on 20th August 1881 at the Registry Office, Richmond.

In 1894 he was a potter of Montague Street, Footscray, when his youngest daughter Ethel Margaret Merrick (my grandmother) was born. James assumed the middle name of Bond for the births of some of his children, but I have yet to find out where this supposed family name originates from. James Bond Merrick is a well-known Victorian potter, but I have not found much on his potting fame.

He is not located in the 1899 Electoral Roll, however two different entries for James Merrick appear in Brunswick after this date, one of which is at 41 Wilson Street, Brunswick, in 1904. A third James arrived in Brunswick in 1910 - James T. Merrick - at 15 Goodman Street, the next generation moving in to reside in Brunswick.

Margaret Merrick is remembered by several of her grandchildren as an active old girl who liked her drop of beer. To sate her desires she was known to have hocked anything she could lay her hands on - tablecloths, silverware and whatever - for another jug or two. At one time she broke her leg climbing over a fence to get a jug of beer.

James Bond Merrick and Margaret O'Mahoney had nine children

born in different parts of Victoria and NSW: Maud Christina Merrick (b. 1880), James Thaddeus Merrick (1881-1967), Lillian Myra Merrick (1883-1970), Mary Merrick (1884-1885), Doreen Merrick (b. 1888), Annie Merrick (b. 1890), John Merrick (b. 1892), Ethel Margaret Merrick (b. 1894) and William Charles Merrick (1898-1977).

Six are known to have reached adulthood, and four have descendents today, but none of these are 'Merricks'.

Select Bibliography

Archives

Ashby-de-la-Zouch Museum, Leicestershire
Leicestershire, Leicester and Rutland Record Office, Leicester
The Royal London Hospital Museum, London

Newspapers

Aberdeen Evening Express
Illustrated London News
Leicester Chronicle
Leicester Daily Mercury
Leicester Journal
Leicester Mercury
Leicestershire Mercury
Lloyd's Weekly Newspaper
London Daily News
London Evening Standard
Morning Post
Northampton Mercury
Nottingham Evening Post
Pall Mall Gazette
Perry's Bankrupt Gazette
Shoreditch Observer
St James's Gazette
Supplement to the Northampton Mercury
Tamworth Herald
The Era

The Star

The Times

Yorkshire Gazette

Books

A Labrador Doctor by Sir Wilfred Thomason Grenfell (1929)

Articulating the Elephant Man: Joseph Merrick and his Interpreters by Peter W. Graham and Fritz H Oehlschlaeger (1992)

Capturing Jack the Ripper: In the Boots of a Bobby in Victorian England by Neil R.A. Bell (2014)

Commercial and General Directory and Red Book of Leicester and Suburbs 1875

Dame Madge Kendal by Herself by Madge Kendal (1933)

Education in Leicestershire. 1540-1940 Edited by Brian Simon (1968)

Health, Medicine and Society in Victorian England by Mary Wilson Carpenter (2010)

Home Sweet Home: A Century of Leicester Housing 1814-1914 by Dennis Calow (2011)

In Sickness and in Health: A History of Leicester's Health and Ill Health 1900-1950 by Clive Harrison (1999)

Indoor Paupers: Life inside a London Workhouse by 'One of Them' by Peter Higginbotham (Kindle Edition 2013)

Jack the Ripper, the Celebrity Suspects by Mike Holgate (Kindle Edition 2013)

Leicester Trade Directory 1870

Life in a Victorian Workhouse by Peter Higginbotham (Kindle Edition 2013)

Measured by Soul: The Life of Joseph Carey Merrick (also Known as 'The Elephant Man') by Jeanette Sitton and Mae Siuwai Stroshane (2012)

Medicine and the Workhouse. Edited by Jonathan Reinarz and Leonard Schwarz (2015)

Medieval Leicester by Charles Billson (1920)

Memories of Thurmaston (2007)

Stoughton: Images of a Village (2000)

Tales of Old Leicestershire by Marian Pipe (1991)

The Autobiography of Joseph Carey Merrick

The Duties of Servants: The Routine of Domestic Life (1894)

The Elephant Man and Other Reminiscences
   by Sir Frederick Treves (1923)

The Penny Showman: Tom Norman, Silver King.
   With additional writings by his son George Norman (1985)

The Slums of Leicester by Ned Newitt (2009)

The Spectacle of Deformity: Freak Shows and Modern British Culture
   by Nadja Durbach (Kindle Edition 2010)

The Story of Leicester by Siobhan Begley (Kindle Edition, 2013)

The True History of the Elephant Man by Michael Howell
   and Peter Ford (Kindle edition, 2011)

The Workhouse Cookbook by Peter Higginbotham (2008)

The Workhouse Encyclopaedia by Peter Higginbotham
   (Kindle Edition 2013)

Thurmaston National School 1844-1868 (1979)

Treves and The Elephant Man. Compiled by Jonathan Evans, Archivist,
   The London Hospital (2003)

We Are South Highfields: Life in our Area Past and Present (2012)

Working Class Life in Leicester: The Joseph Dare Reports
   by Barry Haynes (1991)

Online Resources

Convict Records of Australia: www.convictrecords.com.au

Genealogy: ancestry.co.uk

Joseph Carey Merrick tribute website: www.josephcareymerrick.com

National Fairground Archive: www.sheffield.ac.uk/nfa/index

Podcast: Joseph Merrick, The Elephant Man with Jeanette Sitton
(25 July 2015): www.casebook.org/podcast/listen.html?id=108

The History of the Workhouse: www.workhouses.org.uk

The History of Vaccines: www.historyofvaccines.org

The Music Hall and Theatre History Site: arthurlloyd.co.uk

Index

225